VIERENTIA BEUKES

Keeping and breeding
BIRDS

A GUIDE FOR SOUTH AFRICA

δελος

CAPE TOWN

COVER PHOTOGRAPHS: Cordon Bleu (*top left*), Fischer's lovebird (*top right*),
scarlet macaw (*bottom left*) and red-crested cardinals (*bottom right*)

P. 4: Plum-headed parakeet.

© 1993 Delos
28 Wale Street, Cape Town

Also available in Afrikaans as *Boer suksesvol met voëls: 'n Handleiding
vir Suid-Afrika*

Translated by Jan Schaafsma
Photography by Vierentia Beukes
Illustrations by Jan van Tonder
Cover design and typography by Linda Vicquery
Typeset in 10 on 12pt Plantin by Martingraphix, Cape Town
Printed and bound by Toppan Printing Company, Hong Kong

First impression 1993

ISBN 1-86826-263-4

Contents

1. Look before you leap — 5
2. Building an aviary — 7
3. Providing water and food — 15
4. Plants, perches and nests — 17
5. Feeding — 22
6. Buying birds — 27
7. Sexing, the egg and hand-rearing — 31
8. Combating diseases — 35
9. The parrot family — 44
10. Finches and waxbills — 63
11. Show canaries — 76
12. Show budgies — 80
13. Ornamental waterfowl — 83
14. Pheasants — 93
15. Quail — 97
16. Wild doves — 100
17. Fancy pigeons — 103
18. Breeding for colour — 107
19. Caged birds — 109
    Index — 110

Look before you leap

Breeding and rearing birds lifts weary spirits and gives interest to bored people, is therapy for the depressed and companionship for the lonely. Birds bring back something of nature – something basic, beautiful, clean and fresh – into the life of modern man.

However, before you plunge headlong into aviculture, it is wise to sit down and take stock. A bird in an aviary is completely dependent on its owner. It is certainly not everybody's idea of fun to look after a bunch of birds year in and year out, day in day out, on Saturdays, Sundays, Christmas and New Year.

Not only is it cruel towards birds to neglect them, but good breeding results cannot be achieved under such circumstances. Dark, dirty aviaries, with slimy water and only seeds for food, inhabited by listless, lice-infested birds with poor plumage, are a sorry sight. If you do not have the required time or enthusiasm, do not take up aviculture at all, but if you must, keep the operation small.

Remember something else too: For many years birds have been caught in the wild and exported to other countries for bird lovers. Aviculturalists often claim that they have saved certain bird species from extinction and, in some cases, this is undoubtedly so.

However, the unfortunate truth is that many bird species breed so poorly in captivity that bird fanciers cannot even supply their own needs; one example is the strawberry finch. Aviculturalists are consequently forced to buy birds and, with such a voracious market, birds are caught in great numbers in the wild, with the result that many species are threatened with extinction. Aviculture and other factors such as the destruction of habitats – the greatest culprit – are therefore partly responsible for the fact that many species, certain macaws, for example, are hovering on the brink of extinction.

Many countries have now placed a ban on any further exports of their birds. The aim of the Convention on International Trade in Endangered Species of Wild Fauna and Flora (CITES) is to control the international trade in birds, among others. The convention has drawn up lists of highly endangered species, less endangered species, and so on. For example, trade in birds listed in Appendix I is absolutely forbidden. Trade in birds listed in Appendix II and III is allowed only if the dealer has obtained the necessary permits.

Certain airlines have already agreed not to transport any birds caught in the wild. In future, therefore, only birds bred in aviaries, or smuggled birds, will move between countries. This means that aviculturalists will have to rely on birds they can breed themselves, as the supply of birds from the wild is decreasing. Aviculturalists must therefore do everything in their power to achieve success in breeding the more difficult species in particular, and in large enough numbers to supply their own needs as well as those of pet shops.

Something else you should guard against, is weakening the birds you own. Particularly as a result of inbreeding, caged birds such as cockatiels and budgies (which have been bred by man for many years) are smaller than the same species in the wild, and fertility problems are often encountered. It is common practice to breed brother and sister. In the case of extremely expensive species, for example Kings and Queens of Bavaria, it is common practice to buy one pair (themselves often a brother and sister), and to breed the offspring, who are also brothers and sisters. (Uncontrolled inbreeding is not the same as careful line breeding, which is done to breed a particular characteristic such as a new colour.)

The world-famous Pheasant Trust of Norfolk, England, is of the opinion that at least 10 pairs of birds should be kept to prevent inbreeding. When birds are simply too expensive and/or rare to permit the keeping of so many pairs, the owner should try to exchange birds with other enthusiasts. For example, hire a male for the duration of a season and pay 'stud fees', as is done with dogs and stallions. For this a computerised database with information about rare and expensive species available in South Africa is a necessity. Such a database should be available at a central point, for example a bird club. Anybody wishing to know where to obtain a certain species would then be able to extract the information from the database for a small fee.

The breeding of rare birds in captivity should be encouraged, provided this remains in the hands of experts who manage to get the birds to breed. This can make a major contribution towards saving these species from extinction and even increasing their numbers. Breeders of such birds should be registered internationally and should be permitted to exchange birds across international borders in order to ensure fresh blood. At present this practice is forbidden by regulations which curb the trade in birds in order to save certain species from extinction, but which have not succeeded in curbing the smuggling of rare species.

Instead of concentrating on shows, bird societies should rather encourage breeding for the pet market as well as the breeding of extremely rare and threatened species on an organised basis. This is a much more important function than attempting to breed the prettiest mutation of a lovebird species. For many birds threatened by the destruction of their habitat, an expert aviculturalist's aviary may be the only place where they will survive. This is the case with the New Zealand parakeet, which is a threatened species in its natural habitat, but which breeds so well in aviaries that there are literally thousands available and it has even become one of the cheaper species.

In South Africa there are many bird clubs, all of which fall under a national council. A bird club is a rich source of information. This is where members' problems are discussed and informative lectures are presented. Most clubs also organise shows. Although clubs already exist in most of the large urban centres, anybody can establish a club wherever a need for one exists. Beginners are urged to join a bird club.

This guide describes the management of exotic bird species. Indigenous birds are subject to a permit system as well as inspections by officials from the Department of Nature Conservation.

For this reason they are not very popular among aviculturalists, command poor prices and are seldom kept by the average aviculturalist.

Consideration should, however, be given to placing South African species threatened by extinction in the hands of knowledgeable aviculturalists, as many of our own species, too, may in future survive only in captivity.

1 A fine round aviary for a bird collection. At least two-thirds of a round aviary must be protected from the prevailing winds.

3 An example of handsome, neat aviaries with plants, rockeries and fishponds which will be a credit to any garden. Aviaries like this are usually built for their aesthetic appeal and house a collection of birds. Birds kept in these aviaries must be selected with care so that they do not eat all the plants or kill one another.

2 This is a neat aviary with one large flying area in front and four separate shelters behind. Each shelter is partly covered with asbestos sheeting painted white, which provides the birds with privacy. The fact that the shelter is divided into four separate compartments prevents unnecessary fighting. Entry to the aviary is gained by means of a walk-in behind the shelters.

4 These aviaries are strictly for breeding, with only one pair of birds in each compartment. The flying area is in front, and at the back is the shelter containing the nests.

2

Building an aviary

Design

Aviaries normally form part of the garden, even if they are situated in the back yard. As regards building plans, you can give your imagination free rein – aviaries may range from showy enclosures with small gardens and lawns, ponds, rockeries and waterfalls, to simple yet neat and functional designs. Aviaries cobbled together from old crate planks, corrugated iron, plastic or hessian spoil the appearance of the garden, do not do the beautiful inhabitants justice and may even reduce the value of the home.

The only thing of real importance in the design of the aviary is that it should give the birds enough shelter. For example, a round aviary is suitable only if the aviary is sheltered from the prevailing wind along at least two-thirds of its circumference by a wall, asbestos sheeting, reeds, grass, fibreglass, corrugated iron or something similar.

Aviaries consist of a flying area (flight) with or without a roof, and a shelter with a roof at the back of the aviary. The shelter protects the birds from the wind, rain and cold. This is where they sleep and normally also breed, as their nests are suspended within the shelter. Furthermore their food is placed inside the shelter so that it cannot become wet. In the case of finches, who are quick to fly out through an opened gate, a 'double door' for a single aviary or a 'safety passage' in front of an entire row of aviaries is essential. This consists of an enclosed passageway or extra cage in front of the gate to the aviary. You enter the extra cage, close the gate behind you and then open the gate of the aviary itself. Should a bird escape, it cannot go any further than the extra cage or safety passage, where it can then be caught.

Siting

Aviaries partially enclosed on three sides should preferably face north. If an aviary faces east, west or south, there should be, in addition to the shelter, a partially uncovered flying area so that in winter the birds can sit in the sun from early morning.

In the beginning the aspirant aviculturalist can often afford only one or two aviaries. Once the bird bug has bitten, however, any profits from the birds are usually spent buying more birds – this calls for more aviaries. Be sure to site the very first aviary in such a way that there is enough room to attach the next one to it, so that the aviaries eventually form a neat whole.

Display aviaries

Breeding aviaries and display aviaries are not the same thing. Aviaries built to show off birds to their best advantage and incorporating rockeries, plants and housing a large variety of bird species do not necessarily produce the best breeding results.

With the exception of some small species such as grass parakeets, parrots and parrot-like birds cannot be kept in display aviaries because they will chew all the plants to ribbons, unless the aviaries are particularly large. For the back-yard aviculturalist such large aviaries are normally not possible. In the case of most of the larger parakeets, and certainly all of the parrots, only one pair per aviary should be housed or else they will fight to the death.

If a variety of species are kept in one aviary, they may pester one another, pull apart each other's nests and fight. Pheasants and ducks, living on the ground, may kill and even eat baby finches and doves that can't fly. It is also extremely difficult to keep such a large planted aviary free of mice – and mice spread diseases and eat eggs and chicks.

However, display aviaries do have their rightful place. After a hard day's work it is soothing to relax near or even inside such an aviary. The aviary enhances the garden, and if the birds kept in it are selected with care, you can even achieve interesting breeding results. See p. 29 for information about the species which can share an aviary.

Plans

First draw the aviary plan on paper and accurately calculate the dimensions. Then determine how much material you need. Study photos 1, 2, 3 and 11 and figs. 1-6 for ideas about designs.

Frames

An aviary usually consists of a wooden or metal frame covered in wire. The material for the shelter (e.g. asbestos, fibreglass or corrugated iron sheets) is normally fixed to the frame on the outside of the wire cage. The frame and the type of wire used should be suited to the birds. For the larger members of the parrot family, who will happily chew through wire if possible, the wire and frames for the aviaries should be far more robust than for finches. In South Africa aviary frames are usually constructed of iron piping or sometimes angle iron (for large birds such as macaws).

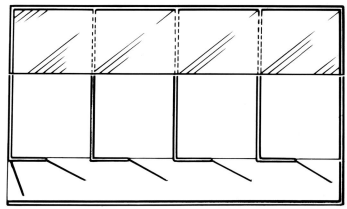

Fig. 1 Plan for a row of aviaries (as seen from above) which can be extended at a later stage. In front is the safety corridor which leads to the gates of the individual aviaries. There is no roof over the flying areas. At the back are the shelters covered with roofs. The food, water and nests are placed in the shelters. A row of aviaries such as this should preferably face north.

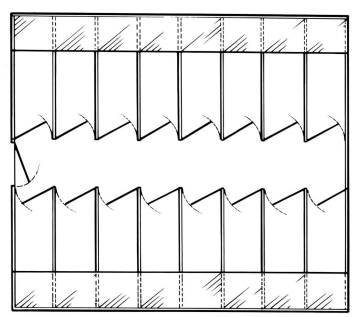

Fig. 2 Plan for a double row of aviaries. The safety corridor, which gives access to the gates of all the aviaries, is in the centre. There are no roofs over the flying areas. The roofed shelters are at the back.

Wooden frames are suitable at the coast, as they do not rust. However, some parrot species will chew a frame like this to pieces with great relish. In the case of finches, doves, ducks, most parakeets, quail and pheasants, wooden frames are perfectly adequate. Use 5 cm × 5 cm wood for the frame of a small aviary and 10 cm × 10 cm for larger aviaries.

Painted metal frames are long-lasting. Round or square-sectioned steel pipe with a minimum diameter of 2 cm is suitable for aviaries for most bird species. Steel pipe of a larger diameter makes for a neater and more durable frame,

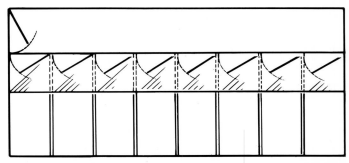

Fig. 3a and **3b** Plan for a row of aviaries with an access corridor at the back, i.e. behind the shelters. Access to the individual aviaries is through a wooden door. There is a hatch in the wooden door with a food tray below it on the inside of the shelter. In the morning the food is placed on the tray through the hatch. It is therefore not necessary to open the door and enter the aviary every time the birds are fed.

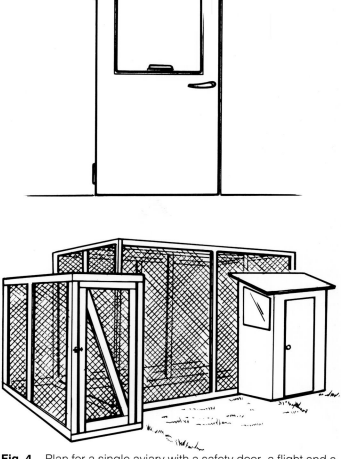

Fig. 4 Plan for a single aviary with a safety door, a flight and a separate room which can be closed in very cold weather to keep the birds inside. Access to the room is through a separate door. There is a window in the room to provide light. Such a plan is suitable for regions where the winters are very cold, or for delicate birds such as Gouldians.

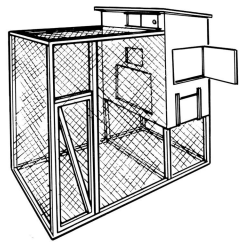

Fig. 5 Another plan for a single aviary without a safety door and a small separate section where the birds can be enclosed during very cold weather. Access to the enclosed area is through a hatch. Food and water are pushed through the hatch. There are glass windows to provide light. Such a plan is suitable in areas where the winters are very cold or for delicate birds such as Gouldians.

Fig. 6 A plan for an aviary in regions where the winters are very cold. Access to the aviary is through a gate in the flight. The birds are not restricted to the shelter, but the shelter is very well protected against wind from all sides. There are glass windows in the shelter, as the birds will not enter the shelter if it is dark.

but is more expensive. Aviaries for macaws, true parrots, cockatoos and other birds with strong beaks require thicker piping or even angle iron, as do the frames of very large aviaries. Weld the sawn-off ends of pipes closed to prevent water from entering and causing rust.

Template
If more than one aviary is to be built to the same pattern and size, first construct a basic template out of angle iron and then place a piece of iron piping in it before sawing it. This ensures that the various pieces will be sawn to the correct length each time. It's so much easier than measuring each piece of piping separately.

Portable aviaries
Sometimes an aviculturalist has to move house or is forced by some other circumstance to sell the aviaries. It may be a good idea to construct the sides as well as the roof in the form of separate sections. Attach the sides and roof with binding wire instead of welding them together. When you need to move, all it takes is a snip through the binding wire – the sides and roof can then be taken apart and transported separately (see photo 5).

Dimensions

Birds need room to fly. It is better to construct long, narrow aviaries rather than small round ones or very small square ones. The larger the birds, the larger the flying area that is needed. Finches can be kept in aviaries of 1-2 m long × 1 m wide × 2 m high.

The smaller parakeets and parrots such as conures, grass

parakeets and lovebirds need a flying area of at least 4 m long. Lovebirds will also survive in smaller aviaries providing not too many are kept together.

The larger parakeets and parrots need a flying area of about 6 m or more in length in order to help them stay fit. In the case of large birds such as macaws, cockatoos and amazons, of which only one pair is normally kept in an aviary, the width of the aviary can be only 1 m, while the height can vary from 2-4 m.

Wire

Chicken wire, welded wire mesh or even diamond mesh wire is suitable for aviaries for birds such as cockatoos, galahs and macaws. However, diamond mesh wire open-

5 One method of building aviaries is by means of loose frames which are simply tied to one another with binding wire. These aviaries can be moved quite easily.

ings are so large that snakes and mice can easily enter, causing great damage to eggs and contaminating the food.

Ordinary 12-mm chicken wire is the cheapest, suitable for most bird species (except macaws and cockatoos) and is used most often. Chicken wire is either woven first and then galvanised, or galvanised first and then woven. Both types are available commercially, but pre-woven galvanised wire is more rust-resistant. Wire which has been galvanised before being woven tends to crack where it was bent during the weaving process, and tends to rust at these cracks.

Chicken wire has a lifespan of about ten years if it is painted regularly. After this period a hailstone can quite easily punch a hole through it, resulting in the loss of your birds. Bright paint such as silver reflects light and makes it more difficult to see the birds properly. Darker paint such as green or black makes the birds more visible. When wire biters are accommodated in the aviary, it is important to use paint which does not contain lead, as this is poisonous. Every time you paint, use a different colour, so that you can spot any areas you may have missed out. Chicken wire should be repainted every two years.

Welded wire mesh is expensive, but is excellent for aviaries. It looks neat, is sturdy enough to require little support and is easier to fit than chicken wire because it does not stretch as much. Wire mesh stands up well to any assault by parrot-like birds. It lasts longer than chicken wire, particularly if it is painted regularly. Furthermore it is proof against dogs trying to get at the birds. A mesh of 12 mm × 12 mm is suitable for small birds, while bigger openings are fine for the larger parrot species.

Slack in chicken wire

Chicken wire stretches, sags and soon looks untidy. It must therefore be stretched tight over the frames. Do this as follows: thread stiff fencing wire along the edges of the chick-

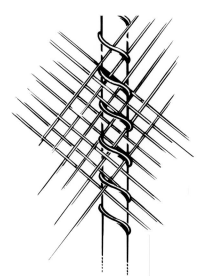

Fig. 7 This is how chicken wire is fixed neatly to a frame with binding wire.

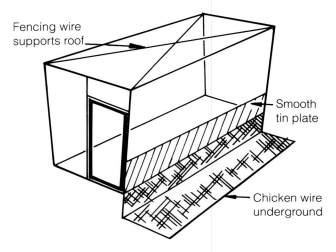

Fencing wire supports roof

Smooth tin plate

Chicken wire underground

Fig. 8 This figure shows how mice, rats and snakes can be kept out of an aviary. A smooth piece of tinplate is fixed to the outside of the aviary for about 60-70 cm. Furthermore the chicken wire can be dug into the ground vertically and then bent horizontally. Two lengths of wire are crossed to support the wire over the roof.

6 With home-made apparatus such as this the aviary wire can be stretched tight. The hooks on the left and right are hooked into the chicken wire. At the end of the crank there is a support which rests against the pipe over which the wire must be stretched. By turning the crank, the hooks (and the wire) is pulled closer to the pipe. This is more effective than a rake.

en wire for strength. Hook the tines of a rake through the edge, over the fencing wire and pull the chicken wire tight over the frame. Tie the wire to the frame with strong binding wire (see fig. 7). To prevent the chicken wire (which forms the roof) from sagging, two lengths of thick fencing wire can first be stretched diagonally across the roof (see fig. 8).

Rats, mice and snakes

Make it more difficult for these pests to get into your aviary by fixing smooth tinplate 60-70 cm high on the outside of the bottom part of the aviary. You can also place fine mesh

7   The gate to an aviary must preferably be low so that it is difficult for the birds to fly past your head suddenly. This aviary
door, which forces you to stoop while carrying pails of food, is
unnecessarily low.

Fig. 9   A simple latch for an aviary gate. If the latch is properly
balanced, it will close by itself. This is handy when you enter the
aviary carrying an armful of food containers. It is locked with a
padlock.

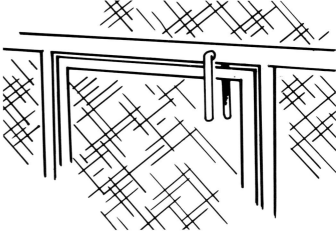

Fig. 10   A simple method for keeping a gate closed, especially
if the gate leads to a safety corridor. A hole is drilled in the top
framework and a U-shaped piece of iron about 10 mm in diameter
passed through it. The U-shaped latch falls into place easily.

chicken wire vertically into the ground to a depth of about
40 cm and then bend it out horizontally (see fig. 8). This
will not keep out small field mice or small snakes, but will
deter those dangerous rats which kill even large birds.

Gates

An important point to keep in mind is that the gate should
not be much higher than your head. If the gate is low
enough to force you to stoop slightly on entering, so much
the better. This is particularly important in the case of
aviaries housing small, quick birds because they can fly past
your head in a flash. On the other hand, the gate should not
be so low that you have to bend almost double upon entering the aviary while carrying a bucket of food (see photo 7).
   A gate with a spring which closes the gate automatically,
is also very handy and has prevented many an escape. See
figs. 9 and 10 for methods for closing gates.

Foundation

If the aviary has a concrete floor, and you want to scrub it
regularly, the wire cage must be put on a foundation of

bricks (see photo 8). This looks neat and keeps the frame
and wire from rusting where they come into contact with
the water used for scrubbing. Of course there must be an
opening in the foundation through which the water can
drain away. This opening should be screened with wire to
keep out rats and mice.

Floors

Aviaries usually have concrete or earthen floors, which
both have advantages and disadvantages.
   The biggest advantage of a concrete floor is that it can
regularly be scrubbed and disinfected thoroughly. In this

11

8 Here the frames of the aviary rest on a brick wall. This prevents the frames from standing in rainwater and rusting, or rats and mice from digging a hole under the wires. The gates are low so that it is difficult for the birds to suddenly fly past your head. Note that the gates shut very securely. Greenstuff is planted directly in the aviaries.

way diseases such as coccidiosis can be controlled. Bird droppings, seed husks, wilted greenstuff and so forth can also be swept up with little trouble.

A disadvantage of a concrete floor is that it is bitterly cold in winter although a layer of sand or straw on the concrete can alleviate the problem. Concrete floors look clinical and unnatural – place plants in pots on the floor for a more natural look.

An earthen floor is cheaper than a concrete floor, is warmer and looks more natural. Grass, weeds and greenstuff can grow in an earthen floor. These in turn attract insects, which are beneficial to finches.

The disadvantage of an earthen floor is that a high concentration of harmful bacteria can build up in the soil because bird droppings are not removed. After a few years diseases such as scour (diarrhoea), tuberculosis and coccidiosis can sweep through the entire bird colony and destroy all the birds.

The soil in an aviary can be partly disinfected by digging agricultural lime or salt into it twice a year. Earthen floors can also be kept clean by spreading a thick layer of sand on top. This layer of sand is removed three or four times per year and replaced with clean sand.

Spread fine gravel on the earthen floor where the water containers are positioned. This absorbs the moisture in which bacteria that cause diseases flourish.

Shelters and roofs

The shelter is usually placed to one side of the aviary. It must be large enough so that all the birds in the aviary can sleep under it without crowding. The shelter must have a roof and be enclosed on at least three sides. It is also essential to suspend a sheet so that it partly covers the open side or use some other method of deflecting any cold wind which may blow into the open side (see fig. 11 and photo 9).

In your choice of material for shelters and roofs the climate must be taken into account. In South Africa asbestos sheets are a popular choice because they are quite strong and do not become excessively hot or cold. Corrugated asbetos sheets can be used for the roof. These are bolted onto a crossbeam or part of the roof frame. In the warmer regions it is a good idea to leave an opening directly beneath the roof between the roof and the wall. Warm air rises, and the opening allows the air to escape, so that there is a crossdraft of air (see photo 10). If a shelter becomes too hot, the female may leave the nest or the eggshells may become so dry and hard that the chicks cannot hatch. In extreme heat the chicks may die in the nest.

A hole in an asbestos sheet can be repaired by placing a piece of sacking over it and covering it with cement.

Corrugated iron is suitable in cases where the climate is mild, in other words neither too hot in summer nor too cold in winter. A corrugated iron roof can become extremely hot in summer.

Glassfibre sheets, in particular the coloured type, look neat. Translucent fibreglass sheets are often used to

9 A shelter with a plain piece of asbestos in front of the nest is adequate in the warmer regions of the country.

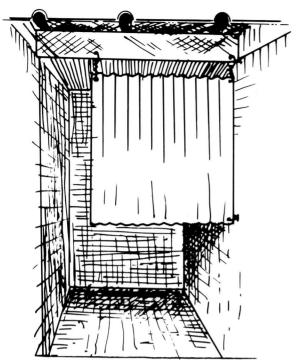

Fig. 11 A simple method for keeping wind and rain out of a shelter is to suspend a piece of asbestos or fibreglass sheeting in front of the shelter. The nests and perches are placed behind the sheeting. A shelter like this is adequate in parts of the country where the winters are not very cold.

enclose virtually the entire roof and sides of an aviary, to the benefit of birds such as gouldians which are sensitive to the cold. In the Cape, where extreme cold is often accompanied by rainy weather (a deadly combination), such fibreglass roofs and walls are very efficient. Reject fibreglass sheets often cost only half the normal price.

Wooden shelters and roofs are also suitable for smaller birds such as pheasants, doves and quail, but the parrot family can quickly make a meal of the wood. Of course brick walls are particularly neat and tidy, but quite expensive and naturally not portable.

Precast walls are easy to erect, look neat and can be erected on the outside of a wire aviary. Stone walls always look good, particularly in the case of a display aviary.

A grass or reed roof looks natural but, apart from the fire hazard, also provides an excellent shelter for mites and lice. It must therefore be regularly sprayed against these pests.

Heating aviaries

In Europe and the colder areas of the Americas it is common practice to heat aviaries or to provide them with a shelter which can be closed completely. The birds remain in the shelter for the entire winter and are only released into the flying area in fine weather.

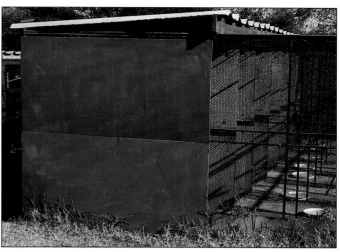

10 This photograph shows one method of roof construction for a row of breeding aviaries. Almost half the aviary space is sheltered by means of asbestos sheeting. The roof does not rest directly on the side walls, but is slightly lifted by means of a beam so that a cool wind can blow into the shelters. In winter these gaps are stopped up.

Because South Africans do not experience six-month winters with thick snow, we are inclined to think that our winters are not particularly cold. As a result it is usually regarded as an unnecessary luxury to heat our aviaries.

Yet there are large parts of the country where the temperature often drops to below zero, where sudden cold fronts accompanied by rain move in and aviculturalists sustain great losses. This is particularly true of birds which do not sleep in nests, but spend the winter on perches. Even in a warm place like Pretoria it is a good idea to provide extra heat during the coldest days.

Providing a little heat in an aviary is relatively simple. The idea is not to make the aviary nice and snug. In aviaries where the temperature is always maintained at an even level the birds do not become hardy and this often results in weakened birds. When such birds are sold to someone who leaves them outside, the buyer is likely to suffer a number of fatalities, which will give the seller a bad name. The purpose of aviary heating is simply to ensure that the temperature does not fall to near freezing point and to protect the birds against bitterly cold wind. Icy cold wind with rain is a fatal combination, causing great losses which may be prevented. Birds can be protected against the worst cold weather in the following ways:

☐ Enclose the entire shelter or aviary with fibreglass sheets. These block the wind but let through the light, so they are particularly useful for this purpose. If money is a problem, the aviary can be temporarily covered with sheets of plastic, canvas, fertiliser bags, gunny sacks, grass or even newspaper. By keeping out only the icy wind birds can be saved.

☐ Ordinary infrared lamps or the more expensive type used

11 Smart aviaries like this one are suitable in regions where it becomes very cold, or to acclimatise freshly imported birds. The fronts of the aviaries are closed off with glass, and ventilation is provided by means of windows closed off with chicken wire. The temperature is thermostatically controlled in these aviaries.

for piglets will save the life of many a bird. Remember that warm air rises. Do not site perches only below the lamp, but above it as well. There should be enough perches for the birds to move away if they feel too hot. In a very large aviary more than one lamp will have to be suspended in the more sheltered areas, for example in the corners where the walls meet. One extension cable with a number of electric sockets can supply a whole row of aviaries with electricity.

☐ Cheaper than infrared lamps, although less efficient, are a number of 25-watt bulbs at the back of the shelter. Suspend the bulbs near the perches.

☐ Asbestos heaters placed in the aviary during the coldest periods of the year can also prevent unnecessary deaths.

☐ Where there is no electricity, an enterprising aviculturalist can fix a number of water pipes to the inside of the aviary; these water pipes are then connected to a slow combustion stove.

☐ Always hang a 25-watt night light in each aviary and switch it on at night (if electricity is available). A good place to hang it is low over the food. If the birds are disturbed at night and fly about, they will be able to find their roosting sites again. Also, if a bird feels cold and sick, it will seek the heat of the bulb and you will notice the sick bird more easily.

A prospective aviculturalist who knows that the winters in his area are long and cold, may wish to build aviaries in the European style (see figs. 4, 5 and 6).

Protection from heat

Although more birds die from cold than from heat, certain parts of the country become so hot that you should make provision for this as well. The eggs dry out and chicks in the nest suffer or may even die, or the female feels so hot that she leaves the eggs. Take the following steps against excessive heat:

☐ Do not build the roof of the shelter directly on top of the shelter's walls, but lift it slightly so that a cooling breeze can move through the shelter. If the winters are cold (e.g. in the Bushveld), the opening between the walls and the roof is temporarily stopped with sacking or newspaper during winter.

☐ Ensure that the nests never hang directly in the sun.

☐ Spray the birds with a fine mist of water on very hot days. They enjoy this tremendously!

3

Providing water and food

Water supply

Fresh, clean water is of the utmost importance. To have birds drinking murky, green water polluted with droppings is simply asking for trouble. This is why every aviculturalist would like to find a safe, easy method of providing water. Water can be supplied in the following ways:

☐ A container, deep enough for birds to bath in it as well, must be scrubbed daily to remove the algae and droppings and then filled with fresh water. Flower pot saucers make excellent baths and containers for drinking water. Place the container in the shade, because this retards the growth of green algae. Do not add swimming-pool chlorine to the water to try and make it remain fresh for longer. These containers require the most effort, but are the cheapest and keep the birds in fresh drinking and bathing water.

Plastic, glass or ceramic dishes are the easiest to clean. Avoid metal dishes because of the possibility of rust.

☐ A deep water container placed upside down in a flat basin is available commercially (see fig. 12). This type of water container is filled only once every few days. Small

Fig. 12 A water dispenser like this can hold enough to last a few days. However, it does not provide room for the birds to bath.

birds can bath in it, but large birds such as parakeets and parrots cannot. It is a good system which is fairly safe and which saves you a good deal of work.

☐ Install a tap in the aviary with the spout upwards (i.e. the tap is upside down). Leave it at a permanent trickle, but not so much so that the water runs onto the ground and causes a soggy mess.

In this instance the birds can always drink clean water from the spout, but they cannot bath, which for most birds is very important. A platform or perch must be installed near the tap for the larger birds.

Unfortunately this system needs constant water pressure and it is precisely on very hot days that nearly all the neighbours begin watering their lawns simultaneously with the result that the water pressure drops, the tap stops dripping, and the thirsty birds have nothing to drink.

Place a thick layer of gravel beneath the tap to combat the sogginess and mud. The germs that cause diseases thrive in wet places, as do internal parasites.

A better plan is to open the tap wide enough for a constant trickle of water to run into a small cement pond built around the tap. The pond provides a place for bathing and can be beautified with rockery rocks or even ferns and bamboo, if finches inhabit the aviary.

A variation on this theme is to allow the tap to drip permanently into a large water bowl. The water bowl or cement pond must be scrubbed regularly.

☐ Aviculturalists with larger budgets can buy systems designed for poultry which allow a whole row of aviaries to be supplied with water nipples. However, this does not solve the bathing problem.

☐ If the aviary is built on a slope, a water furrow can run from one section to the next. This is fine as long as diseases do not break out. As soon as this happens, they will spread to all the sections within a very short time.

Food supply

Food containers

Birdseed is placed in shallow, open containers or in self-feeders. When shallow containers are used, it often seems as if there is ample food in the containers, but closer inspection will show that this consists mainly of husks. In the case of a deep bowl the problem is compounded; the husks lie on top of the seed and the birds cannot get at the seeds.

Food containers must therefore be stirred every few

days, and you must ensure that there is enough food between the husks.

Self-feeders

Self-feeders or seedhoppers are available in various shapes and sizes. You can buy beautiful wooden self-feeders shaped like a house with a roof for the garden. These are also suitable for aviaries containing finches, but parrot-like birds will soon reduce the wood to splinters.

Self-feeders or hoppers have the advantage that the husks do not accumulate on top of the seeds. Some have a tray underneath to catch the husks, but unfortunately such a tray makes a marvellous hiding place for a mouse; its larder is right above its head!

Although self-feeders do save time and trouble, an aviary with self-feeders cannot be left unattended, because the seeds often stick and then feeding is not possible. Before you realise what has happened, the birds are dropping because of hunger.

The self-feeder must stand or hang straight. If it is angled backwards, the seeds will not flow; if angled forward, the seeds spill out. Self-feeders must be checked at least three times a week to ensure that they actually do feed (see fig. 13). Seeds enriched with oil such as cod liver oil are sticky and may not flow through the feeder. Allow these seeds to stand for about a week to give the oil time to soak in before placing in a self-feeder.

When siting the food containers, the birds' habits must be taken into account. Most parrots such as macaws, cockatoos, Senegals and Amazons take off slowly and deliberately. In nature they are therefore easy prey for their enemies and as a result the birds feel unsafe on the ground. This inborn fear remains nascent in caged birds and they prefer not to find their food on the ground.

Preferably place food for parrots, and even parakeets, high up in the aviary. If the food is placed on the ground they will descend to eat, but they will be in such a hurry to fly up again that they may eat too little, and in the end you are stuck with skinny parrots.

On the other hand most waxbills, many finches and even lovebirds are quite happy to forage for food on the ground. Particularly when new finches arrive in an aviary, scatter food on the floor to ensure that they do not starve to death before discovering the seed dishes.

However, because mice and rats contaminate the food on the ground with droppings, urine and germs, it is common practice to place finch and waxbill food high up in the aviary as well. A food table with a single central support planted in the soil is ideal to thwart rats and mice.

12 A self-feeder like this one has the advantage that the husks do not accumulate on top of the seeds. The glass in front allows one to see immediately how much food is left. This type of feeder must be checked twice a week to make sure that seed is indeed being fed through.

Fig. 13 A home-made self-feeder. At the bottom is a tray in which the empty husks are collected.

16

4

Plants, perches and nests

Plants

The aviary has been completed and the master builder stands back to admire the fruits of his labours spanning many weekends and nights – but something is missing. It all looks so bare, clinical and cold, just like a laboratory.

The question is this: to plant, or not to plant? This is not easy to answer. Plants, rockeries, tree stumps and ponds can beautify the aviary, but may not always be practical.

One of the simplest ways of beautifying an aviary is to pave the surrounding area with slate or bricks, for example, or to plant grass, shrubs and flowers. If the exterior is beautiful, the bareness inside will not bother you that much.

It is difficult to beautify aviaries for parrot-like birds with plants because these birds can destroy most plants with ease. This is not always the case as most parakeets and parrots will only eat the branches of the trees and shrubs on which they sit. Clumps of grass and other low-growing plants are usually left alone.

Aviaries for such birds may therefore be planted with lawn or lucerne, oats or sorghum and if the birds do eat the greenstuff, it will do them good. A few rockery rocks or perhaps a pretty pond or stumps of wood can all help to beautify the bare aviary and to create a more natural atmosphere.

Among the parrot-like birds the problem children are the lovebirds and quakers. They will strip anything green to line their nests. A pond, fountain and a few rockery rocks are about all that can withstand the assaults of these birds. Lovebird chicks are strong flyers and it is unlikely that they will fall into the pond. Do not plant succulents with thorns. In a finch aviary you are free to give full rein to your gardening instincts.

In Europe and America, where it is cold, people think nothing of enclosing an entire verandah with glass and fine mesh. In this artificial tropical climate they grow plants such as delicious monsters, rubber plants, ferns, etc. as tall as the ceiling. Then they let loose a number of finches. And what a beautiful sight it is!

However, our finch aviaries are mainly sited out of doors. Some people build their finch aviary over and around an orange or loquat tree, or some other evergreen.

Many shrubs, in particular the various cypress species which have many small branches, are popular nesting places and are well suited to a finch aviary. Thick creepers such as jasmine also provide excellent nesting spots. Bamboo, reeds, ferns, grass and even weeds are advantageous in a finch aviary. They all attract insects which provide the finches with food.

Birdseed such as wild millet, millet and spray millet makes excellent ground cover. (Spray millet is an imported long-eared millet available from pet shops.) Protect the young plants with chicken wire. The finches will eat the leaves projecting above the wire without destroying the young plants. The birds also enjoy eating the half-ripe ears.

Concrete floors can be beautified by placing one or more shrubs in pots in the aviary. The pots are easy to move when the aviary is scrubbed. Avoid poisonous plants and seeds such as castor oil, oleander and syringa, as well as plants with thorns.

There are disadvantages to a thickly planted aviary: it cannot be scrubbed clean, but the worst problem is mice and rats who breed faster than finches and eat their fill of finches, their eggs and chicks. Rats get in through the wire while still small and grow to adulthood inside the aviary. They can cause the most dreadful damage to a finch aviary, being quite capable of wiping out an aviary of 200 finches within a few weeks.

Some bird species, particularly diamond finches, like to tunnel deep into a shrub in order to nest. They are so stupid, though, that they often become entangled in the shrub and cannot find their way out. When the aviculturalist starts searching the shrub in the great hope of finding a nest, he only finds a few pieces of bird biltong instead of chicks. In an aviary with diamond finches, dense shrubs are therefore not the answer.

Perches

There should not be so many perches that the birds have no flying room, or crash into the perches when they fly. Place perches at both ends of the aviary or in the corners, but not in the centre.

Provide thin as well as thick perches in the same aviary so that the birds' feet get exercise and their claws wear down. If all the perches are the same size, the birds' feet become stiff after many years and arthritis can develop because the feet are always in one position. Thick perches help the claws to wear down. Perches should be made from natural branches and not from even, smoothly sanded wood.

Don't use metal perches for parrots because in winter the birds can freeze to death or lose their toes. Use perches made of hard wood, such as lead wood.

Mice

Where mice and rats are a problem, perches must be suspended from the roof by two wires so that a mouse cannot jump onto them. Use washing line coated with plastic so that the birds can clearly see the wires and won't fly into them.

The food containers must also be protected from mice by fixing the self-feeders to a smooth wall and placing loose bowls on a table with one central support.

It can be difficult to eradicate mice already inside the aviary, particularly if there are plants inside the aviary. The birds themselves may spring any traps or eat poisoned food put out for the mice. Rather use plastic pipe with a diameter of about 3-4 cm and about 20 cm long. Lay the pipe on the ground and push the rat poison to the middle of the pipe. The mice will crawl into the pipe and eat the poison, but the birds will not. There should be no other food for the mice in the form of seed scattered on the floor or seed hoppers within their reach.

Nests

Before you buy birds for the new aviary, their nests must be ready. Lovebirds and many finch species sleep in nests and will therefore fare much better if the nests are ready when they are let loose in a new aviary.

The nests which the bird fanciers supply for the birds are often a far cry from what the birds would pick for themselves in nature. Certain members of the parrot family prefer to set up home in a hollowed-out anthill or a hole in the ground, while we expect them to move into a neat wooden box high up in the air. Plum-headed parakeets, for example, will often dig a hole in the ground beneath the food dish and breed there.

Budgies prefer a nest without nesting material, but with a hollow in the bottom to keep the eggs from rolling around. Special budgie nests are available commercially (see fig. 14). Any other nest such as a calabash or hollow stump is also suitable. There should be a perch in front of the opening, preferably outside as well as inside the nest. Remember to drill holes in the sides for ventilation.

Budgie nests are suspended at about shoulder height, which makes it possible to see inside. The nests can be suspended close to one another like blocks of flats, as budgies are quite tolerant of neighbours. However, there should be twice as many nests as there are pairs, or the birds will be inclined to fight fiercely.

During the breeding season in the spring and autumn the nests must be inspected regularly to remove any dead chicks.

Cockatiels' nests are available commercially. These are wooden boxes of about 30 cm × 30 cm × 30 cm. An opening with a perch close to it, a lid or front that can open, and a

13 A calabash makes a really good nest for small birds. It is airy and far less sweaty than a tin and also is not as cold in winter.

14 You can easily make a row of nests for budgies or lovebirds from a few long planks and crosspieces.

number of airholes in the sides are all that is required. Buy a nest with a slightly hollow bottom so that the eggs won't roll around. If the bottom is flat, it should be covered with a layer of wood shavings with a hollow in the centre for the eggs. Sometimes a cockatiel lays a great many eggs – seven to nine, or even more – and then the eggs are all over the nest. Some of them become cold and the chicks die inside the eggs.

The problem can be solved by placing a racing pigeon nest on the bottom of the cockatiel nest. Fill the corners of the box with wood shavings. As the racing pigeon nest is made of cardboard, it is discarded after every brood.

A good buy is a wooden nest with a loose bottom which

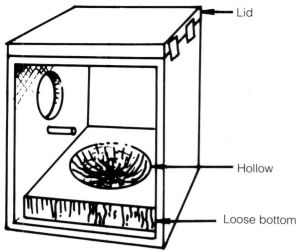

Fig. 14 A budgie nest. The loose bottom can be removed, washed and disinfected after each set of chicks. Suitable dimensions are 15 cm × 15 cm × 22 cm high.

15 Far left is a deep nest for parrots and parakeets. The nest opening is reinforced with tinplate to prevent the birds from chewing it to pieces. On the inside there is a ladder which leads to the nest opening from below so that the chicks can climb out. However, this nest is much too small for large birds such as cockatoos, macaws and Grand eclectus. The L-shaped nest (right) with the sliding lid is used mainly for Gouldians and sometimes for lovebirds. Other finches will also make their home in such a nest.

The nest below right is suitable for cockatiels, lorikeets and smaller parakeets. The two nests in the centre on top of the large nest are suitable for budgies, finches and lovebirds. The lid of one of the nests lifts up and the front of the other slides upwards so that one can inspect the eggs and chicks. At far right there is a nest made from a natural tree stump.

can easily be removed and is washable. The nests should not hang directly in the sun, because the eggshells can dry out and the chicks can't hatch. It can also become so hot that the female leaves the eggs or the young chicks die.

Parrots and parakeets get nests with shavings placed inside. In this material the birds can make hollows to their liking. The nest should be large enough to ensure that there is enough room for the tails of long-tailed species such as ring-necked, red-rumped or Stanley parakeets.

Some of the larger parrot species such as the cockatoos and Grand eclectus make their nests very deep down in a hollow tree trunk. You should provide them with a very deep box. Some aviculturalists fill the box almost to the top with shavings, which the birds then remove to the required depth. Others place only a thin layer of shavings in the bottom of the box. Both methods work well. If the nest is deep, there should be a ladder made from wire mesh, for example, so that the chicks can climb out. If not, they could remain trapped inside the nest. In the case of a very deep nest, for example an agave tree stump or hollowed-out tree trunk, there should be a spy hatch near the bottom so that you can check regularly whether there are eggs or chicks and whether the chicks are getting enough to eat.

Because parrots are given to chewing their nests, particularly around the entrance, this opening should be reinforced with smooth tinplate. Apart from hollowed-out tree trunks and agave trunks, wooden barrels can also be used to create an interesting natural nest. Cockatoos – inveterate chewers who will gnaw through wood and thin wire – can be given a metal rubbish bin or 50-litre drum for a nest. Macaws are given a 200-litre drum placed on its side.

Quakers are an exception to the rule of having shavings in a wooden box. They do nest in wooden boxes, but prefer to build a giant nest from thin pieces of wood and grass in any suitable place. Ensure that they have a tree with a firm fork. In the fork build a flat table out of wire or planking on which the quakers can build their nest. If no tree fork is available, construct a table in one of the corners of the aviary, preferably under cover. Supply enough sticks and twigs as well as thick grass such as tambookie grass, or even leaves and branches with leaves.

Brush-tongues breed well in an ordinary cockatiel nest in which a thick layer of shavings has been placed. The chicks remain in the nest for a long time and because the birds' droppings are watery, the nest and chicks sometimes become badly soiled and the ammonia which is released burns their eyes. Remove the shavings every week or two and replace with fresh dry shavings. The parents should be tame enough to allow such interference without abandoning the nest.

Another method is to replace the wooden bottom of the nest with chicken wire (see fig. 15). A thick layer of charcoal is placed on top of the chicken wire to absorb moisture. Because the charcoal will blacken the chicks, a piece of sacking made from natural fibre, a double layer of muslin

16 These agave stumps serve as nests for parakeets.

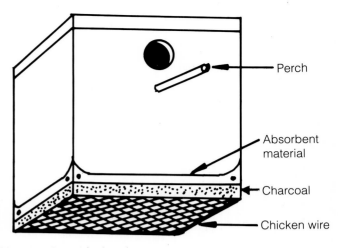

Fig. 15 A nest for brush-tongues

Labels on Fig. 15: Perch · Absorbent material · Charcoal · Chicken wire

17 Lovebirds are colony breeders. In this case the nests are suspended above and alongside one another like blocks of flats. Wooden nests which hang outside, like these ones, may become too wet when it rains a great deal, or become very hot in the sun. Place a roof over the nests for shelter.

or any absorbent material is placed on top of the charcoal. This material is fixed to the sides with thumbtacks and will prevent the chicks from becoming soiled.

Lovebirds like using wooden boxes, but not shavings. They build an intricate nest of finely chewed grass, reeds, leaves, lucerne, papyrus or anything else that is available. They must continually be provided with new nesting material. A budgie, cockatiel or finch nest is suitable.

In a large aviary with many lovebirds you can place a whole bale of straw on the ground. *Eragrostus curvula* is good, but teff hay is softer and therefore better. Green nesting material is preferable as this brings dampness to the nest, which helps to prevent the eggshells from drying out and becoming too hard for the chicks to hatch. The moistness carried to the nests by the birds after a bath, as well as the birds' own sweat, is normally enough to keep the eggshells soft, except during extremely warm and dry weather. This is why it is essential for all birds to be able to bath.

Finches and waxbills: Finches use a wooden box filled with nesting material. An ordinary budgie box is suitable for smaller finches and waxbills. A special L-shaped wooden nest with a lid that slides open is used for gouldians (see photo 15). Such nests are available commercially. Hang the nest against a smooth asbestos or tinplate sheet so that mice cannot reach it.

A large jam or fruit juice tin cut open halfway on one side is very popular among finches. Suspend the tin from the roof with wire so that the mice cannot reach it. Use thick wire coated with plastic, e.g. washing line, or else the birds may fly into the wire and injure themselves (see photos 18 and 19).

Some finches such as zebra finches will build a grass nest on top of an open canary nest. Hollow containers such as the cardboard holders for wine bottles, calabashes with one side cut open or hollowed-out coconuts are also suitable.

A large wire bag made of diamond mesh wire and tightly stuffed with grass or hay is sometimes used. Make hollows in the grass with your fist. The birds crawl into these and build a nest inside the bundle of grass. Unfortunately a wire bag full of grass is also a very good hiding place for mice, who may then eat all the small birds.

18 A clever aviculturalist has taken a fruit juice tin, spruced it up with a wooden roof and a perch – and, hey presto, he has a neat finch nest.

19 This is how a large tin is cut open at the top to serve as a finch nest. Because tins sweat easily and become unhealthily wet inside, holes must be pierced in the tin. Suspend it from thick wire (such as washing line) so that the birds can clearly see the wire and do not fly into it. A nest suspended from a wire in this way is safe against mice and rats.

Waxbills and many finches will often ignore such pretty artificial nests and prefer to build their own nest of grass in any dense shrub in the aviary.

Once again such shrubs are good hiding places for mice. Their presence is indicated by a strong mouse odour.

Mice sometimes bite off only the finches' heads – up to a dozen in one night. Field mice (musk-shrews) are normally the ones with such a predilection for bird brains. Mice also eat the chicks and eggs and contaminate the food with droppings and urine. It is therefore important that finch nests be made as mouse-proof as possible.

Finches need a great deal of nesting material. Soft green grass, lucerne and carrot tops are quite flexible and make excellent nests, but are not always available. A bale of teff hay is soft and many a finch nest will be built from it.

Nesting material can be placed in a rack or spread on the ground. Do not make the holder for the nesting material out of chicken wire. Birds sometimes become entangled in it.

A supply of pillow feathers is also welcome, although not essential. Sprinkle all the nests with a lice and mite powder and place a handful of grass in the box or tin to give the birds the right idea and to save them some effort.

There should be about twice as many nests as breeding pairs. Birds like to have a choice. The various nests should not be suspended too close together as fighting, even to the death, can occur when finches have to defend their nests against other finches.

Waxbills such as strawberry finches, orange-cheeked waxbills and red-eared waxbills have special nesting needs. They do not like breeding in artificial finch nests, but prefer breeding in thick clumps of grass or dense shrubs. We have a poor record of breeding results for waxbills, and one of the reasons is that it is not easy to meet their particular nesting needs. One method to encourage waxbills to breed is as follows:

Place pots with dense cypress-type shrubs in the aviary, or hang bunches of tambookie grass or 'slangbos', bound at the top and bottom, in various places in the aviary – breast high for strawberry finches and orange-cheeked waxbills and low on the ground for red-eared waxbills. Large pots with substantial tufts of grass growing in them can also be placed inside the aviary, or if the aviary has an earth floor, this can be planted with tufts of grass.

Release a number of zebra finches in the aviary. Supply straw, hay, green grass and feathers and soon the zebra finches will make nests in the shrubs or grass. Remove the zebra finches and release the waxbills in the aviary. They will move into the zebra finch nests, finish them off to their own taste, e.g. by building a nest for the male on top of the bottom nest and, it is hoped, begin breeding.

5

Feeding

What do I feed my birds? This is a subject about which bird fanciers can talk at length and with great differences of opinion. The ideal is to provide the birds with the same food they eat in nature, but this is rarely possible.

Fortunately birds are fairly adaptable as regards their diet. Rice-eating birds, for example, can successfully switch over to millet.

Unfortunately fertility is often impaired and bright plumage fades when the deviation from the birds' natural foods is too drastic.

Try, therefore, to keep as closely as possible to the birds' natural diet; if this is not possible, provide them with the best possible replacements. A well-fed bird has a strong resistance to diseases, breeds well and sports a sleek and shiny plumage.

It serves no purpose to keep birds and then fail to feed them properly.

The diet of most birds consists of seed, which normally forms their staple food, as well as supplements, rock salt, minerals, shell grit and greenstuff and also grit to help them digest the food in their crops.

Waxbills and finches also need live food, while brush-tongues require a special diet, which is discussed separately on p. 26.

Aviculturalists often become excited about what they regard as the 'right' mixture of seed or supplements for their birds. However, the important point is to provide a variety, so that the birds can choose what they want. Birds' feeding habits change from time to time. In between breeding they will usually eat more seed, but when chicks are being reared, they will prefer bread soaked in milk or water or other soft rearing food.

It is wrong to prepare a seed mixture for birds from which they cannot extract the individual substances they want. For example, many aviculturalists prepare a supplement which consists of peanut butter mixed with a number of substances such as ProNutro, sugar, oats porridge and other foodstuffs.

This means that the birds are compelled to eat the rich peanut butter while they are really after the oats porridge, or that they have to eat this rich mixture whether they want to or not, because there is nothing else to eat. In this way birds can become obese, which in turn can lead to infertility.

Rather present the birds with the various foods separately, even if they are placed in the same bowl. Do not mix them. This gives the birds the opportunity to choose for themselves what they wish to eat.

Seed mixes

Birds are fairly adaptable as regards their seed intake and can tolerate the substitution of one type of seed with another. In the recipes that follow, the percentages are not critical, as the birds pick what they want for themselves. For example, the quantity of expensive canary seed can be reduced, or half the mixed birdseed can be replaced by grass seed, or Niger seed can be added. The important thing is that there should be a variety of seed because seeds differ as regards the amounts of vitamins, proteins and oils they contain, and the birds must have a choice according to their needs. The birds' needs as regards seed differ from time to time. For example, cockatiels with chicks often eat more fine seed than cockatiels without chicks.

When a variety of seed is placed in a single dish and presented to the birds, it often leads to wastage. The birds choose what they want and simply scratch out the rest. Rather place different seeds in different containers. Sunflower seed, budgie mix and peanuts for parrots can, for example, be placed in three separate containers.

Always ensure that the seeds you buy have not been treated for insects or fungi, but are meant specifically for birds. Seed sold for sowing is often fumigated with a poisonous substance.

Guidelines for suitable seed mixes:

Lovebirds: 25% sunflower seed, 10% oats, 10% sorghum, 5% canary seed and 50% mixed birdseed (white, yellow or red millet). The composition of this mixture can be varied within reason.

Budgies: 25% white millet, 25% yellow millet, 25% red millet, 25% canary seed. Because canary seed is so expensive, it is often omitted.

Parakeets: 70% budgie mix, 25% striped sunflower seed, 5% oats or sorghum.

Parrots: 20% budgie mix, 25% sunflower seed, 25% oats, 10% sorghum, 10% crushed maize, up to 10% peanuts. Also present parrots with pumpkin pips if available.

Finches: 25% white millet, 25% yellow millet, 25% red millet, 25% canary seed. A great variety of other seeds can be added in small quantities. The following is also a good mixture: 20% canary seed, 20% red millet, 20% yellow millet, 20% white millet, 10-15% Japanese millet and 5-10% other seed such as lucerne, turnip, radish, rye, lettuce and linseed.

Wild grass seeds in a separate dish make an excellent extra. Gouldians should always have Japanese millet in a separate dish as an extra.

Larger finches such as cardinals: 10% sunflower seed, 10% oats seed, 5% canary seed, 25% white millet, 25% yellow millet, 25% red millet.

Supplements

A seed mixture alone is inadequate to keep birds in good health, and without the necessary supplements they will become ill and eventually die. Extra supplements must be provided to fill hungry stomachs, particularly when there are chicks. Supplements supply essential vitamins, minerals and protein.

Supplements consist of greenstuff such as lettuce, parsley, fresh lucerne and weeds; peanut butter; bread; hard-boiled egg; fruit such as apples, pears, oranges, bananas and pawpaws; dried fruit such as raisins; vegetables such as raw carrots, peas in the pod, lettuce, spinach, cucumber and particularly raw green mealies; dog pellets or dogfood cakes, laying meal or growth meal for chicks. Nuts are expensive but essential for many of the parrot species.

The fruit and vegetables must be fresh and wholesome. Overripe fruit you do not wish to eat yourself will not do for the birds either. If fruit is scarce or unobtainable, tinned fruit can be offered. Birds unfamiliar with certain types of food may refuse such food for several weeks. It is important, however, that they learn to eat what is good for them. This is particularly the case with young birds that are used to being fed by their parents. Persist in offering them the rejected food. This is also important in the case of imported birds that are in the process of switching over from their natural diet to the types of food we can provide for them.

The droppings of birds that eat a good deal of fruit and vegetables become more watery. Some aviculturalists then think that the birds have had too much fruit to eat and this has caused scour (diarrhoea). However, this is not the true diarrhoea which indicates an illness, and can be regarded as normal. On the other hand, rotten and fermenting fruit can cause an upset stomach and cause the birds to fall ill due to bacterial infection.

The simplest supplement is brown bread soaked in water. Bread soaked in milk is better, but the milk soon goes sour and can then cause bacterial infections. The bread should not be very fresh, as fresh bread forms an indigestible lump in the stomach and may even cause the death of young chicks.

One of the very best supplements for virtually all birds, whether breeding or not, is the following mixture: mashed hard-boiled egg, minced meat or bone meal, chopped greenstuff such as spinach or grated carrot, and whole-wheat bread. No more should be given than the birds can finish in one hour, or the egg and meat will go off and cause scour and fatalities. Carrots, enough for quite a few days, can be minced in a meat grinder and kept in the refrigerator. Two days' supplies can be mixed at the same time and half of it kept in the refrigerator for use during the next day. If this is too expensive, the egg and meat can be omitted in aviaries where there are no chicks; those aviaries are still supplied with whole-wheat bread and chopped greenstuff.

Rearing mixture: This is sold by pet shops and is a good supplement for all birds. Mix it with water. The nutritional value can be increased by mixing mashed hard-boiled egg with it.

Egg: Hard-boiled egg mixed with bread, porridge or putu is an excellent supplement for all birds. After all, small birds develop from an egg – muscles, bones and all internal organs. Egg therefore contains most of the elements necessary to allow birds to grow. It has only one disadvantage, namely that it is a good growth medium for bacteria in warm weather. For this reason, supply only as much as the birds can eat within an hour.

Peanut butter: This is an excellent supplement and you must try to induce all birds to eat it. This is particularly desirable in the case of parakeets, parrots and brush-tongues. Peanut butter is rich in protein and contains a large variety of minerals and vitamins, as well as oil which maintains the feathers in a good, shiny condition. When birds have learnt to eat it, they like it a great deal.

Dog meal: Most birds benefit from an intake of animal protein. The most convenient way of supplying this is to place dog meal, laying meal or poultry growth meal in the aviary. This type of meal also contains vitamins, minerals and salt. The meal should not be allowed to become wet or old. Replace the bowl of meal at least once a week if it is not finished. Sometimes the birds select only certain parts of the meal and leave the rest. This does not mean that they should not get any more dog meal – what they do eat is all that they need. Mynahs and parrots can be fed soaked dog cakes or dog pellets. Brush-tongues can be taught to eat soaked dog meal, particularly if it has been slightly sweetened.

ProNutro: ProNutro is an excellent supplement. ProNutro makes things much easier for South African aviculturalists, particularly when hand-rearing small birds. Hand-rearing chicks is discussed in chapter 7.

Seed sprouts: Birds like seed sprouts, particularly when there are chicks. Finches will always greedily gulp down sprouted seeds. Any seed can be used to make sprouts.

Small seeds such as millet and Japanese millet is used for small birds, while larger seeds such as sorghum, oats and sunflower are more suitable for the parrot family. This is how you make seed sprouts:

Place the seed mixture in a holder and cover with water. This causes the seeds to swell. Place the holder in a warm place, e.g. a sunny windowsill, near the stove or near the motor which drives the freezer or refrigerator and where warmth is emitted.

After about 18 hours the seeds are placed in a sieve. An ordinary flour sieve is fine. Thoroughly rinse the swollen seeds with water.

Place the sieve with seeds in a warm place, e.g. a sunny windowsill. The seeds must become dry, but must not dry out. Shake them every now and then or turn them carefully with your hands so that the inner parts can also become dry. As soon as the sprouts have burst forth from the seed husk – after about 6-24 hours, depending on the temperature – the sprouts are ready. Place them in a container, cover with a lid and place the container in the refrigerator. Feed the sprouts to the birds over a period not exceeding two or three days at the most.

If the swollen seeds begin fermenting or smell bad at any stage, or if hairy fungi begin growing on them, discard them and start afresh.

Minerals: The most convenient way of supplying minerals is to buy a mineral mixture for racing pigeons. This is available from most pet shops. Place it permanently in a small container in the aviary. If you prefer to make your own mineral mixture, mix finely ground charcoal, fine oyster shell, bone meal or dicalcium phosphate plus iodised table salt in more or less equal parts.

Vitamins: If birds receive a good variety of greenstuff and supplements, it is unnecessary to add vitamins. However, extra vitamins are necessary when birds are under stress, such as during deworming, moulting, particularly during illness, when a pair is constantly breeding or has laid a large number of eggs, when it is very cold or during winter when greenstuff and fruit are unobtainable. When birds are sold and find themselves in a strange environment, they suffer a great deal of stress. Newly imported birds in particular must be supplied with extra vitamins and minerals.

Vitamins meant for poultry and which are added to the drinking water are suitable for birds. During stressful periods these can normally be supplied for five days in a row, or otherwise permanently one or two days a week. Of course a product which contains both minerals and vitamins is even better.

Eggshells: Of course all eggshells from the kitchen go to the aviaries. In aviaries with concrete floors a sod of clean earth is placed on the floor for waxbills and quail in particular (but finches as well) to peck and scratch in.

Bone meal: When the butcher saws a carcase, bone fragments, being a mixture of bone and meat, remain on the saw. As long as this is fresh, it is an excellent supplement for birds as it contains a great deal of calcium, phosphate and other bone minerals as well as protein. Boil it and feed it to all the birds.

Coarse grit: Clean grit or sand helps to grind down the seeds in the crop. Clean river sand is often available from nurseries. Unfortunately river sand is fairly smooth and therefore not the best for grinding seed in the crop. Fine granite grit is better.

Shell grit: This is commercially available and is used for chickens. It provides valuable minerals such as calcium.

Rock salt: Some owners provide rock salt, but if the birds are supplied with pigeon minerals, this is not necessary.

Spray millet: Books on aviculture published abroad often mention that spray millet is good for birds. This is not the millet grown in South Africa, but plants with particularly long ears containing a particular type of millet seed. The dried ears are imported and are available from pet shops, but are much too expensive if you keep a great many birds.

Branches: Parrots in particular like to chew branches and it is important that they get fresh branches, preferably every day. This not only supplies certain vitamins but also keeps them occupied, so that they are less inclined to pluck their feathers out of frustration. Be careful not to use poisonous branches. Shrubs growing in the garden are not necessarily safe. Willow branches, sugar cane and the unsprayed branches of all fruit trees can be offered with safety.

Animal protein

One of the greatest problems is to supply birds with fresh animal protein. This is particularly the case with finches. Most finches switch over to a high percentage of worms, spiders and other insects in their diets when they have chicks.

Even parrots eat worms when there are chicks in the nest. Crop analyses have shown that parrots and brush-tongues in the wild eat flower buds and bark, and in the process they also accidentally ingest insects. Although the general opinion is that parrot-like birds are not meat eaters, they do have a need for it.

Waxbills in particular need large numbers of live insects. Without insects they will not breed, or if they do, they will not be able to rear their chicks. However, it is difficult to supply birds with live food, and this is one of the greatest stumbling-blocks in the way of successful aviculture.

Live food in the form of grasshoppers, crickets, beetles, termites, young ants, caterpillars, spiders or flies is undoubtedly among the best of supplements, in particular for finches. In the case of waxbills it is essential for good breeding results.

Unfortunately the provision of live food is one of the most difficult tasks for the aviculturalist and one which is often neglected through sheer lack of time. This is also one of the main reasons why finches sometimes breed so badly or why the chicks die before they become adults.

Mealworms: Mealworms are a real boon to the aviculturalist needing live food for his birds. Mealworms are sometimes advertised in newspapers or agricultural magazines. If not, you have no option but to buy a start-up supply from another aviculturalist.

Place the mealworms in a drum, tin or box partly filled with bran. Place potatoes, apples and lettuce or beetroot leaves in the bran to supply moisture. The mealworms eat the bran and also the apples and potatoes. If the bran becomes wet and messy, there are too many potatoes or apples in the culture. The bran must remain dry.

Close the holder with a double layer of muslin. This allows air in, but prevents the tiny acarida moths which occur in spoilt grain from laying their eggs in the bran. The worms (mites) of these moths are deadly to the mealworms.

Mature mealworms change into pupae, which in turn become beetles. The beetles lay eggs and the next generation of mealworms hatch from these eggs.

The entire process lasts about six to nine months. The warmer the temperature and the mealworm culture, the quicker the worms progress through all their stages. As the worms and beetles grow, they moult. The new skin is white and soft and during this stage they are particularly suitable for the birds. When the worms' skins are brown, they are very hard and indigestible. (This is one of the reasons why birds' intake of mealworms must be limited.)

Small finches should not get more than about two worms per day. When there are a large number of birds in an aviary, it is best to place the worms in a good number of different places so that the stronger and greedier birds do not grab everything.

If the worms are fed to very small birds such as waxbills, it is better to chop them into pieces, as the worms are fairly large. Worms with hard skins can be boiled and the contents squeezed from the skin, or they can be finely chopped so that the birds can get at the soft parts. A greedy bird often swallows a whole worm, skin and all, and can then suffer from acute indigestion.

The black beetles are not fed to the birds. They are very hard and should preferably be used to produce eggs and keep the worm culture going.

Termites and ants: In some regions of South Africa aviculturalists are much more fortunate than their counterparts in Europe or America. We have anthills, and we should use this bounty from nature to the full.

Birds do not eat the small red ants, but do eat the eggs and the young white ants you find in the breeding chambers deep in the nest. Birds also do not eat the soldiers of termite nests, but they love the eggs and young termites that are found deeper in the nest.

Dig deep into the nest to reach the honeycombed breeding chambers where the eggs and young ants are found. Store these combs under a wet sack in the shade. The young ants and eggs remain alive for a long time and this reduces the need to drive out for a supply to only once every one or two weeks.

The birds, particularly waxbills, should get ants or termites every day if possible. If the ants or termites are scarce, three times a week will also help. Birds that receive ants as part of their diet should be dewormed regularly because the ants sometimes act as intermediary hosts for certain worms which contaminate caged birds (see chapter 8 for deworming).

Fruit flies: Fruit flies, too, are a good source of live protein. Place one or more deep tins (a petrol or oil can of 5 litres) in the aviary.

Place overripe fruit or fruit peels in the bottom of the tin and close it off with chicken wire so that the birds cannot get at the fruit. In a day or two fruit flies will fly about above the tin, and small birds will catch them with glee.

Maggots: Suspend wet meat above a piece of chicken wire stretched across a container. Place moist bran in the holder. Try to keep the meat moist while it rots. With luck bluebottles will lay their eggs in the meat. After a while grubs hatch out of the eggs and eat the putrid meat. At this stage the maggots are black on the inside because they are full of rotten meat, and are therefore not suitable food for the birds.

Eventually the maggots fall through the chicken wire into the container with moist bran, where they eat the clean bran. As soon as the insides of the maggots no longer appear black, they can be given to the birds.

Grasshoppers: At certain times of the year grasshoppers are plentiful. Catch them and feed them to the birds.

Another method of supplying the birds with live insects is to plant plants in the aviary. This will attract insects which can be caught by the birds.

Certain bird species such as Pekin robins can be supplied with insects by allowing them to fly about outside the aviary. As soon as the chicks have emerged from the shells, the aviary's gate can be opened so that the parents can fly about freely outside in order to catch insects. The birds will always return to the chicks, unless a cat, owl or hawk spirits them away.

In conclusion: All birds of the parrot family and common finches get seed, some or other high protein supplement, a mineral mixture, shell grit and coarse grit. The supplement must contain protein such as hard-boiled egg, peanut butter, dog pellets or dog meal, or ProNutro.

Smaller parrot-like birds like budgies and lovebirds will often refuse fruit and eat only greenstuff. Larger parakeets will eat fruit as well, while parrots eat everything going (including meat and the furniture).

Waxbills, strawberry finches and Pekin robins must get live food together with the above diet. Mynahs live mainly on dog pellets and a great deal of fruit, but will also eat seed. The diet of rare and exotic species such as touracas and toucans, which have to be fed frogs and mice, is not discussed.

Brush-tongues

In Europe and America people feed their brush-tongues nectar which they prepare from honey dissolved in water, with other food elements mixed with it. This is generally not done in South Africa.

There are various ways of feeding brush-tongues. One is to use ProNutro as a staple food. The ProNutro is mixed with water to make a thin porridge and then sweetened with sugar or honey. ProNutro contains a great variety of essential vitamins and minerals as well as a good quantity of proteins together with the necessary fat and carbohydrates.

Because honey contains vitamins and minerals, it is a better sweetener for the ProNutro than sugar. However, it is expensive, particularly if you need to feed a large number of brush-tongues. If enough fruit is supplied, it does no harm to replace the honey with sugar.

Be careful not to sweeten the food too much because oversweetened food can lead to the birds contracting the deadly fungal infection, *Candida albicans*. This fungus, also called thrush, is a white growth in the mouth and throat which thrives on sugars. *Candida albicans* can cause great distress and even death and is extremely difficult to eradicate once it has taken root. The food must therefore be only slightly sweet, not syrupy. Of course the ProNutro must be freshly mixed every day. Two-day-old ProNutro can go bad and cause scour in the birds.

A second popular feeding method is to give the birds soaked dog pellets. The pellets must be presented fresh every day, as harmful fungi can grow on the damp meal, or it may otherwise ferment and turn sour. The advantage of dog meal is that it has a high protein value and also contains the necessary vitamins and minerals. In nature brush-tongues also take in essential worms and insects when they eat flowers. The protein in dog meal compensates for this to a certain extent.

A staple food of ProNutro or dog meal is, however, not sufficient to keep brush-tongues in good condition. Good fresh fruit, particularly apples, pears or grapes, must supplement the daily diet. Raisins soaked in water, and dates, are welcome delicacies.

Some brush-tongues like eating seed, despite the belief that they do not do this. Brush-tongues who are not familiar with seeds learn to eat them when they are available. Place a small bowl with mixed seed (a parakeet mix is suitable) in the aviary. They are partial to sunflower seeds, but will also eat other seeds.

When there are chicks, bread soaked in water or milk must be added daily. Normally the breeding pair eats more seed when there are no chicks, but as soon as there are chicks, they switch to bread and milk.

Peanut butter is an excellent supplement. Newly acquired birds, as well as young birds fresh from the nest, will ignore the peanut butter for weeks on end before they learn to eat it. However, it is worth persevering until the birds have learnt to eat it. Peanut butter contains many vitamins, minerals and proteins, as well as oils that help to keep the birds' feathers in good condition.

The aviary must always contain a bowl with minerals which also contains salt. A mineral mix meant for pigeons is commercially available. It is suitable for placing inside the aviaries of all birds.

In conclusion: Brush-tongues' staple food is ProNutro mixed with honey and water, or wet dog meal. Provide this freshly mixed every day. Supplement the staple food daily with a variety of fruit, peanut butter and bread soaked in milk. Seed and a mineral mixture must always be available. Replace this every two weeks or earlier if it is dirty. This diet will keep brush-tongues healthy and breeding well for years.

Because fresh food and fruit must be provided every day, this may cause problems when you wish to go away, even for a long weekend. You can, however, go away for a few days even though there is nobody to look after the brush-tongues.

Place whole apples or pears in the aviary so that their insides are protected by the peel – they will not dry out so quickly. A bunch of grapes will also last a few days. Place a thick slice of fruitcake (with plenty of fruit) in the aviary. Given the apples, fruitcake and seed – which is in the aviary at all times anyway – the birds will be able to manage on their own for a few days. (This is another reason why the birds should learn to eat seed.)

However, it is not wise to do this while there are chicks, because they could die of hunger.

6

Buying birds

How do you buy birds?

The aviaries are all ready and the nests have been hung up. Now the birds have to be bought. Our avid aviculturalist trots off to the nearest pet shop dealing in birds or a breeder who has birds for sale. Bird fever is at its highest: his judgement is distorted by excitement and desire and he clinches his deal – how good or bad, will only be apparent to him later.

How is he to get the birds home? No problem, a brown paper bag with holes in it is just the ticket! The poor birds – finches, normally – are shoved into the paper bag, carefully placed on the front seat of the car and the new aviculturalist drives home, highly pleased with himself.

At the stop street he peeps into the bag to make sure that the birds are not too hot, and zip – one or more of the birds flits out. We have always known that, like time, money flies, but in this instance our bird fancier has the opportunity of seeing with his own eyes how his money flies away. At home he carefully opens the paper bag, but horror of horrors – most of the remaining birds are lying dead on the bottom, asphyxiated. No, this is not the way to buy birds; you must buy or build a travel box.

Travel boxes

A travel box can be used again and again and will normally give you many years' service. Of course travel boxes must have no sharp nails or wires on the inside. They must provide enough shelter for frightened birds to hide away, i.e. they must be largely of wood with only a small area of wire

at the front for light and air. A handle on top of the travel box is handy. A few holes must be drilled in the sides for air, particularly if it is a large box which will contain many birds (see photos 20 and 21).

The water containers in the box are fixed with wire to ensure that they do not move about. The edges of the tins are crimped over to ensure that the birds do not cut themselves. To prevent the water from slopping out, a round piece of foam rubber with a hole in the centre is placed on top of the water. Less efficient, but better than nothing, is a wad of cotton wool in the water container. If the water slops out, the birds can still obtain some moisture by pressing their bills into the wet cotton wool.

If the road is long, place half an orange in the box. If the box contains finches, the segments must be cut so small that, if they roll about, they will not injure the birds.

There should rather be too much food and too few birds in a travel box than the other way round. The longer the journey, the fewer birds there should be in a box. Large and small birds must travel apart, otherwise the large birds will bite the smaller ones and injure or even kill them. Certain species, in particular brush-tongues and parrots, may even bite their own kind to death in a travel box.

When birds are dispatched by train or aeroplane, the receiver's telephone number must be clearly indicated on the box as well as on the waybill so that the station can trace

21 A travel box with enough room for a good number of birds which have to be transported over long distances. Note the perches on the inside. The front is slanted so that the air supply cannot be cut off when two boxes are placed with their fronts facing. Rows of holes on the sides provide fresh air. Tins with crimped edges for water are fixed to the wire end so that the birds can spot them easily. A flat door is screwed over the travel box's opening with four screws.

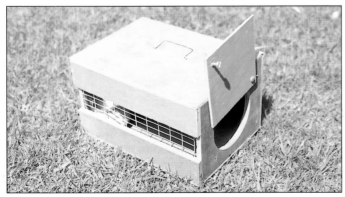

20 This is the standard travel box in which small numbers of birds are transported. This travel box is also suitable for transporting one or two birds by aircraft.

22 A bird with a bad bite can be securely held in this manner. The thumb is inserted behind the attachment of the lower bill to the skull. Try not to throttle the bird!

the receiver. It is of the utmost importance that the sender informs the receiver of exactly when he can expect the birds.

Always ensure that the birds will make the correct train or postal connection. Do not send birds by train just before the weekend, as far too many birds die because they had to spend a weekend at a station without being collected or because they were too late for a particular connection.

Parrots need a travel box made of thick, sturdy wood. What is important is that the inside of the box should be smooth so that the bird cannot find any spot to start biting. It is a great disappointment to go to the station to collect an empty travel box with a hole in it while the expensive parrot is flying about somewhere over the Karoo.

Capture net

A capture net consists of thick wire bent into a circle and attached to a handle. The wire is then wrapped with strips of foam rubber to ensure that the birds are not knocked senseless by the wire. A bag of light, gauzy material is then fixed to the wire in the manner of a wind sock. Capture nets are often available commercially. Just make sure that the wire of the capture net you buy is covered with foam rubber.

Where do you buy birds?

In the first place birds can be bought from dealers in birds. Such dealers buy South African-bred birds from breeders or import birds and then sell this supply to aviculturalists. Normally the dealers have a great variety of birds available, and they advertise in newspapers and magazines, particularly agricultural magazines, among others.

One disadvantage of buying birds from a bird dealer is that aviculturalists often sell birds which won't breed to these dealers. These non-breeders, as well as older birds,

are then eventually offered to the novice. Another disadvantage is that such a collection point for birds from many sources is, of course, also a collection point for diseases from a great variety of aviaries. The aviculturalist must therefore ensure that the birds he buys are healthy and not obviously old.

On the other hand the dealers often obtain large stocks of young birds from breeders and such young birds are a very good buy. Sometimes one of a breeding pair dies and the dealer then obtains the other for sale. Such an odd female or male can also be an excellent buy.

The imported birds for sale from dealers have advantages as well as disadvantages. Imported birds must be acclimatised carefully as they have usually spent weeks in very sheltered circumstances in the quarantine station. They have usually adapted to South African food. Rather buy imported birds in summer when there is no danger of sudden cold. It is also preferable to give them extra vitamins for a week or two. Imported birds are a good source of new blood.

Birds can also be bought directly from breeders. Of course the variety offered by a breeder is smaller than that of a dealer, and there could be problems with inbreeding. Always be wary of so-called breeding pairs. Unless an aviculturalist is selling all his birds because of his own poor health, pressure of work or having to move, he will not normally sell his good breeding pairs. Often the old birds and non-breeders are the ones being disposed of. Rather buy young birds, even if you have to wait a year or two before they begin breeding. Of course the very best buy is a breeding pair together with their young.

Pet shops are also a source of good imported or young locally bred birds. Be aware of the same traps, i.e. that you may be offered old birds or non-breeders, or birds which have contracted diseases.

Things to note when buying birds:

Are the aviculturalist's aviaries reasonably clean? Are the drinking containers clean? Do the birds appear healthy or ill? Stand back from the aviary a bit so that the birds are not disturbed by your presence and then judge their appearance. Are they sitting with feathers puffed up and their eyes closed? Of course if it is very cold all birds puff themselves up, but their eyes should remain bright and alert.

Are the feathers nice and smooth, or are they tatty? A bird with smooth feathers is a healthy bird. Moulting birds (usually about January), newly imported birds and birds in small cages (in which they are inclined to bite each other) often have tatty feathers. In such cases that is not necessarily an indication of disease. Nevertheless, examine a tatty bird carefully.

If the birds' eyes are bright and they move and sit normally, they may be caught and examined more closely. First of all examine the vent. If this is wet, leave well alone and do not buy! Before the bird itself dies of scour, it will infect all the other birds in your aviary and contaminate the aviary itself. Never buy a bird showing signs of diarrhoea.

However, birds which often get greenstuff or fruit may have soft or even slightly watery droppings, which must be distinguished from true diarrhoea. A bird with diarrhoea proper has feathers which are badly smeared. A slight wetness can be the result of greenstuff.

Feel the bird's breastbone. If the bird is very thin, it may suffer from some malady or have been poorly fed. Such a bird has a much reduced ability to resist the shock of adapting to a new aviary. Therefore buy only birds that are nicely plump.

If the bird is plump, its eyes are bright and the vent is dry, you can just about produce your wallet. But just examine the bill before you do. An old bird's bill is often rough, scaly or full of fine cracks. The bill must be normally shaped and smooth. Look at the joints of the legs and toes. There should be no sign of swelling or arthritis. Blow open the bird's feathers and look for lice. A badly infected bird has a very low resistance and such a bird unnecessarily transports lice to your aviary. In all cases it is a good habit to dust newly bought birds with louse powder before placing such birds in your own aviary.

Now place the bird in the travel box and watch it until it has calmed down. Sometimes a bird is injured during the process of capture. If a wing has been broken, it will hang limp. If it has knocked its head against the wire or has been banged with the capture net, it will sit with its eyes closed and may even die within a few hours.

Shock and injuries during capture are some of the reasons why birds sometimes die shortly after they arrive at a new aviary. Other causes are that they do not know where the feeding or water containers are, or that the settled inhabitants of the aviary chase away the newcomers to such an extent that they get no opportunity to eat.

When releasing new birds into an aviary, the food and water must be clearly visible. Scatter some of the food on the ground.

Birds can also succumb from the cold during the first night because they could not find a suitable place to sleep. Birds used to sleeping in boxes, such as finches and lovebirds, are particularly prone to this. Birds must therefore be released into a new aviary early in the day so that they can get to know the aviary before it gets dark. During winter new arrivals in particular must be protected from the cold.

Imported birds

An imported bird has normally suffered, whether it was captured in the wild or was hatched in the breeding aviaries of Europe. In the first place it endured a long journey in a small travel box among a press of birds where the strong ones bite and bully the weaker ones. Sometimes the birds suffer from hunger and thirst during the flight, which is sometimes delayed and may last up to a week. Then they suffer more crowding in small rooms in the quarantine station lasting three or four weeks.

In Europe birds are often bred in heated rooms. Others originate in the tropics. They are all susceptible to the cold and during winter in particular they cannot simply be released into an open aviary. During nights of sudden cold they will die, and therefore they must first acclimatise. However, this is no reason to avoid imported birds. With a bit of initial care the aviculturalist can enjoy the advantages of imported birds, e.g. new blood or new species. It is not unusual for imported finches to begin breeding within three weeks of their arrival.

Buy imported birds only in late spring to early autumn while the weather is still warm. Should you buy such birds in winter, it is best to keep them indoors until spring, or, in regions of the country where it becomes very cold in winter, to place them in a heated aviary which is protected from cold winds. Add a multivitamin supplement to their water for five or ten days. The kind given to poultry is suitable.

Do not put the birds onto antibiotics without good reason. This is done only if there are really sick birds. The reason is that antibiotics not only kill the bacteria that cause illnesses, but also the essential bacteria that occur in the bird's alimentary canal, and this in turn can lead to scour. Furthermore it is very likely that the imported birds have already been treated with antibiotics before or after they were imported.

As soon as the birds are settled in their new environment, they must be dewormed. Also give special attention to their diet. Imported birds must be strengthened and a full diet with a variety of foodstuffs is the answer. All that is necessary is special care for two to three weeks. Thereafter the imported birds will give their owner many years of joy.

Which bird species mix well?

The beginner often thinks that you buy a good variety of birds and release all of them together into one aviary. However, this often does not work at all. Even birds of the same species often do not get on well with one another and will fight to the death in the limited space of an aviary.

The size of the aviary is of crucial importance. Birds that fight in a small aviary may co-exist quite peacefully in a larger one. However, most kinds breed best if there is only one pair of that species in an aviary. An extra male, in particular, can interfere to such a degree that breeding cannot take place at all.

Zebra and Bengalese finches and many of the lovebird species such as Fischer's, black-masked and Madagascar lovebirds are colony breeders and will tolerate more than one pair to an aviary, but even in their case breeding results decline if the aviary becomes too crowded.

It is impossible to give all possible combinations that may be grouped together, as there are far too many bird species. Sometimes a few of the so-called peaceful species will unaccountably become aggressive and start causing trouble against all expectations. At other times so-called troublemakers such as cardinals will live together with smaller birds quite peacefully as long as there is ample room.

Meek species such as gouldians should preferably not live in a mixed collection, unless they share it with quail. Quail adapt well to most bird species because they occupy the space on the floor and do not compete with the birds in the air for nests and perches.

Birds in the same aviary must be of equal strength or otherwise should not need to compete for the same food and nesting facilities. This means that meek cockatiels or grass parakeets that eat sunflower seed and do not use grass for their nests will fit in well with finches that eat fine seed and make grass nests. However, the wingbeats of larger birds may badly frighten smaller birds, particularly if there is little flying space.

The beginner can place one or more pairs of the following species together: diamond doves, pygmy doves, zebra finches, Bengalese finches, canaries, grass finches, Cordon Bleus, Amadiens, diamond sparrows, African silverbills, red-eared waxbills, orange-cheeked waxbills, spice finches, Chinese quail, any of the grass parakeets, budgies and cockatiels. A large number of waxbills and finches can also be added to this list.

Limit the number of zebra and Bengalese finches because they often interfere with the nest-building of other species. Do not place pheasants or ducks in an aviary with finches or doves. The first day or so after finch and dove chicks have emerged from the nest, they cannot fly and the pheasants and ducks regard them as tasty snacks.

Lovebirds such as Fischer's and black-masked lovebirds interbreed and therefore only one species should be kept to an aviary. Three-coloured and red-headed parrot finches interbreed and so do the grass finches such as long-tailed and Heck's grass finches and Parson finches.

Certain parakeets can live together in a large aviary, although it is common practice to keep only one pair to an aviary. An aviary of 10 m × 10 m can easily house a number of species from the following list: grass parakeets, cockatiels, ringnecks, canarywings, redrumps and plumheads. The ground can be occupied by singing and Californian quail *or* one pair of pheasants. (Pheasant males fight each other to the death during the breeding season. An aviary may therefore accommodate more than one female, but never more than one male.) Quail and pheasants cannot live together, because the pheasants eat the quail chicks.

Some of the larger parakeets such as Princess of Wales,

moustached and Alexandrine parakeets should rather be kept one pair to an aviary, unless it is very large.

When an aviary is in balance, in other words when each bird has found a niche it can call its own and has made peace with its neighbours, this balance is easily disturbed by a newcomer. The established inhabitants can quite easily peck the newcomer to death or harass it to such an extent that it never gets a chance to eat. This is a major cause of deaths within the first two or three days after new birds have been bought. In such case a finger is unfortunately often pointed at the seller who has 'cheated' or 'sells poor birds'.

It helps a lot if an aggressive chaser is removed from the aviary for a few days to give the newcomer a chance to settle down.

Aggression against what the birds regard as an intruder often results in birds such as diamond sparrows and lovebirds pecking chicks which have just emerged from the nest to death. This happens when too many lovebirds live together. It can often be avoided by keeping together in one aviary only two pairs which know each other well. If not, the chicks must be removed as soon as they climb out of the nest and placed in a small cage in which a good deal of food has been scattered. Also provide them with soft food such as bread soaked in water, or canary rearing mix. They will begin eating by themselves, because lovebirds are quite mature when they climb out of the nest.

If you notice that the chicks cannot eat enough by themselves, place them in a small cage with about 1,5 cm × 1,5 cm gauge wire. Put food and water in the cage and place the cage in the aviary with the parents. Good parents will feed the chicks through the wire, while other birds will not be able to peck them.

How many birds in an aviary?

The golden rule is: the fewer, the better. A great many birds cooped up together will always fight for perches, space, nests, food or females. This detracts from breeding results and causes injuries and even fatalities.

Each bird must have a nest where it can sit peacefully without constantly having to chase away other birds which perch too close to its nest. The average backyard aviary of 1 m wide × 3 m long × 2 m high can house at most four pairs of finches or other small birds, and perhaps a pair of quail on the floor. Another combination is one pair of grass parakeets, one pair of doves, one pair of finches and one pair of quail.

7

Sexing, the egg and hand-rearing

Sexing

Sex determination is the bane of aviculture. Unfortunately it is also the cause of many a dispute and suspicion between buyer and seller when a supposed female turns out, at the next moulting, to be a young male. In the case of many birds, e.g. the brush-tongues, the two sexes look so much alike that it is only by surgical means that the sex can be determined without any doubt.

A few veterinarians perform surgical sexing. The bird is anaesthetised and an endoscope is inserted into the abdomen. With the aid of a light the sex organs are then examined. There is a small risk that the bird may die from the anaesthetic or because of bleeding. When birds are very young, the method is not totally accurate either. However, it is the best method available and the reason why parrots are presently breeding in captivity with much greater success than before.

Surgical sexing is not available everywhere, which means that other methods have to be used as well. With practice you can determine the sex of a bird fairly accurately, but nobody can ever really guarantee it. In the case of expensive birds such as parrots it really is worth the trouble to find a vet who can perform surgical sexing.

How to determine the sex

Lay the bird on its back in your hand. The legs must be relaxed and not wedged tight against anything. Using the tip of the finger, gently feel where the two pelvic bones come together just in front of the anal opening (see photo 23). In the male the ends of the bones almost touch and they are hard and relatively rigid, except in the case of young males, where the bones are still soft and pliable.

In females the ends lie further apart. In the case of a bird as large as a lovebird part of the forefinger can be inserted in between the two pelvic bones of a female. The tips of the bones are often soft and can move slightly so that the egg can pass through with ease.

It is important that the birds subjected to this test should always lie in the same position, because differences in pressure on the legs will change the size of the opening between the pelvic bones.

Young males may sometimes be mistaken for females because their pelvic bones are still soft and pliable. You also come across individuals where you cannot clearly determine whether they are male or female. Still, this remains one of the best tests for sexing.

Small bird species such as finches cannot be tested in this way.

Another method is to compare heads and bills. In the case of most adult birds the head of the male is broader and the bill more robust, larger, heavier and coarser (see photos 24 and 25).

An additional method is to hold the bird (usually a finch) on its back in one's hand. The legs must be totally relaxed. The legs of a female are sometimes held parallel while those of a male form a slight V.

Blow onto the vent. Sometimes this causes the bird to push downwards. If a tip appears, it is a male.

Watch the birds through binoculars. In this way you can determine which males are courting which females. The

23 This is how the finger is gently inserted between the pelvic bones to determine the sex of the bird. With practice you will learn to discern the difference between males and females.

24 The male (right) of this outstanding Fischer's lovebird breeding pair can be recognised by, among other things, its broader forehead. The larger beak confirms that it is a male.

25 Here it is clear that the beak of the male (right) is larger and coarser than that of the female. The entire head of the male is also heavier and larger.

males dance, puff themselves up or bring bits of grass. Carefully observe the supposed male or female to recognise some or other mark on the bird so that you can catch him or her in the aviary.

Another method is to place a female in an open cage in amongst a flock of birds. Males will court her through the wire, while other females will merely have a look and then fly away.

In the same way as there are large females and small males among humans, we find them among birds. The relative sizes of the birds are therefore not necessarily an indication of their sex.

In the case of bird species where the males and females look alike, depth of colour is often an indication of whether it is a male or female. For example, the red on the breast of a male Peter's twinspot is often brighter and more widely distributed than in the case of a female, but once again this cannot be regarded as an absolute indication. In the case of Senegals the orange on the breast and belly often differs from one individual to the next, and it is incorrect to assume that all those with deeper orange on the breast are males. In the case of Senegals surgical sexing is the only accurate method.

Infertility

One breeds birds without taking into account their own preferences. When a pair refuses to breed, they are either both of the same sex, or they do not like each other. Exchange them for other birds and observe what happens.

It could also be that the male is infertile. The female will then lay eggs and brood, but the eggs will not hatch. If the female is infertile, the male will court and may even mate, but there will be no eggs.

It is better to start afresh with new birds than to try and stimulate an infertile bird by means of feeding; the causes of infertility are many, e.g. an infection in the female's oviduct.

The egg

When birds lay eggs with poor shells, or misshapen eggs, it can often be corrected by means of improved feeding. Give the birds eggshells, shell grit or laying meal to eat.

If eggs are ready for hatching, but no chicks emerge, the problem may be with the shell. (There may also be other reasons, e.g. that the female has abandoned the nest because of fright, heat or lice.)

Too much calcium results in a shell which is too hard. When the water contains too much calcium, particularly when a well-meaning breeder adds extra calcium to the water, the birds have no choice but to take in the calcium, even though they may have no need for it. Rather supply the calcium in the form of eggshells, shell grit or laying meal so that birds can choose for themselves whether they want to eat it or not.

Too little calcium results in an elastic shell which will not crack when the chick pecks at it.

Dry eggshells do not crack. Broody birds must have the opportunity of bathing and taking moisture into the nest with their feathers. Finches and lovebirds must have green nesting material, which also helps to provide moisture.

Fresh eggs sink in water. Eggs that are partly on their way to hatching float half-way and old rotten eggs float on top. Unfortunately eggs close to hatching also float on top and many beginners destroy 'old' eggs because they float on top, only to discover that they were close to hatching.

An unfertilised egg's shell looks more translucent than that of a fertilised egg. When you observe an egg close to hatching by holding it up to a bright light, a dark spot will be clearly visible inside the egg.

Birds usually lay a certain limited number of eggs and then begin to brood. If the eggs are removed before or shortly after the female has begun to brood, she quite often dutifully begins to lay again.

In this way you can 'milk' her to persuade her to lay much more than she normally would. The eggs are then hatched by other, less valuable birds.

It may happen that such a 'milked' female may continue to lay eggs – eventually mostly infertile ones – until she collapses. Do not, therefore, overdo the 'milking'. It is a good idea to allow the female to brood after she has laid twice her normal quota.

Remember that females lay eggs even if no male is present. However, these eggs will be infertile.

Foster care

Experienced aviculturalists swop eggs (and chicks) among their various birds. Whether the breeding pairs will raise foster children or not depends a great deal on their temperament.

Usually the foster mother's own eggs are removed, unless they are just as close to hatching as the stranger's ones. If her chicks hatch long before the foster children, she will stop brooding. One or two days' difference is still acceptable.

Finch eggs or discarded finch chicks are given to Bengalese and zebra finches and African silverbills to raise.

The eggs of birds of the parrot family are placed under cockatiels. However, cockatiels will often get rid of a brightly coloured foster child when its feathers appear. In this case hand-rearing is the only option.

The chicks of budgies and lovebirds can be exchanged.

Red-rumped parakeets are good foster mothers for brightly coloured chicks. They themselves are so brightly coloured that they will even raise green chicks very well.

Most parrot species breeding for the first time are too stupid to know what their chicks are supposed to look like and will rear strange chicks until adulthood.

Young discarded chicks can also be placed among foster parents' own chicks. With a bit of luck the female may feed them along with her own, as long as the chicks are all roughly the same age.

The younger the chicks are when placed in the care of the foster mother, the better the chances are that she will adopt them.

Nest deaths

There are various reasons why bird parents will abandon their eggs or chicks:

☐ It is too hot. If a nest hangs directly in the sun, the female may no longer be able to stand the heat and may simply abandon the nest. This can also happen during the hottest time of the year.

☐ Lice: If the nest is crawling with lice and the female is also infested, no aviculturalist can expect her to sit still on a nest.

☐ Mites: When these blood-sucking pests converge on brooding birds at night, the birds get out of the way. (See chapter 8 for the control of parasites.)

☐ Exhaustion: The phenomenon of parents abandoning their chicks often manifests itself when they begin raising their third or fourth brood of the year. This happens particularly when there is only seed available and they have to feed a whole bunch of screaming chicks by dehusking the seeds one by one, eating them and then feeding them to the chicks. A variety of soft foods such as bread, grated carrots and hard-boiled egg, which can be ingested without too much trouble, will help a great deal to head off such occurrences. Take away the nests and/or males after two broods – even if only for about eight weeks' duration – to give the female a break.

☐ Cold: Young birds are prone to dying of cold. Their metabolism has not yet developed sufficiently for them to maintain their own body temperature. In winter it is still bitterly cold at 08h00, and if the female has left the nest at 07h00, perhaps because she was disturbed by humans, the chicks can die of cold within 15 minutes. It is not a good idea to enter an aviary containing a brooding female or one with small chicks on bitterly cold days before the day has warmed up.

☐ Fright at night: Cats leaping onto the roof of an aviary at night cause a great deal of damage. The birds fly up from their nests in fright and cannot find their way back in the dark; the next morning all the chicks have died of cold, or the embryos are dead. This can also happen during a heavy thunderstorm or hailstorm. It is a good idea to let a 25-watt night light burn in every aviary.

☐ The aviculturalist fusses around the nest too much.

☐ Other birds bother the breeding parents, who constantly have to leave the nest in order to defend it against intruders. If other birds prevent the parents from returning to their nest after they have eaten, they may also become discouraged and give up trying. Ensure that there is enough flying space near each nest so that birds can brood in peace.

Kicking out chicks

Finches in particular are sometimes prone to kicking their chicks out of the nest. When the chicks are about eight to ten days old, the male kicks them out of the nest because he wants to mate and build another nest and the chicks are in his way.

In the case of most finch species the female will raise the chicks on her own if the male is removed. As some males help with the brooding, they are removed only once the chicks have hatched.

It sometimes helps to have a good number of additional nests in the aviary. While the chicks are being raised in one, the parents can begin preparing another one.

Sometimes it is of no use to remove the male. In such cases the female is the one who kicks out the chicks, particularly if she is young or exhausted. If the aviculturalist knows in advance that certain parents never feed their chicks or will kick them out of the nest, it is best to give the eggs or young chicks to other birds to rear.

Hand-rearing

When young birds are kicked out of the nest, or when the parents do not feed them enough or simply leave them to their own devices, many bird species can be hand-reared with great success. However, it requires a good deal of time and particularly patience, and the birds must be treated extremely gently at all times.

Warmth is an abandoned bird's first need, particularly if it is still naked. A young bird is very vulnerable to death from cold, particularly if placed in a cardboard box on its own. Keeping such birds warm can be a big problem.

The best idea is to place the chick on a piece of cotton wool in a cardboard box. Suspend a weak light bulb above the box. Take care that it does not become too hot, particularly if the chick is still too young to move away. It is a good

26 An ideal hospital cage or incubator for young birds which are being hand-reared. The temperature is thermostatically controlled.

idea to place a lid on the box, if possible – in their natural environment the chicks live in a dark nest. Never place a chick, particularly one without feathers, directly in the sun; it can become dehydrated and die within an hour.

Feeding

Very young birds only a few days old can rarely be raised successfully. Sometimes the parents simply feed the chicks too little, but do not discard them entirely and one or two additional meals are all that is necessary to save the chick.

ProNutro or infant porridge mixed with water and a little milk, with added hard-boiled egg and a vitamin/mineral mixture, is normally used to hand-rear small birds. Milk is not actually a natural food for birds, but it does provide essential animal protein. Because most birds are fruit eaters, a drop or two of orange juice can be added. Pro-Nutro absorbs water for some time, and what is at first a watery porridge can turn into a thick, sticky goo two minutes later – enough to choke a young bird or cause it much discomfort in its crop. Therefore mix the ProNutro very thinly, also because it is the chick's only source of moisture.

Young finches take only a few hours to learn to open their beaks when you lift the lid off the box in which they are kept. The porridge can then be pushed down their throats with the back of a teaspoon. It can also be placed in a syringe and squirted into the birds' open beaks.

Although the porridge will ensure that the birds grow, it lacks animal protein. To compensate, a mealworm can be fed to each chick every day. Mealworms have hard skins, so cut off the head, allow the worm to slide down the finch's beak a short distance with the open end downmost, and squeeze the contents from the skin. The contents of the worm can also be mixed with the porridge.

Egg constitutes almost the ideal food for young birds. Raw or hard-boiled egg yolk mixes well with ProNutro and will compensate for a lack of insects.

Birds which open their beaks by themselves, or eat from a teaspoon by themselves, can be fed with a coarser mixture than ProNutro. Mix rearing mixture, which is available from pet shops, with mashed hard-boiled egg, a few drops of orange juice and a drop or two of multivitamin preparation. Ensure that the mixture is moistened well with water, as the bird has no other source of water. Experienced aviculturalists often make their own mixture which works very well.

It is more difficult to feed young parrot-like birds than finches, because they do not open their beaks themselves. They can often be taught to eat from a teaspoon. If not, buy a 10-cm³ or 20-cm³ syringe (the type with which injections are given). Fill it with watery ProNutro, insert the spout (without the needle, of course) in the bird's beak and squirt the porridge into the beak. Birds quickly learn to eat in this way. Do not spill porridge onto the bird, because it dries hard, and the only way of removing it is to cut off the feathers. If porridge is spilt, it must be wiped off immediately.

Older finches which have been abandoned will no longer open their beaks for a teaspoon. This causes problems. Older parrot-like birds, too, snap their beaks shut and refuse to be hand-reared. In such cases force-feeding is the only solution.

For this purpose you buy a bicycle tube valve (a thin rubber tube). Slip this over the spout of the syringe, wet the rubber tube with water or liquid paraffin, force open the bird's beak and gently insert the tube as far as its crop. Slowly squirt the porridge into the crop (use your finger to feel the crop) until it is well filled. A crop will not burst if it is filled with too much food; the excess could spill over into the throat and the bird might inhale it and choke.

You quickly learn how to insert the tube into the crop without causing any damage. If it does not slip in easily, it may be that you have inserted it into the windpipe. If you squirt in the porridge now, the bird will die immediately. A tube inserted into the gullet usually moves freely.

Very young birds need to be fed a little every two hours, and older birds about every four hours. In the latter case the meals are larger. Nearly grown chicks can make do with three large meals a day. Hand-reared parrots are normally very tame and make good pets. They often prefer human company to that of their own species.

27 Young parrot-like birds can often be taught to eat from a teaspoon, but if you find this too difficult, it is best to fill a syringe with thin porridge and squirt it into the bird's beak. They soon learn to open their beaks for the syringe.

8

Combating diseases

There are a number of diseases which can sweep through an aviary like wildfire and destroy virtually an entire avicultural operation within a short time. At a lower intensity these diseases can cause slow, chronic losses. Fortunately many of these diseases can be combated by keeping the aviaries and food and water containers clean. These diseases, therefore, are directly under the control of the aviculturalist.

A regular dosing programme for the birds and a disinfection programme for the aviaries will solve a great many problems even before they have taken root properly. Warmth allied with moisture creates a suitable environment for worms, fungi, lice and bacterial infections. A set programme for controlling diseases is essential, particularly in the summer rainfall areas. Such a programme is set out on p. 43.

Bacterial infections

Paratyphus

The salmonella group of bacteria causes diseases in birds. In man it causes certain kinds of food poisoning and gastro-enteritis. Various types of salmonella bacteria can also infect birds. The symptoms of the disease depend on the type of salmonella infection they have contracted. Paratyphus is a disease caused by salmonella infection.

The bacteria are transmitted by rats and mice which leave droppings in the birds' food containers, and also by wild birds leaving droppings on the roof of the aviary. If these droppings fall inside, the aviary becomes infected.

Paratyphus can also enter an aviary from infected birds. Seed can be infected with the bacteria by rats and mice on the seed merchant's premises. Commercial bird food containing hard-boiled egg which becomes infected at the packing centre can also bring the disease to the aviary.

It is clear why very few aviaries are completely free of paratyphus.

Symptoms

Birds may die quite suddenly without showing many symptoms, or a watery yellow-greenish or sometimes grey and blood-flecked diarrhoea may be present for a few days. The birds sit puffed up, shiver, soon become thin and may show signs of nervous affliction, e.g. jerky movements and convulsions.

Death usually occurs within a few days to two weeks after the infected food has been eaten. Depending on the type of salmonella which has affected the birds, they may become mildly ill with a few deaths every few days, or up to 90 per cent of the birds may be wiped out within about ten days. Most of the deaths occur among young birds because the older birds will already have built up some resistance.

Unfortunately birds are often only carriers of the disease, in other words they themselves show no symptoms, but they do pass a great many of the paratyphus bacteria in their droppings. In this way eggs are infected through their shells, and the chicks die inside the eggs before they are hatched.

Chicks in the nest are infected in the same way, and the result is a nest full of dead, squashed chicks. If large numbers of nests contain dead chicks, there are large-scale deaths of chicks in the eggs, young birds seem weak and sweaty and diarrhoea occurs, you can almost be certain it's paratyphus.

Diagnosis

It is not possible to make a proper diagnosis without laboratory tests. For an accurate diagnosis samples of droppings as well as the organs of dead birds must be examined at Onderstepoort. Dispatch recently dead birds which have rapidly been cooled in a freezer or refrigerator to Onderstepoort by express post. The address is: Poultry Division, Onderstepoort 0110. Remember to supply your own name and address, as well as a covering letter in which the symptoms are described.

Prevention

Prevent rats and mice from getting to the food. Suspend the food containers from wires, or place them on a one-legged table above ground level, or fix the food dishes to a smooth wall or asbestos or corrugated iron sheets.

Feed the birds only with fresh boiled eggs or eggs kept in a refrigerator. Ensure that no rats or mice get at the bags containing seed. Buy seed only from dealers with clean premises.

Because the birds may be symptomless carriers of the disease and continually drop bacteria onto the floor of the aviary, it is, unfortunately, virtually impossible to keep an aviary free of paratyphus. Try to keep the concentration of bacteria on the floor as low as possible. Scrub the aviary regularly with a wide-spectrum disinfectant to keep the level of the germs as low as possible. Wash the food and water containers regularly, particularly if there are droppings in the food.

Treatment

If an acute outbreak of the disease occurs, treat the birds for ten days with furasolidone or spectinomyacine as prescribed for chickens. Furasolidone is available – without a prescription – from shops which sell animal medicines.

Coccidiosis

The coccidiae are a large group of protozoa that, among others, infects birds. The *Eimeria* genera, which occur in the mucous membranes of the alimentary canal, are particularly harmful.

The birds swallow the oocysts of the protozoa. After a development cycle in the mucous membranes of the alimentary canal (which can cause severe damage to the intestinal wall), another oocyst is formed and passed in the droppings. The oocyst has a strong wall, is very tough and can exist in the open air for a long time, particularly if it is wet and dark.

If birds continually ingest small numbers of oocysts, they develop a resistance and do not become ill. When the oocyst colony becomes too large, the symptoms of the disease manifest themselves.

Symptoms

The clearest symptom is diarrhoea, which may be bloody. The birds die soon afterwards. Young birds in particular die from coccidiosis. By keeping the aviary floor, food and drinking containers extremely clean, the infection can be limited to such a degree that it presents no danger.

The illness can be acute, with a great number of quick deaths. It can also be chronic, in which case the birds will simply become thin over a period of time and languish.

Coccidiosis is not as prevalent in aviary birds as is generally suspected. Aviary birds seldom contract it to the same degree as poultry. However, if aviaries are overcrowded, if a great deal of droppings accumulate on the floor, fall into the drinking water and dark, warm, damp spots are found in an aviary, it does occur. Young birds, which have not developed immunity, usually succumb in such circumstances.

Prevention

Scrub the aviaries regularly, particularly during humid, hot weather. Unfortunately the oocysts are resistant to most disinfectants. Cement aviaries can be scrubbed with Ucarsan, formalin (1%), or iodine preparations mixed with soap which destroys the oocyst.

It is difficult to disinfect soil aviaries. You can sprinkle an iodine preparation on the ground once or twice a year. If the birds do not take in too much when pecking on the ground, it is not harmful. About once a year 1% formalin can be sprinkled on the floor and allowed to soak in. However, caged birds are sometimes inclined to eat from the floor, and an intake of formalin can be harmful. This can be prevented by spreading a thick layer of clean soil or sand on the floor of the aviary. In any case the latter is an excellent practice to help prevent diseases. Do this three or four times a year and remove the soiled sand before clean sand is spread over. Also spread fine gravel where the water containers are placed. This helps ensure that water splashed on the floor can filter down without causing wet, muddy spots.

Treatment

Various remedies are available for coccidiosis in chickens. Treat the birds about three or four times a year – particularly during the warm, wet summer months – for about one to three days with one of the remedies at a concentration as prescribed for chickens. This is a good preventative practice. If an outbreak of coccidiosis does occur, the birds must be treated for the full prescribed period.

By regularly cleaning the aviaries, many other, less deadly diseases than paratyphus and coccidiosis can be kept in check. Examples of such diseases are *E. coli* infections, tuberculosis, pseudo-tuberculosis and fungal diseases such as candida and aspergillosis.

Internal parasites

Many types of worms and flukes infect birds. Of these roundworms and tapeworms are the main culprits. In pigeons up to 18 types of tapeworm and 28 different types of flukes can occur. However, roundworms are the most common infection in birds. Some of them have an interme-

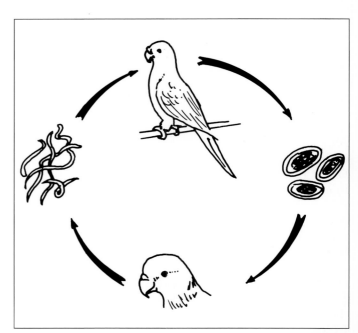

16 The roundworm life cycle. Birds infected with these worms pass the eggs in their droppings. The eggs are then eaten by other birds, the eggs hatch in the birds' intestines and the larvae develop into adult worms which in turn begin laying eggs.

diary host, others not. Beetles, worms, chickens, snails, ants or earthworms can serve as intermediary hosts. This means that the birds are infected with the roundworms when they eat the beetles, snails, ants or earthworms.

Many of the worms and flukes cause little damage to the birds, as long as they occur in low concentrations. Only when they are present in high concentrations do they weaken the birds.

The effect of such infections on the birds can be attributed to other causes than the worms themselves. Some of the parasites cause anaemia which weakens the birds. In the case of others it is rather the poisonous substances secreted by the parasites which harm the birds. In the case of a serious infestation the liver ducts, the windpipe and even the alimentary canal can become clogged by the parasites. A heavy infestation lowers the resistance of the birds so that they become very susceptible to other diseases.

It is a hopeless task for the ordinary aviculturalist to determine accurately which internal parasites are infecting his birds, and it is better to keep in mind general preventative measures. Internal parasite infestations and their consequences can, to a large degree, be controlled by the aviculturalist himself.

Clean, new aviaries are often infected by birds from the wild who sit on the wire and pass droppings into the aviary, by intermediary hosts such as snails and beetles which crawl into the aviary, or by buying infected birds. Aviaries with soil floors and aviaries with many plants usually make good breeding grounds for internal parasites. Particularly in the case of soil floors the eggs of internal parasites accumulate until the aviary is badly infested.

The various stages of internal parasites, e.g. the eggs, stay alive particularly in wet, muddy and shady spots such as are found underneath and next to water containers, until they are picked up by the birds. Wet areas around the water containers contaminated by bird droppings are ideal places for birds to become infested with roundworm.

Combating

Aviaries with cement floors must be scrubbed and disinfected about once a month during wet, warm months. During the cold, dry months once in two or even three months is probably adequate.

Aviaries with plants and soil floors cause more problems. Once a year the entire aviary can be sprinkled with a solution of copper sulphate. One gram of copper sulphate in a watering can with a capacity of about 10 litres will control fluke infestations. If fluke infestation is high, the aviary can be sprinkled with a copper sulphate solution more often. Soil floors can be disinfected more thoroughly by digging in lime once a year. Lime is of some use as a disinfectant.

The best method to clean soil floors is to dig up the top layer of soil once or twice a year and spread about 3-6 cm of clean building or river sand over the floor. This looks neat, is clean and absorbs rainwater quickly so that no puddles remain. Furthermore birds like to scratch and 'bath' in the sand.

Apart from the fact that the build-up of the worm and egg concentrations in the aviary should be kept as low as possible, the birds must also be dosed against internal parasites. Unfortunately there are few remedies on the market which are specifically registered for birds.

However, aviculturalists use remedies meant for poultry, ostriches or even sheep in order to deworm their birds. The treatment usually causes no harm and is effective against the parasites. Should an aviculturalist lose an expensive bird because he has used a remedy which was not registered for birds, he cannot hold the manufacturers liable for the loss.

Roundworm

Treat the birds about three or four times a year for roundworm and wire worm. If the aviaries are badly infected, this can be done more often. Any remedy which contains piperazine, e.g. Predazine, is suitable. Use the remedy in accordance with the prescription for chickens. Such remedies are obtainable without a prescription.

Antipar is a worm remedy for human use, but aviculturalists often use it. It is available from chemists without a prescription and the dosage is one teaspoon per litre of drinking water for two days.

A remedy registered only for ostriches, but which is used by breeders of birds with good results, is levasol hydrochloride 2,5% (e.g. Tramisol or Ripercol). The dosage is one teaspoon per litre of drinking water for two days. Another remedy which can be used is thiabendasole, also with a dosage of one teaspoon per litre in the drinking water for two days.

Some aviculturalists inject a dosage of about 3 ml of the prepared medicine directly into the crop. This can be done only in the case of fairly large birds such as cockatiels. For this purpose a rubber bicycle valve can be fixed to the front of a syringe, lubricated with water, glycerine or oil and inserted into the crop. Some aviculturalists use a teat needle meant for cows or a thin copper tube fixed to the spout of the syringe, and insert this into the bird's crop. However, this has potential for injuries and is not recommended. For the ordinary aviculturalist a remedy in the drinking water is efficient enough.

Gapeworm

Gapeworm is a particular type of roundworm. This parasite is picked up directly from the ground when the birds eat infected earthworms or snails. To reproduce, the parasite attaches itself to the bird's windpipe. This causes intense coughing and the secretion of mucus, as well as a gasping for air. If you open the bird's beak the worms can be seen at the opening of the windpipe.

Thiabensole and tetrasole are effective against this par-

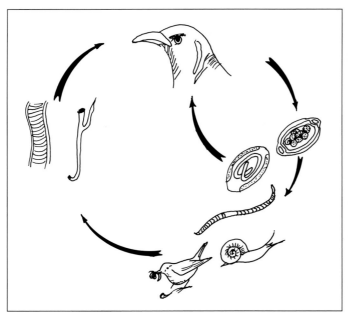

17 The gapeworm life cycle. The host is a bird. The worm eggs are passed by the bird and eaten by an intermediate host such as a snail or earthworm. The cycle is completed when the intermediate host is eaten by a bird. The worms grow to adulthood inside the birds and then attach themselves in pairs to the lining of the windpipe.

ticular type of roundworm. Once again the warning must be issued that these remedies are not registered for birds and that aviculturalists have no legal recourse when using them.

Liver and other internal flukes

Unfortunately you can do little in the case of liver and other internal flukes. The remedies presently available to combat these flukes in sheep and cattle, such as tetrachlorine ethylene and hexachlorine ethane, are very poisonous to birds. No controlled experiments have as yet been done with the very latest remedies, and at this stage they cannot be recommended for birds. Flukes require moisture and warmth and the incidence of infestation is highest in waterfowl. Keep the ponds clean and the areas around the food containers dry.

Tapeworm

A large variety of tapeworm occurs in birds. The head and neck of a tapeworm attach themselves to the inside of the intestine. The body segments of the tapeworm are full of eggs (by means of self-fertilisation). As soon as the eggs are ripe, the segments detach and are then passed together with the bird's droppings.

If a bird eats the eggs directly, the tapeworms cannot develop inside the bird. The eggs must first be eaten by an intermediary host such as an insect. A bladder-worm then develops inside the intermediary host. When this host is swallowed by the bird, the actual tapeworm develops inside the bird.

Seedeaters are therefore less prone to tapeworm infestations than birds who eat insects.

Because caged birds do not get a great many insects to eat, it seldom happens that they become badly infected with tapeworm. However, it does sometimes happen that birds in dirty aviaries become badly infected with tapeworm.

This can also happen when birds are fed infected ants (although not all ants are infected with tapeworm).

Unfortunately no medicine is available which kills both roundworm and tapeworm. Treat caged birds for tapeworm about two or three times a year with a tablet meant for pigeons. The tablet (e.g. Droncit) contains praziquantel and is available without prescription from shops dealing in animal medicines. Dovalint, which contains niciosamide, is also suitable.

One quarter of a tablet for small birds and up to one tablet for large birds is sufficient. The tablet (or part thereof) is pushed down the throat. Some aviculturalists also use Dicestal (which is actually meant for dogs) for their birds. However, Dicestal causes broken feathers and is not recommended for birds.

Lintex L is completely soluble in water and you can use it for tapeworm. The dosage is two teaspoons per litre of water. In summer give it for one day and in winter for two days (when the weather is cold, the birds drink less water). Aviculturalists must, however, note that this remedy has not been registered for birds.

The dosages of some remedies must be calculated according to the weight of the birds. To help in this regard, the following weights are given for a number of bird species:

Zebra finch: 10-16 g
Java sparrow: 24-30 g
Budgie: 30-60 g
Lovebird: 50-70 g
Cockatiel: 100-120 g
African grey parrot: 300-380 g
Japanese quail: 18-42 g

External parasites

Lice and mites can severely damage an avicultural operation. A number of external parasites live on birds. The parasites as such do not kill the birds, but can irritate them to such an extent that they leave the nest. The parasites can also cause anaemia by sucking the birds' blood. The birds become weak and susceptible to other diseases. Because lice and mites move quite freely from one bird to another, they can also spread diseases among the birds.

Lice

More than 40 louse species have been found on poultry. Many of these species, as well as a horde of other lice, also flourish on birds.

Lice are small, flat insects which can lie flat against the skin. Some lice live only on the bird's head, others only on the wings, etc.

They lay heaps of eggs which clump together. In favourable, warm circumstances one pair of lice can produce 100 000 offspring within a few months. They spread from one bird to the next when the birds sit close together for warmth. If the aviary is overcrowded with birds, the louse population spreads extremely quickly.

Bird lice live mainly on the outer layers of the skin and feathers, although a few species bite until blood emerges, and then live on the blood.

Symptoms

Lice cause restlessness, loss of appetite, an inability to sleep and irritation. Brooding birds cannot sit still and often leave the nest.

Despite the great number of different louse types, one kind of treatment is fortunately suitable for all of them.

Mites

Mites are nasty, bloodsucking creatures with eight legs. They can cause great damage among birds and their chicks because they are bloodsuckers. A type of mite commonly found in aviaries is the *dermanyssus gallinae* mite.

These mites are grey, but when they are full of sucked blood, they are red. When they have drunk their fill, they congregate in cracks in the wooden nests, perches or construction material of the aviaries in crawling masses. They normally sleep here during the day. At night they seek out the birds and once again drink their fill. This is why you never see them on the birds by day; you can remain unaware of their presence for some time. It also does not help a great deal to dust the birds against the mites; the entire aviary must be sprayed. If you shine a torch into the aviary or nest at night, you will see the mites crawling about – usually red and full of blood.

If young birds just emerging from the nest are too weak to fly, or fall over when they walk, you can start looking for mites. The mites suck so much blood that the birds become dangerously anaemic and then have little resistance to other diseases.

Treatment

Treat the birds and aviaries simultaneously. In this way not only lice and mites are killed, but bedbugs, ticks and other creepy-crawlies that bother the birds as well. Aviaries must be cleaned routinely two or three times per year and sprayed with remedies that kill the lice and mites. If there is an infestation, the aviaries must be sprayed more often.

Spray the aviaries, the insides of the nests, all cracks, dark corners and splits in the wooden frames of the aviary thoroughly with Karbaspray or Duramitux or something similar. Burn nesting material, clean the nest well and place fresh nesting material in the nest. As these remedies are very poisonous to birds, instructions regarding mixing, etc. must be carried out accurately. Of course all food and water utensils must be removed before you spray.

If there are chicks or eggs in the nest, a little Karbadust powder can be sprinkled underneath the nesting material so that it does not contaminate the chicks. Then skip that nest while cleaning the rest of the aviary. As soon as the chicks have left the nest, clean the nest thoroughly and burn the nesting material. If at all possible, it is best to catch the birds and remove them from the aviary before cleaning it. Cleaning the aviary is a major task, but it is important to do so.

If the aviary has a cement floor, the spray must immediately be rinsed off, otherwise the birds will peck at it when the spray has dried, and may then die.

One aviculturalist sprayed his aviaries every weekend with Karbaspray, and every Monday his birds staggered about. (Karbaspray poisons the nervous system.) Only once the help of a vet was called in was the mystery of the birds' Monday illness cleared up.

If the aviary has an earthen floor, this can cause serious problems, as the poison accumulates in the soil. It is best to soak the earth floor with a hose after the aviary has been cleaned so that the poison can drain away. Poison on the walls and inside the nests usually does not cause problems, as the birds do not eat there.

Mites and lice are usually bothersome during the warm summer months, and this is the best time to spray the aviaries.

At the same time treat the birds themselves by dusting them. Do not use the spray remedy used for the aviaries on the birds. This remedy is highly concentrated, is absorbed through the skin and the birds may die.

Various powders registered for use on birds are commercially available. Such remedies may contain karbaril (e.g. Karbadust).

Ensure that you are using the powder meant for birds and not the one for gardening. The latter is also very concentrated and can cause the birds to die.

Even when the powder is meant specifically for birds, the birds can be affected if too much of the poison is absorbed through the skin. Dust them lightly and do not, under any circumstances, rub the powder into the skin. Shake off the excess powder. If the birds subsequently become shaky, keep them quiet in a dark place until they seem to have recovered, and next time remember not to apply so much powder. Any powder breathed in by the birds can also cause symptoms, so apply the powder neatly and carefully.

A Pulvex treatment in spray cans which is registered for caged birds is also available. It is not necessary to spray the birds until they are dripping wet. There is almost no chance that they will catch cold – just avoid spraying them on a cold, rainy day.

It is always a good policy to sprinkle a little louse powder in the bottom of all nests before nesting material is placed in the nest.

Knemidocoptes mite

Budgies often display scabby noses and faces. The bare parts around the eyes, too, are often covered in rough, horny, wartlike skin.

In the case of canaries you sometimes notice that their legs and feet have become thick and rough. This phenomenon also occurs in birds in the wild and is caused by the *knemidocoptes* mite which penetrates beneath the skin.

The bird develops a crooked, horny bill as a result of the damage the mite does to the growing tissue. The various parts of the bill then grow at different speeds and the beak becomes crooked, or curls.

If you examine carefully the horny growths on the budgie's face with a magnifying glass, you will notice that the entire area is full of holes where the mites have tunnelled into it. The horniness is a secretion of the badly damaged tissue.

Treatment

Because these mites are so common, it is important to treat the disease at an early stage. Brush just about any insecticide onto the affected parts.

The various types in spray cans which are meant for flies and mosquitoes are suitable.

The poison can be sprayed directly onto the legs, but in the case of the face it is better to brush it on carefully so that it does not get into the eyes or is breathed in unnecessarily.

One treatment is not enough – repeat every few days for three weeks.

28 The devastation that can be caused to a budgie's face by the *knemidocoptes* mite.

Sternostoma tracheacolum mite

This mite occurs in the respiratory canals. Canaries and Gouldians are particularly susceptible. They lose their voices, have trouble breathing, cough and sneeze, lose sleep and eventually die.

Treatment

Place the bird in a cardboard or wooden box. If this does not have a lid, drape a towel over it. Now blow malathion powder into the box. A plain hypodermic syringe without the needle can be used for this purpose. The idea is for the bird to breathe in the malathion so that the mites can be killed. There is the danger that the bird may die from the malathion, so a light dusting is adequate – after all, the bird must be able to breathe. Its fluttering will further distribute the powder throughout the box. Leave the bird to breathe the powder for about five minutes. Repeat after four or six weeks.

Ticks and bedbugs

Ticks and bedbugs sometimes bother birds. The treatment is the same as for other external parasites: dust or spray the birds, burn the nesting material and spray the aviary thoroughly.

General infections and injuries

Scour, pneumonia and general infections

Scour is symptomatic of a number of diseases. It is an impossible task for the aviculturalist to diagnose precisely which disease the bird suffers from, and this is really unnecessary. Thanks to modern broad-spectrum antibiotics you are able to treat a wide variety of diseases at once. This also holds true for respiratory and other infections.

If birds appear seedy and sit puffed up, with or without scour, it is time to act. It is, therefore, always wise to have at hand one of the broad-spectrum remedies. Some remedies are only available with a veterinarian's prescription. Obtain a good supply in advance.

Treatment

Remove the bird from the aviary and place it in a small cage in order to facilitate treatment and prevent the disease from spreading. An ill bird always feels cold, so keep the cage in a warm place.

Give the bird (as well as any of its companions who may already have been infected) any of the following remedies: Tylotad Plus, Baytril, Polibiotic, Doxibiotic or Oxyvital. Some of the remedies also contain furazolidone which will curb paratyphus if this is present. The dosage is normally 1-2 g per litre of water for four days, but the dosages may differ. If instructions are included, follow these scrupulously.

Birds receiving medicine should always be given extra vitamins. Sometimes this has already been included in the remedy.

A word of warning about the use of antibiotics. These remedies not only kill the harmful bacteria in the alimentary canal (and the rest of the body), but also the useful bacteria. Without the useful bacteria in its alimentary canal a bird can fall ill. It is therefore wrong to treat birds with antibiotics for simply any reason, e.g. sudden cold weather.

It is not recommended that birds are treated routinely once a month with a diluted antibiotic, as is sometimes done. Weak preparations given too frequently provide the bacteria with an opportunity to build up immunity. When you do need to use the remedy urgently, it no longer has any effect. It is therefore important to give it at the full strength and for the recommended number of days in order to ensure that all harmful germs are eradicated.

Although sulpha drugs are effective in the case of a great variety of bacterial infections such as diarrhoea and pneumonia, they can cause problems in the case of birds because the dosing cannot be controlled. Sulpha drugs are normally dissolved in the drinking water. In very warm weather the birds may drink a great deal of water, take in too much of the sulpha drugs and sustain kidney damage. This can be so serious that they may die. Try to avoid the use of sulpha drugs during a heat wave.

When disease has broken out in an aviary, the food and drinking utensils and – in serious cases – even the aviary itself must be thoroughly scrubbed with Ucarsan, or otherwise the birds will simply pick up the germs again. Ucarsan destroys spores, fungi, yeasts, numerous bacteria and some viruses.

Egg blockages

The anatomy of birds shows some design faults: The alimentary canal, which is full of excrement, the urine ducts and the sexual orifice all run into one another and end up in one opening, the cloaca. (Unlike humans, female birds have only one ovary and one oviduct. This is situated in the left side of the abdomen.) The bacterially loaded excrement so close to the single oviduct often causes problems in the form of a light or heavy infection of the oviduct. Such an infection is one of the commonest causes of egg blockages and, in the long term, treatment is not particularly successful. When a female sits puffed up and appears to be trying to express something all the time, turn her upside down and feel under the breastbone, then across the soft part of the belly to the cloaca. Normally you will soon feel where the egg is stuck. This happens because the affected irritated muscles of the oviduct contract and do not allow the egg to pass through.

Other causes of egg blockages include the weakening of the muscles in the oviduct, e.g. in the case of old birds or caged birds getting no exercise. It also happens when the egg is particularly large or misshapen, or when the female is exhausted because of excessive or out-of-season breeding.

Obese birds can also experience trouble in laying eggs, as can thin, ill birds that are too weak to express the egg.

A poor diet is of much less importance than is generally accepted, because it normally leads to non-ovulation and no egg is therefore formed.

An egg that is stuck is a real emergency and time is of the essence. The egg must be removed, or the bird will die. The general practice among aviculturalists is to place the bird in a very warm box or even to hold her over steam. However, steam is dangerous because it can burn the bird, and is not recommended at all. Warmth is of value, particularly on a cold day. The extra heat can help to relax the oviduct. In more severe circumstances it does not help a great deal, and while you are rushing about trying to provide the heat, much time is lost and the bird's death becomes a far greater possibility.

In the case of a valuable bird it is preferable for a veterinarian to remove the egg. If the egg blockage is very deep, you can do very little about it. If the egg is close to the cloaca, the chances that you can do something about it are naturally so much higher.

Treatment

Between contractions, push the egg back up into the oviduct with the fingers. Insert a little KY jelly, baby oil or liquid paraffin into the cloaca and see whether the egg will emerge with the help of the lubricants. If nothing happens, a thoroughly boiled (sterilised) bent hairpin can be gently inserted between the egg and wall of the oviduct. The bent part of the hairpin is then hooked over the egg and the egg extracted. At all times work carefully and gently.

If the egg still does not emerge, it must be broken. Sometimes this will kill the bird immediately as a result of shock, but often it works quite well.

The procedure is as follows: Insert the end of a sterilised hypodermic needle or blunt tapestry needle into the oviduct up to the egg – without piercing the oviduct with the needle! Of course this can only be done if the egg is very close to the opening. The content flows out by itself and the bird ejects the pieces of the shell.

Only as a last resort is the egg to be crushed by exerting pressure on the stomach with the fingers. This causes a great deal of pain and shock and the bird often dies.

Because of the broken shell and the fiddling with the hairpin, the oviduct will now be lacerated inside, and an infection is likely to be the bird's fate. It is therefore important to inject an antibiotic directly into the oviduct.

Veterinarians have the correct medicines, but the aviculturalist forced to apply emergency treatment by himself must use what he has at hand. Eye drops containing antibiotics (but not antihistamine) can be injected into the oviduct. Use a syringe without a needle, or you will pierce the oviduct. Sterile antibiotics meant for injections can also be used. Such remedies are often found on farms. Antibiotics meant for mixing with water so as to be drunk are not as suitable, as this is not sterile. Place the bird in a hospital cage and give it antibiotics in the drinking water for about five to eight days.

Bumblefoot

Bumblefoot sometimes occurs in birds. Usually the cause is a small injury or scratch on the skin underneath the foot into which any of a variety of bacteria can find their way to cause infection.

A swelling in the form of a hard round pad develops underneath the foot. Because the bird is constantly treading on the foot, necrosis or dying off of the tissue in the centre of the swelling occurs.

The swelling then exhibits a dark or black spot. Pus will form later and the foot becomes extremely painful. Because the bird is constantly treading in dirty soil, it is difficult for the foot to heal.

Fig. 18 This shows an example of bumblefoot. A swelling in the form of a stiff, round pad occurs underneath the foot.

Treatment

Wait until the infection is ripe, in other words until it feels soft and the pus moves. Cut open the swelling, squeeze out the pus and disinfect with an iodine solution. A powder such as terramycin eye powder or a solution containing antibiotics is also suitable, as are ointments for human use which contain antibiotics or sulpha drugs. Then wash the whole foot well with an antiseptic, place clean cotton wool on the wound and dress the foot in such a way that the toes project, or else the bird will fall over!

Place the bird in a small box with a thick layer of soft, clean grass or soft sawdust on the bottom. Keep it in the box until it has shown signs of healing. If the foot is red and hot, the bird must also be given an antibiotic in its drinking water. Clean the foot twice a day, sprinkle antibiotics on the wound and dress it again.

Sometimes paratyphus infection manifests itself as bumblefoot. It is essential that the bird is then given a preparation which contains furasolidone.

Terramycin eye powder is an excellent remedy for ani-mals. Always keep some in the house, as it can be sprinkled onto any open wound.

Broken bones

A bird's bone structure is much more porous than that of any other animal. It helps keep the body weight down for flying, but at the same time the bones are much more prone to breakage. When a frightened bird flies into a wire, it can easily sustain a fractured skull, or may break its back or neck. If a small bird such as a finch breaks a bone in its leg and this is a simple fracture, i.e. no bones have pierced the skin and they are not crushed or splintered, the leg can be set.

Treatment

Manoeuvre the bones into position carefully so that they line up properly. Wind a thin layer of cotton wool around the leg, make a splint from a matchstick or the thick primary feathers of a larger bird and fix it to the leg with sticking plaster.

Another method is to use the type of synthetic adhesive used for wood, porcelain, metal, etc., spreading it over the cotton wool and keeping the leg straight until the adhesive is hard. Put the bird in a small cage so that it cannot move about much.

The cage must have smooth sides, or else the bird may try to climb up the wire. The leg must be used as little as possible. A cage as for caged birds, with long strands of smooth wire instead of chicken wire, is suitable.

Fix newspaper to the outside of the cage so that the bird cannot see out and become frightened by people moving around it.

If the splint does not stay in place, remove it and wind some sticking plaster fairly tightly around the leg. Leave the bird in peace in its cage for two weeks.

If the leg is badly crushed and bone has pierced the skin, cut it off with a pair of scissors, sprinkle antibiotic powder on the wound and simply leave the bird alone. It is quite amazing how well birds get by with one leg and how quickly they recover from having a leg cut off.

A larger bird, such as a parakeet, can be treated in the same way. Use a piece of thick cardboard for a splint. Plaster of Paris is too heavy. Very large birds with thick legs, such as parrots, can be treated with plaster of Paris. Remember to twist some cotton wool around the leg first before the plaster of Paris is mixed with water and spread over the cotton wool.

A valuable bird with a broken leg should be left in the care of a veterinarian.

Broken wings

In the case of a broken wing a veterinarian will be able to provide the best help (as always). It is difficult to ensure that a broken wing grows back properly, and often the wing remains useless after the operation. Unfortunately we don't all have a veterinarian at our beck and call, and usually the value of the bird does not always justify the expense.

Treatment

A fractured wing, where bones have not been forced out of position and do not pierce the skin, is brought to its normal folded position.

Tie the ends of both wings to the base of the tail feathers using a long piece of sticking plaster. Now wind a long piece of plaster around the chest and the front parts of the wings so that both wings are held against the body.

If it is a large bird and the wings can still move, wind another long piece of plaster over the back and the centres of the wings and then loosely over the belly. If it is wound too tightly across the belly, the bird cannot breathe.

Put the bird in a small box for two or three weeks. It should be able to see very little, remain calm and not be disturbed by people or cats.

Programme to combat diseases

The following is a suitable programme which may be followed by aviculturalists from year to year to safeguard birds against certain diseases:

August (This is the start of the breeding season.)
Treat for roundworm.

Dust birds for lice.
Spray aviaries and nests for mites.
Burn old nesting material and provide fresh, clean material.
Scrub the aviaries or spread clean sand on the floor.

November

Replace dirty nesting material after the first set of chicks.
Dust the nests for mites and lice before the new nesting material is added.
Scrub the aviaries or remove the top layer of soil and spread fresh sand on the floor.
Treat birds for roundworm and coccidiosis.

January

Treat aviaries and nests for external parasites such as lice and mites. Dust the birds.
Treat for coccidiosis.

February

Treat for worms.

April/May

Clean aviaries and nests after the breeding season.
Hose down the aviaries and nests and dust the birds. Clean the floors.
Treat for worms.

June/July

Clean the floors.

9

The parrot family

Parrots and parrot-like birds (*psittaciformes*) are found worldwide in the warmer regions. Africa is home to a good variety of psittaciformes, but South America, the Far East and Australia boast a wealth of these exotic birds.

All psittaciformes have hooked bills and peculiar mallet-shaped tongues. Parrots were among the earliest bird species captured by man and kept in cages, probably because they have the habit of becoming quite domesticated and imitate the words of their owner. Sailors first brought colourful parrots to Europe, where they were unknown, but where they soon became very popular. During Roman times ringnecks in particular were very popular. Because they were rare and very expensive, they were seen as status symbols.

There is something exotic about parrots and parakeets. For centuries images of these birds have been used to decorate tapestries, wallpaper, fabrics and screens.

Formerly parrots were always transported by ship – a slow process – and many died because of ignorance regarding their feeding and care. For the past 30 or 40 years, however, birds have been transported by aircraft and fewer losses are suffered. As a result an enormous international trade in birds has developed, to such an extent that, together with the destruction of their habitats on an unprecedented scale, this has led to many species being almost wiped out in their natural state.

It is therefore of the utmost importance that aviculturalists must treat the rare parrot-like birds in their aviaries today like gold and do everything possible to encourage them to breed, because birds in the wild are becoming scarcer by the day. Fortunately it is generally easier to feed parrots than most of the other bird species, which often need an extremely specialised diet such as flower nectar or particular types of insects.

Aviculturalists seldom use the birds' scientific names. Because this guide is meant for South African aviculturalists, the names in local use are given. Some birds are known in South Africa by one name, while they may be known under another in America, for example.

Psittaciformes are divided into two main groups, namely birds with thick tongues such as the seed-eating parrots, and birds with brush-tongues that eat nectar, such as the lorikeets.

Both these groups are further roughly subdivided into birds with short tails and birds with long tails. Birds with thick tongues and short tails are generally called parrots such as the African grey parrot and the large variety of Amazon parrots from South America. Birds with thick tongues like those of parrots, but with long tails, are known

as parakeets. Examples of parakeets are Indian and African ringnecks, Princess of Wales from Australia and the much-loved plum-headed parakeets.

Brush-tongues are a special, unique group of psittaciformes because – in their natural state – they live mainly on nectar, pollen, flowers and fruit. Their tongues are specially adapted to this diet, with papillae on the tongue that stand erect as soon as the tongue is extended, to roll the pollen into small balls and to lap up the nectar.

Short-tailed brush-tongues are known as lories, e.g. the chattering lory. Long-tailed brush-tongues are known as lorikeets, e.g. Swainson's lorikeet.

However, there are exceptions to this general division by the layman; nobody calls the giant macaw a parakeet just because it has a long tail.

The beginner usually starts off with budgies and cockatiels. As soon as he/she has mastered these, the next step is often to buy the cheaper parakeets such as red-rumped, plum-headed, ring-necked and grass parakeets. More expensive species such as conures and rosellas are added later, while some aviculturalists graduate to the Princess of Wales, Barabands, Grand eclectus and rock peplers.

Some of our top aviculturalists own birds that can cost up to R50 000 or more a pair. Some of the most expensive birds in the country are the macaws, cockatoos, galahs, Twenty-eights and Kings and Queens of Bavaria.

Disadvantages of the parrot family

Before you invest your money in parrot aviculture, think first about the following:

☐ Some psittaciformes (e.g. quakers) have harsh screeching voices and can cause trouble with the neighbours. Others, such as red-rumped parakeets, have soft and even melodious voices. Therefore always choose the right birds for your particular circumstances.

☐ Most psittaciformes cannot bear others of their kind in the same aviary and will kill one another. There are exceptions, for example some lovebirds, who are colony breeders. Each breeding pair must therefore have its own aviary and this requires a great deal of capital per breeding pair.

☐ Because many of the parrot species are wirebiters, the aviaries and their frames must be constructed from strong, and therefore expensive, material. If this does not suit your pocket, you must choose from among the brush-tongues, long-tailed parakeets and smaller parrot species which can be accommodated in ordinary chicken-wire aviaries.

□ One pair of psittaciformes needs more living space than one pair of finches.

□ Many psittaciformes, particularly the true parrots, must become quite mature before they will start to breed.

□ It usually costs a great deal more to buy psittaciformes than finches.

In spite of the possible disadvantages, however, psittaciformes are the most popular birds in aviculture. They are easy to feed, display beautiful colours and have interesting personalities.

Lovebirds

The aviculturalist today has at his disposal an interesting variety of lovebirds. These miniature examples from the ranks of the parrot family are particularly popular among beginners because they are colourful and easily obtainable and most species breed easily.

All true lovebirds originate from Africa. There are nine different species. The best known to South African aviculturalists are the Fischer's, black-masked, Nyassa and rosy-faced lovebirds.

In South America you find even smaller parrots than the lovebirds from Africa. They are called parrotlets, but are not generally encountered in South African aviaries.

Lovebirds look just like real parrots, apart from being much smaller and often more colourful, maturing more quickly and usually breeding very well. Because they interbreed freely, only one species is kept per aviary. Most lovebirds are colony breeders and many pairs can be kept in one aviary, with the exception of the rosy-faced lovebird and its mutations. These will kill, with the greatest of pleasure, all other lovebirds unless the aviary is very large.

As is the case with all birds, breeding results are poorer when too many birds are forced to live together in one aviary. Lovebirds become very tame and may sometimes even learn to talk a little, but then they have to be isolated from their friends. It requires more effort to teach them to talk than in the case of a budgie.

It is important to remember that because they sleep in nests, such nests must be available for them throughout the year. There must also be a choice of more than one nest. The fact that they sleep in their nests means that they are better able to withstand sudden cold and wet weather than other birds.

It is often extremely difficult to determine their sex. By observing them over a period of time, the beginner aviculturalist will eventually notice that the male is usually larger and more robust than the female. It is best to buy more than two birds and from their behaviour draw a conclusion about whether they are males or females.

Even if they feed each other, it does not mean that they are a pair. Birds of the same sex will sit close together and feed each other if birds of the opposite sex are not present. Although it is normal practice to keep one male per female, the male will breed with two or even three females and help to care for the chicks if there is a shortage of males.

Lovebirds build an unusual nest and provision must be made for this. They use an L-shaped finch nest, a cockatiel nest or even a budgie nest. Inside such a nest they build an intricate laying area out of finely chewed leaf and grass material. Palm leaves, reed leaves, papyrus, kikuyu or any other type of grass is suitable.

Because they continually renew their nests, it is important to have large quantities of fresh green nesting material always available. The green material is moist and helps to prevent the eggshells from becoming so hard that the chicks cannot hatch.

About twice a year, particularly after a set of chicks has been reared, you must clean the nest and scrub it with disinfectant, sprinkle louse powder on the bottom and then place a handful of leaves or grass in the nest. There should be at least twice as many nests as pairs, or the birds will fight to the death.

Because they breed so regularly, proper feeding is important. The first sign of nutritional deficiencies is the appearance of light flecks on the birds' wings. Later the feathers will fall out and the birds will crawl about on the ground. Some species will literally breed themselves to death if they are not properly cared for and the males are not removed during the winter. See chapter 5 for the feeding of lovebirds.

Parakeets

Parakeets are parrot-like birds with long tails. Because they have elegant lines and beautiful colours, they are very popular. They are less inclined to chew wire than parrots, reach maturity sooner and can therefore begin breeding sooner. In general they breed more freely than true parrots and a greater variety of parakeets is considerably cheaper than parrots. However, they do not breed as well as cockatiels or budgies. In the case of most parakeets one or at the most two sets of chicks per year, usually early in summer, constitute a good breeding record.

Most parakeets tolerate only one breeding pair of their own species per aviary. Were you to place another pair in the same aviary as a breeding pair, they would fight to the death unless the aviary was very large. They can share an aviary with doves, pheasants, quail, ducks and occasionally large finches, provided the aviary is roomy.

Grass parakeets are among the prettiest of the smaller parakeet species and include names such as the Turquoisine, Elegant, Splendid and Bourke parakeets – all popular aviary birds. They are small and elegant and hail from Australia, where they were once threatened with total extinction. In an effort to save them, all exports from Australia were banned, but so many were still being smuggled out that the export or import of, e.g. Turquoisines and Splendids, was banned worldwide. It has had the positive result that their continued existence in Australia has probably been ensured.

This ban on the movement of grass parakeets also has disadvantages: In South Africa aviculturalists are doing well with them, perhaps because we are also situated in the southern hemisphere and the breeding season and climate correspond to those of Australia. However, because there is no export market for Turquoisines and Splendids at present, their prices have fallen to such an extent that bird owners no longer breed them in large quantities. Yet South Africa could make a great contribution towards ensuring the continued existence of these birds and supplying the eager European market with them.

Precisely because they are no longer so expensive and are such lovely birds, they are a good choice for the aviculturalist wishing to buy interesting stock.

The rosellas are a beautiful, brightly coloured group of parakeets well adapted to life in an aviary. Among them are the Pennants and the cheaper golden-mantled, Stanley's and mealy rosellas. The rosellas all come from Australia. They have soft, melodic voices and caring for them presents no particular problem, although they are aggressive towards other birds. They can be kept in an aviary with ordinary chicken wire as long as the wire is not rusted. They breed well and are hardy, and therefore suitable for the beginner.

The conures are a group of parakeets from South America. Some are available for reasonable sums, while others, such as the Queen of Bavaria, are extremely expensive. Conures are noisy, with harsh screeching voices, and an aviculturalist in the city must take this into consideration. They breed reasonably well and are good pets. They can be kept in aviaries made from ordinary chicken wire, as long as the wire is not rusted. Conures become restless when they breed and are quick to leave the nest at the slightest movement. They require privacy when they breed. See chapter 5 for the feeding of parakeets.

Parrots

Parrots were previously known as extremely reluctant breeders. The breeding of African grey parrots was regarded as a special achievement. Since surgical sexing has become more generally available, two birds of the same sex are no longer kept together for years under the impression that they are a breeding pair.

A true breeding pair requires a great deal of patience, as it takes a good number of years before parrots reach maturity and can begin breeding. It is a good idea to combine parrot aviculture with other birds such as parakeets, who breed more readily, in order to maintain interest.

Parrots cannot be kept in aviaries constructed from ordinary chicken wire. Their aviaries must be made from welded wire mesh or even diamond mesh wire. There must be only one pair to an aviary, because they kill each other.

Parrots are excellent pets and are kept as caged birds rather than breeding birds. It is often extremely difficult to persuade a caged bird to become a breeding bird once more. See chapter 5 for the feeding of parrots.

Brush-tongues

The happy nature and colourful plumage of the brush-tongues are enough to turn many people into highly enthusiastic admirers, in spite of the fact that they must be given fresh food daily, which means that the aviculturalist cannot go away for even a few days without appointing a surrogate keeper.

On the tip of its tongue this bird has a number of papillae which normally lie flat. When the tongue is thrust forward, the papillae stand erect in order to collect liquid food or pollen. This tongue enables the birds to collect nectar, almost in the same way as a cat laps up milk. The natural food of the brush-tongues consists mainly of pollen, nectar in flowers, the flowers themselves, fruit, grass seeds, certain insects and larvae. When kept in aviaries they must be given a substitute diet as you cannot feed them flower nectar and larvae. In South Africa the staple food is sweetened ProNutro mixed with water, or dog meal.

The more popular brush-tongues sport bright and impressive colour combinations. They have marvellous personalities in that they become extremely tame, sometimes fall madly in love with their owners and play delightfully with each other. It is not unusual to find a brush-tongue flat on its back with a stick or piece of grass between its feet, with which it plays like a kitten! A brush-tongue will also flop over onto its back so that you can scratch its belly, and will then play with your hand with its feet and beak. They enjoy bathing and then play among themselves by crawling through the grass.

They can also be released and will return to the nest. Unfortunately people sometimes capture them and, if they are tame, dogs, cats and hawks can catch them. It is not worth the risk of releasing and possibly losing them.

The brush-tongues constitute a particularly large group of birds, but only some of the more colourful species are kept in South Africa. These include the chattering lory, Swainson's lorikeet, dusky lory, fairy lorikeet and a number of others.

Because of their special diet brush-tongues have very watery droppings. This makes them unsuitable as pets in a cage indoors, because they eject a stream of excrement which messes up the whole floor.

It is best to keep them in aviaries with concrete floors, unless the aviary is particularly large. An aviary with a concrete floor can be scrubbed from time to time.

Because the birds enjoy bathing so much, particularly when they are covered in porridge, honey, syrup or fruit juice, water for bathing must always be available. This keeps their feathers clean despite their diet.

Brush-tongues do not tolerate other parrots and will murder fellow-occupants of their aviary with the greatest of pleasure, unless the aviary is particularly large. Their aviaries must be protected against cold wind because they come from warm regions and are susceptible to cold.

Once they have bred, they like sleeping in the nest, and a sleeping nest must therefore be available at all times. This is an excellent habit, as it helps to protect them from the cold and limits losses. See chapter 5 for the feeding of brush-tongues.

Individual descriptions

ABYSSINIAN LOVEBIRD (*Agapornis taranta taranta*)

Origin: Ethiopian highlands.

A beautiful green lovebird which certainly deserves greater attention from aviculturalists. They are less noisy than other lovebirds and can even be kept indoors.

Description: *Male* – Forehead and orbital ring: red. Body: green. Wingtips: brown-black. Tail feathers: green with a broad black band near the ends. Beak: dark red. Eyes: brown. Legs: grey. *Female* – As for the male, but lacks the red on the head. Size: 16,5 cm.

Diet: Seed mix for lovebirds, supplements such as dog pellets, fruit and willow bark if available. When there are chicks, they must also get bread soaked in milk. A mineral mix, shell grit and coarse grit must always be available.

Breeding habits: They build a nest in a finch nest, hollowed-out tree trunk or large calabash. It is preferable to keep only one pair in an aviary, together with other birds such as grass parakeets or finches. If more than one pair is kept to an aviary, there should be many nests so that they have no need to fight over them, because they can easily kill one another.

Give them green kikuyu grass, teff, oats or straw with which to line their nests. Two to four chicks are raised at one time. When the chicks emerge from the nest, their beaks are a dull yellow. They can interbreed with Fischer's and black-masked lovebirds and should preferably not be kept in the same aviary as these species.

AFRICAN GREY PARROT (*Psittacus erithacus*)
PHOTO 29

Origin: Central Africa – from the islands of the Gulf of Guinea and the west coast to western Kenya and north-western Tanzania.

They are very popular because they learn to talk very well and become extremely tame.

South African aviculturalists recognise three kinds. One parrot is large and light grey with a red tail and hails from Zaïre. This is a beautiful bird – sought-after, but scarce. The more common type is smaller and darker grey and also has a red tail. They come from the Congo, amongst other places. Then there is the Timneh African grey parrot,

29 African grey parrot

which is an even darker grey and without the beautiful red tail. The tail of the Timneh is brownish-red. The Timneh is a subspecies of the common African grey parrot.

In general it is believed that the males of all the species learn to talk better than the females, but this is not necessarily so. It is thought that African grey parrots can live up to eighty years.

Description: *Male* – Dark grey. Rump: light grey. Tail: red. Wings: dark grey to black. Head and neck feathers: grey with greyish white edges. Beak: black. Iris: pale yellow. Legs: dark grey. *Female* – As for the male, but often smaller and slighter. Size: 33 cm.

Diet: Seed mix for parrots, a great deal of fruit and vegetables such as green mealies and carrots, nuts, raisins soaked in water, peanut butter, a little meat or bone meal and branches from fruit trees to chew. Also a mineral mixture, shell grit, coarse grit and dog cakes.

Many parrots fall ill and end up at the vet because their owners think that parrot seed is enough for them to live on. This is absolutely not the case. Without a variety of fruit and/or vegetables daily they cannot remain healthy and eventually they will die. Their natural foods are berries, nuts, seeds, fruit and even soft green leaves.

When there are chicks, hard-boiled egg and bread soaked in water must be added.

Breeding habits: It often requires a great deal of patience on the side of the aviculturalist before his African grey parrots will breed. They are only sexually mature at the age of five years. A true pair will breed in a deep parrot nest in which wood shavings have been placed. Three or four eggs are laid. Young birds leave the nest after about ten weeks. The first few days the female feeds the chicks white crop milk. If the young birds are raised as pets, they must be removed from the other parrots, or they will not learn to talk.

AFRICAN RING-NECKED PARAKEET
(*Psittacula krameri krameri*)

Origin: Africa, from Senegal to Ethiopia.

Ringnecks are popular aviary birds and suitable for beginners. They breed readily and are hardy as far as cold is concerned. They will share an aviary with other parakeets, finches or quail, but not with another pair of ringnecks. They can be kept in an aviary constructed from ordinary chicken wire, even though they are fairly large birds.

Description: *Male* – A black ring extends from beneath the beak right around the head. The black ring is edged with pink. A black stripe connects the eyes. Body: Greyish green with a blue sheen on the neck and some of the tail feathers. Underwing: yellowish. Tail: greenish blue with yellow underneath. Beak: rose pink. Eye: There is a red ring around the eye. Males can be confused with females because the black ring around the neck appears only at two years of age. *Female* – She lacks the black ring around the neck, the black band connecting the eyes and pink collar. Size: 42 cm. There are blue, yellow and albino mutations. The African ring-necked parakeet is slightly smaller than the Indian ring-necked parakeet and its colours are also duller.

Diet: A seed mix for parakeets is suitable, and also fruit and vegetables, dog meal and a mineral mixture, shell grit and coarse grit. When there are chicks, bread soaked in milk or water, and mashed hard-boiled eggs, must be added.

Breeding habits: These birds are well suited to life in an aviary and breed once or twice in the spring and summer. The male courts the female for some time. She lays her eggs in a wooden nest in which sawdust has been placed. A cockatiel nest is a little too small as the long tails of these birds get in the way.

A larger parrot nest is preferable. The female lays three or four eggs. Both parents feed the chicks. Young birds can be tamed and kept in a cage. They will often learn to talk a little.

ALEXANDRINE PARAKEET (*Psittacula eupatria nipalensis*)

Origin: Sri Lanka, Nepal and Burma.
Alexandrines look like a larger version of the Indian ring-necked parakeet, with a heavier head and beak. They are more expensive and rarer than the Indian ring-necked parakeet.

They are big and strong and must therefore be kept in aviaries constructed from welded wire mesh. They are hardy, but must be protected from frost.

Description: *Male* – The male is green all over. Only the back of the head and the cheeks show a grey-blue sheen. A black stripe extends from the nostrils to the eyes. A black stripe extends from the lower edge of the cheeks to the lower mandible. Neck band: pink. Tail: greenish blue feathers with yellow tips. Wings: green with a red spot. Eyes: grey with red eyelids. Beak: blood red. Legs: grey. *Female* – As for the male, but lacks the black markings on the face and the pink neck band. Size: 58 cm. There are various subspecies which differ slightly from one another. There is also a blue and a lutino mutation.

Diet: A seed mix for parakeets, supplements such as greenstuff, dog pellets, fruit, peanut butter, a mineral mixture, shell grit and coarse grit. When there are chicks, bread soaked in water, hard-boiled egg and oat sprouts must be added.

Breeding habits: They prefer a deep nest which is large enough to accommodate their tails and is lined with wood shavings. The female lays three to five eggs. Both parents feed the chicks. Young birds raised in a cage can learn to talk.

BLACK-CAPPED OR BLUE-THIGHED LORY (*Lorius lory*) PHOTO 30

Origin: Various islands north of Australia.
The voice of the black-capped lory is such that it can be kept in an urban environment. They can be housed in an aviary constructed from plain chicken wire but, unless it is very large, they must not share an aviary with other birds.

Description: *Male* – General colouring: red. Forehead, crown, neck, breast and belly: black, with a dark purple sheen. Mantle: blue. Wing upper parts: green. Wing underparts: red with a broad yellow and black band. Tail upper parts: red. Tail underparts: olive yellow. Beak: yellow. Eye: orange-red. *Female* – As for the male. Size: 31 cm. Surgical sexing is essential.

Diet: ProNutro with water and honey, or dog pellets. Also fruit, bread soaked in milk, peanut butter and a seed mix suitable for parakeets.

Breeding habits: The female lays two eggs in a wooden box which contains wood shavings (or bran). The chicks hatch after about 24 days. When the chicks have hatched, the shavings (or bran) must be replaced every week, as the chicks soil the nest, the ammonia burns their eyes and the nest becomes soggy. The chicks become very tame and make amusing pets. However, they cannot be kept indoors because they make a huge mess with their watery droppings.

30 Black-capped or blue-thighed lory

31a Black-masked lovebird   **31b** Blue-masked lovebird   **32** Blue-fronted Amazon parrot

BLACK-MASKED LOVEBIRD (*Agapornis personata*) PHOTO 31a

Origin: North-eastern Tanzania.

Description: The description relates to the bird in the wild – there are aviary bred mutations which look different. *Male* – Head: black. Breast: yellow. Back: green. Beak: red. Eye ring: white. *Female* – As for the male. The males and females can sometimes be distinguished because the head of the male is darker than that of the female. Size: 14,5 cm. The blue mask (photo 31b) is a mutation from the black one. In this case all the yellow has disappeared from the bird and what was green before has become blue. (Green is a mixture of blue and yellow.) Furthermore all the yellow parts have become white. There are also a white and a lutino mutation. (The latter is yellow with a pink eye.)

Diet: As for Fischer's lovebird.

Breeding habits: As for Fischer's lovebird.

BLUE-FRONTED AMAZON PARROT

(*Amazona aestiva aestiva*) PHOTO 32

Origin: South America.

The blue-fronted Amazon parrot is one of the best-known and most popular parrots because it talks so well and makes an excellent pet.

With surgical sexing and a great deal of patience an aviculturalist should be able to achieve success with breeding. One pair only must be kept in an aviary constructed from welded wire mesh.

Description: *Male* – Face and throat: yellow. Forehead: blue. Eyes: red. Body: dark green. Shoulders: red. Wings: green. Wingtips: red. There are blue feathers in the wings as well. Tail: green with red. Beak: dark grey. Legs: dark grey. *Female* – As for the male. There are a number of subspecies which differ from each other. Size: 35 cm.

Diet: Parrot seed, lots of fruit and vegetables, other supplements such as peanut butter, dog cakes, a mineral mixture, shell grit and coarse grit. When there are chicks, bread soaked in water or milk as well as mashed hard-boiled egg must be added. Dates, raisins and all kinds of nuts can be given as delicacies.

Breeding habits: Although they breed in a hole in a tree trunk in nature, in captivity they will accept a wooden nest suitable for parrots. The inside of the nest should contain wood shavings. They lay from one to five eggs. Incubation lasts about 29 days, and only the female broods.

BOURKE'S PARAKEET (*Neophema bourkii*)

Origin: Australia.

This is a mild-mannered parakeet with a melodic voice which breeds well and is suitable for beginners. Bourke's parakeets will live in harmony with other small bird species. Their large dark eyes indicate that these birds prefer twilight, which is why they only really come alive late in the afternoon. They form a particularly close bond with their partners and a pair will eat, drink and sleep together in one nest. It is a pity to separate a couple without taking into account their affection for each other. They must be well protected from cold wind and frost.

Description: *Male* – Greyish brown, darker across the rump. Head and neck: brown with a pink wash. Forehead: blue, white around the eyes. Cheeks: rosy. Wings: dark blue with blue. Tail: blue and brown. Belly: pink. Thighs: blue. *Female* – Slightly smaller than the male and her colours are slightly duller. The blue across the forehead is almost lacking, apart from old hens. Size: 19 cm.

Diet: A seed mix for parakeets, supplements such as dog pellets, greenstuff, fruit and peanut butter, a mineral mixture, shell grit and coarse grit. When there are chicks, bread soaked in milk or water, hard-boiled egg and sprouted grass seeds must be added.

Breeding habits: They breed in a cockatiel nest which contains wood shavings or sawdust. This prevents the eggs from rolling about. Because Bourke's parakeets are so mild-natured, the nest should not be close to those of aggressive birds such as cardinals. Aggressive birds will chase them away from their own nests. They can be used to hatch the chicks of other parrots and parakeets, but will not be able to raise them successfully. Strange chicks must not be left with the Bourke's parakeets for longer than the first three days, or else they will die. Thereafter they have to be hand-reared.

BROWN-EARED OR BROWN-BREASTED CONURE   (*Pyrrhura calliptera*)   PHOTO 33

The popular as well as the scientific name differs in various parts of the world. There are also a number of subspecies.

Origin: South America.

As many of the conures do, they become very tame, but they have harsh, screeching voices. They can endure a fair amount of cold. Each pair should preferably be kept alone in an aviary.

Description: *Male* – Body: green. Crown and back of the neck: brown, with a blue and green sheen. Feathers over the ears: reddish brown. Cheeks: green. Neck, throat and breast: The feathers are brown with light brown edges which create the impression of undefined bars. Belly: green with brown in the centre. Wings: green with yellow to the side. Underside of tail: reddish brown. Eye ring: bare and white. Beak: horn-coloured but with white where it attaches to the head. Iris: yellowish brown. *Female* – As for the male. Size: 22 cm.

Diet: A seed mix for parakeets, supplements such as greenstuff, dog pellets, fruit and peanut butter, a mineral mixture, shell grit and coarse grit. When there are chicks, bread soaked in water or milk, as well as hard-boiled egg, must be added.

Breeding habits: If they are a true pair, the female will lay two to four eggs in a cockatiel nest lined with shavings or sawdust. Both parents feed the chicks.

BUDGIE OR BUDGERIGAR   (*Melopsittacus undullatus*)   PHOTO 34

Origin: Australia.

Budgies are the easiest psittaciformes with which to start an avicultural operation. Budgies are gregarious, cheerful, colourful, become tame and even talk a little. For the beginner they are cheap, breed easily, are always in demand and need little space. Budgies give such pleasure that budgie clubs, budgie societies and budgie shows are encountered all over the world.

Colour breeding: In nature a budgie is green, but breeders have managed to breed an astonishing variety of colours. However, there are as yet no red budgies. Breeding the various colours is very specialised. For example, dark green crossed with cobalt results in an excellent cobalt. To retain a soft purple, a budgie of this colour must from time to time be crossbred with a first crossing of olive green crossed with blue (olive green/blue). To retain a good light blue, a light blue budgie must be crossed exclusively with other light blue budgies. When the blue becomes too light, it can be improved by crossing it with the first crossing of light green and blue (light green/blue).

Breeding budgies of various colours is an entrancing hobby. The best way of learning more about this is to join a budgie club.

Show budgies

Show budgies are bred by selection from budgies from the wild. Show budgies are larger than common budgies and must satisfy set standards as regards head and wing posture, the angle of the body in relation to the legs and many other criteria. This requires specialised breeding and a prospective show budgie breeder is advised to join a club.

Description: The description is for the green budgie which is found in the wilds in Australia. *Male* – Nose: blue. Face and forehead: yellow. Undersides: green-yellow. Upper parts: yellow and black bars, six black spots on the throat. Cheeks: purple. Tail: green and blue. *Female* – Nose: brown. For the rest, as for the male. Size: 18 cm. In the case of some mutations the blue/brown sexual difference on the nose has disappeared. It is then difficult to determine the sex accurately.

33   Brown-eared conure

34   Budgie

35   Canary-winged parakeet

Diet: Budgies do not eat larger seeds such as sunflower seed. Enthusiastic budgie owners have their own special feeding methods in which they believe implicitly. A suitable diet is a budgie seed mix (see p. 22), supplements such as greenstuff, dog pellets and brown bread, a mineral mixture, shell grit and coarse grit.

Breeding habits: Budgies are colony breeders and many birds can be accommodated in one aviary. Budgies breed in special budgie nests (see p. 18). Any other enclosed nest, e.g. a calabash or hollow tree trunk, is suitable. There must be a perch in front of the opening, preferably inside as well as outside the nest.

Nests are suspended at about shoulder height. This ensures that one can see what is happening inside. The nests can be suspended close together like blocks of flats, as budgies are tolerant of their neighbours. However, there must be about twice as many nests as pairs, or the birds will fight viciously. During the breeding season in spring, summer and autumn, the nests must be inspected regularly to remove any dead chicks. Because of excessive inbreeding certain problems manifest themselves in budgies, e.g. low fertility, deformed chicks and high fatalities among young birds. It is of the utmost importance to bring in new blood from time to time.

Young birds must be at least eight months old before you breed with them. At three to four years they are already too old to breed well. This means that many old budgies are offered for sale, and the beginner must be wary of this. An old budgie's beak and nose is rough and crisscrossed with tiny cracks.

The serious breeder will separate the males and females in winter. Surplus males in the aviary may interfere when other budgies wish to mate, which may result in infertile eggs. An excess of females will, however, often share the available males. Budgies begin brooding before the last egg has been laid, and chicks therefore appear in a staggered sequence. It is quite normal to have large and small chicks in the same nest. Budgies breed in a nest without nesting material, but the bottom of the nest must be hollow to prevent the eggs from rolling around.

Budgies will raise strange budgie chicks quite successfully. If one nest contains too many chicks, some can be removed and placed in a nest with few chicks.

CANARY-WINGED PARAKEET (*Brotogeris versicolorus*) PHOTO 35

Origin: South America.

There are various subspecies. They are small and can be kept in aviaries constructed from plain chicken wire, together with other small parakeets. They are a bit noisy, but do not have loud voices.

Description: *Male* – Head, back and underside: green. Wings: green, yellow, white and blue. Beak: yellowish. Eye ring: partly covered with feathers. Underside of tail: greenish blue. Upper side of tail: green. *Female* – As for the male. Size: 22 cm. Surgical sexing is recommended.

Diet: Parakeet seed, fruit and greenstuff, dog pellets, a mineral mixture, peanut butter, shell grit and coarse grit. When there are chicks, they must also get bread soaked in milk and mashed hard-boiled egg mixed together.

Breeding habits: They breed in a cockatiel nest with wood shavings in the bottom of the nest. The female lays up to five eggs. Incubation begins after the second egg has been laid. Only the female broods, but the male sleeps with her at night.

CANINDE MACAW (*Ara caninde*) PHOTO 36

Origin: Central South America

The Caninde macaw is rare. Photo 36 is of a Caninde in the wild and was taken in the Amazon. The common blue and yellow macaw offered for sale in South Africa looks almost the same except that its throat is blue and it lacks the black stripe under the beak. Its face is also less bare. The Caninde is probably a subspecies of the blue and yellow macaw.

Macaws are fearful wire-biters and must be kept in a very large aviary constructed from diamond mesh wire. They become excellent pets, but it is cruel to keep such large birds in the small cages they are usually provided with in South Africa. Rather keep a pet macaw on a T-bar. They often screech and can cause problems with the neighbours.

Description: *Male* – Head, wings and back: blue. Belly and underside of tail: yellow. There is a blue spot underneath the tail at its base. Face: bare and white with black stripes. Throat: yellow. A black band runs across the throat to the ears. *Female* – As for the male. Size: 86 cm. Surgical sexing is recommended.

Diet: Parrot seed, vegetables, fruit, dog cakes, meat or bone meal, peanut butter, shell grit, a mineral mixture and

36 Caninde macaw

coarse grit. Give them extra delicacies in the form of nuts, raisins, dates or pumpkin pips. Also give them fresh branches to chew.

Breeding habits: They need a very large nest (the size of a rubbish bin) with wood shavings in the bottom. There must be a ladder inside the nest, and the opening must be reinforced with smooth tinplate.

The female lays two eggs and only she broods, although the male will often climb into the nest. The incubation period is about 25 days.

CHATTERING LORY   (*Lorius garrulus*)

Origin: Indonesia.

These exotically coloured brush-tongues are noisy and have a screeching voice. Keep only one pair per aviary as they will kill other pairs.

Description: *Male* – Body: blood red. Wings: green. Shoulders: yellow. Thighs: dark green. Tail: red and brown. Beak: red. Eyes: yellow. Legs and feet: grey. *Female* – As for the male. Size: 30 cm. Sex must be determined surgically.

Diet: ProNutro mixed with water and sweetened with honey or syrup. Fruit, bread soaked in milk or water, peanut butter and parakeet seed. The ProNutro must be freshly mixed every day. When there are chicks, they will eat more of the bread and milk. When there are no chicks, they will eat more seed.

Breeding habits: They will use a cockatiel nest with wood shavings or sawdust in it. Two eggs are laid. The shavings must be removed every two weeks and replaced by fresh shavings.

When the chicks mature, the shavings must be replaced weekly, because the birds pass very watery droppings and the nest becomes dirty and unhealthy. City aviculturalists who do not have access to shavings can buy bran and place this in the bottom of the nest. The nest must be cleaned thoroughly after every breeding attempt by scrubbing it, sprinkling louse powder on the bottom and putting in another few handfuls of shavings or bran. They normally make very good parents.

COCKATIEL   (*Nymphicus hollandicus*)

Origin: Australia.

Apart from the budgie the cockatiel is the most popular psittaciforme in aviculture. This good-natured, cheerful little bird almost begs to be tamed. It has a clear voice with which it whistles tunes it learns, and mimics words.

Cockatiels are very well adapted to life in an aviary. This is probably because the seed we give them corresponds to a great degree with the dry seed available in their natural environment.

They are an excellent choice for the beginner because it is not difficult to care for them and they breed well enough for the aviculturalist's interest not to flag.

Description: The description is of the common or original grey cockatiel as it occurs in nature. *Male* – Grey.

37   The underside of the wing of a grey cockatiel female shows the white spots which indicate her sex.

Underside: paler grey. Forehead, crest, face and throat: yellow with orange across the ears. Wings: white. Tail: grey on the underside. *Female* – Grey. Cockatiel females are easily identified by the white spots under the wings and the light and dark bars on the underside of the tail (see photo 37). Their orange cheeks are paler than those of the male. For the rest they look like the male. Very young males also display white spots underneath the wings, but the spots usually show clear signs of disappearing from the outside inwards. Size: 32 cm.

Mutation colours

White cockatiels: These are not true albinos, but lutinos. An albino has no colour pigments, whereas a lutino does. This is why some so-called white cockatiels are often almost entirely yellow. White cockatiels have black eyes, yellow faces and crests and orange cheeks. White females display yellow spots under the wings (see photo 38).

Pearls: The wings and back have a spotted or pearly appearance. The spots can occur on a white or yellow base. A deep yellow base is the most attractive and such pearls are known as golden pearls, while those with a white base are known as silver pearls.

There are 'good' pearls and 'poor' pearls. Good pearls show sharp contrasting spots and patterns while poor pearls show hazy, undefined patterns. One breeding pair will not always produce the same kind of pearls and one nest can produce various types of pearls. Parents who have produced poor pearls stand just as good a chance of breeding good pearls the next time as a pair which produced good pearls at their first attempt.

Unfortunately the male loses his pearl pattern after his first moulting and then normally becomes grey. For a year or two afterwards you can usually see that it is a pearl male by the whitish flecks on the back and wings, but eventually he looks just like a normal cockatiel.

The fact that the pearl males lose their beautiful colour

38 White cockatiel

has caused their popularity to wane. However, in the past few years, progress has been made in breeding pearl males which do retain their colour.

Pied: These cockatiels are flecked with white and grey. Great variations occur as regards the size, shape and pattern of the patches. A 'poor' pied is almost exclusively grey, with a white patch here and there. A 'good' pied displays a number of contrasting spots and flecks. The ideal is for the patches to be symmetrical on both sides of the body, but this is seldom achieved.

The bars and grey on the tail of a pied are usually replaced by yellow. Sexing can therefore only be done as long as the bird has orange cheeks, which indicates a male.

Cinnamon or Isabella: The bird is light brown or cinnamon-coloured. The black pigmented dots in the feathers are replaced by brown pigmented dots. When the yellow background is very dark, the bird is particularly beautiful. A light yellow background produces a coffee-and-cream colour. The male is often slightly darker than the female. Other mutations, such as red-silver, also occur.

Diet: A seed mix for parakeets, greenstuff, dog pellets, fruit, vegetables, a mineral mixture, shell grit and coarse grit. In the case of birds that breed often, it is important to always supply shell grit. A mixture of hard-boiled eggs, grated carrots, chopped carrot tops or chopped parsley and whole-wheat breadcrumbs constitute a good daily supplement to the diet of cockatiels with chicks.

Of course the seed mix and minerals must be supplied in unlimited quantities. It is totally wrong to give only so much seed that the containers are emptied within a few hours. In the case of a bird, you cannot see beneath its feathers whether it is becoming thin because it gets too little to eat. Only once the bird has lapsed into a pitiful state is it noticable underneath the feathers. Also try to teach the birds to eat dog meal or laying meal. This will supply much of their protein, vitamin and mineral needs.

Breeding habits: The cockatiel nests that are commer-

cially available are suitable. In the wild, cockatiels nest in a hollow tree trunk. Of course such a hollow trunk looks very good in an aviary.

Do not place the nests in the sun, because the eggshells can become so dry that the chicks cannot hatch, or the chicks suffer or may even die of heat exhaustion.

In nature cockatiels mate after the first rains. This ensures that there will be enough food when the chicks emerge. This instinct is still present in caged birds. Cockatiels become very excited when it rains; they like to bath in the rain and the males begin courting the females.

Cockatiels breed better when there is only one pair to an aviary, unless the aviary is very large. Too many cockatiels in an aviary cause tension which impairs breeding results and lowers resistance to diseases. However, they are tolerant of other pairs sharing the aviary and do not kill one another.

Cockatiels sometimes begin breeding as early as eight months old, but good breeding results can be expected mostly from one year or 18 months onwards. As happens in the case of birds, the first brood is often a failure, but this should not be held against a young pair – they should be given another chance.

Sometimes the female begins laying again before the chicks have left the nest. Often the chicks fare perfectly well even though their parents are busying themselves with the eggs. However, sometimes the parents attempt to drive the chicks from the nest by chewing their crests, biting them or refusing to feed them.

When parents attack chicks in the nest, it often helps to remove the chicks from the nest and place them on the ground. The male will often continue looking after the chicks while the male and female take turns to hatch the new eggs. Should the parents refuse to feed the chicks, they must be hand-reared. Young cockatiels react very favourably to hand-rearing.

39 Coelestial lovebird

COELESTIAL (*Forpus coelestis coelestis*)   PHOTO 39
Origin: The dry west coast of South America.
This is a tiny parrotlet which normally breeds in autumn.
Description: *Male* – Body: green. Face and throat: yellowish green. Wings: dark green and blue. Rump: blue. Tail: blueish green. A blue stripe extends from the eye to the back of the head. Eyes: brown. Legs: brown. Beak: horn-coloured. *Female* – All the blue is replaced by green. The yellow-green on the face and throat is paler. Some females do display a little blue behind the head as well as the blue stripe from the eye to the back of the head, and blue on the rump. Size: 12,5 cm.
Diet: A seed mix for lovebirds, greenstuff, dog pellets and fruit, peanut butter, a mineral mixture, shell grit and coarse grit. When there are chicks, hard-boiled egg and bread soaked in milk are good supplements.
Breeding habits: They make a nest in any hollow. Calabashes, finch, budgie and cockatiel nests with a few wood shavings or sawdust in the bottom are suitable. They do not build intricate nests like those of the lovebirds from Africa.

Four to six eggs are laid, incubation is 17 days and the chicks emerge at intervals of a few days. They leave the nest when they are about 30 days old.

ELEGANT GRASS PARAKEET (*Neophema elegans*)
Origin: South-western and south-eastern Australia.
These pretty grass parakeets must be well protected from the cold as they are not hardy. Elegants have soft, melodic voices and, because they are mild-mannered, they can share an aviary with non-aggressive species such as finches.
Description: *Male* – Back and upper parts of wings: olive green. Forehead: A deep blue band extends across the forehead from one eye to the other. Orbital ring, cheeks and throat: yellow. Breast: gold-olive. Belly: yellow. Sometimes an orange patch occurs in the centre of the belly. Tail: underside yellow, upper parts green-blue and yellow. Undersides of wings: dark blue. Beak: horn-coloured with

a blue sheen. *Female* – Her colours are duller and the band across the forehead is narrower. There is less blue on the wings and she lacks the orange patch on the belly. Size: 23 cm.
Diet: A seed mix for parakeets, supplements in the form of greenstuff, dog pellets, fruit, peanut butter, a mineral mixture, shell grit and coarse grit. When there are chicks, bread soaked in water or milk, and mashed hard-boiled egg must also be given.
Breeding habits: They breed well in budgie, finch or cockatiel nests.

They use no nesting material, but the nest must be lined with wood shavings or sawdust to prevent the eggs from rolling around.

FISCHER'S LOVEBIRD (*Agapornis personata fischeri*)   PHOTO 40
Origin: Tanzania.
An excellent choice for the beginner as this lovebird is an attractive colony breeder which usually breeds very well.
Description: *Male* – Green, undersides a little more yellow-green. Forehead: bright orange yellow. Head: olive. Cheeks and throat: orange with a slight olive sheen. Rump and upper parts of tail: bright blue. Wing feathers: black with green. Tail: centre feathers green with blue tips; outer feathers orange at the base with a band of black, and blue tips. Eyes: brown. Beak: coral red. Legs and feet: dark grey. Orbital ring: bare and white. *Female* – As for the male. Head sometimes smaller and beak slightly smaller. Size: 15 cm.
Diet: A seed mix for lovebirds, supplements such as dog meal, bread soaked in water or milk, grated carrots and greenstuff such as lucerne, a mineral mixture, shell grit and coarse grit.
Breeding habits: They breed in colonies and many nests can be suspended fairly close to one another. They use finch or budgie nests or calabashes in which they make nests using teff, oats, straw or green kikuyu cuttings.

40   Fischer's lovebird   **41**   Golden-mantled rosella   **42**   Indian ring-necked parakeet

Supply almost twice as many nests as there are pairs in order to prevent quarrels.

They raise their chicks well. Just be aware of the fact that they can breed themselves to death. Males must be removed during winter to give the females a rest. Their feeding must be excellent in order to prevent exhaustion.

GOLDEN-MANTLED ROSELLA (*Platycercus eximius cecilae*) PHOTO 41

Origin: Southern Queensland, Australia.

This popular parakeet species with its pretty colours must not be kept in the same aviary with other large birds, as they will kill one another. However, they can be kept in an aviary with small finches. They are not noisy and are suitable for city dwellers. They are hardy.

Description: *Male* – Back: golden yellow and black. Belly: golden yellow with a red sheen. Tail: blue and green. Head, neck and throat: red. Cheeks: white. Thighs: green. Wings: blue. *Female* – As for the male, but her colours are duller. Size: 28 cm.

Diet: A seed mix suitable for parakeets, dog pellets, fruit, vegetables, peanut butter, a mineral mixture, shell grit and coarse grit. When there are chicks, they must also get bread soaked in water or milk, and mashed hard-boiled egg.

Breeding habits: They breed readily in a wooden box large enough for their long tails. Wood shavings must be placed in the bottom of the box. The female lays four to six eggs which are hatched by her only.

INDIAN RING-NECKED PARAKEET

(*Psittacula krameri manillensis*) PHOTO 42

Origin: India, Sri Lanka and Burma.

Description: The Indian ring-necked parakeet is larger than the African ring-necked parakeet and the colours are brighter than the African species. For the rest it looks like the African species. There are blue, yellow and albino mutations.

Diet: As for the African ring-necked parakeet.

Breeding habits: As for the African ring-necked parakeet.

JENDAY OR YELLOW-HEADED CONURE

(*Aratinga jendaya*) PHOTO 43

Origin: Eastern Brazil.

They are beautiful and peaceably inclined towards other birds and also their own kind, but they are noisy. They breed reasonably, as long as you are dealing with a true pair.

Description: *Male* – Head, throat and breast: yellow with an orange sheen. Belly: orange with a green sheen. Back, wings and tail: green. Rump: yellow. Beak: black. Orbital ring: bare and white. *Female* – As for the male. Size: 30 cm.

Diet: A seed mix for parakeets, lots of greenstuff and fruit, dog pellets and also a mineral mixture, shell grit and coarse grit. When there are chicks, bread soaked in water or milk, and mashed hard-boiled egg, must be added.

Breeding habits: Surgical sexing is recommended, or else you can quite easily be stuck with two of the same sex. A true pair will readily breed. The female lays three or four eggs and chases away all birds who venture too close to the nest. They breed in a cockatiel nest containing wood shavings.

LESSER SULPHUR-CRESTED COCKATOO

(*Cacatua sulphurea*) PHOTO 44

Origin: Islands north of Australia, and Indonesia.

Cockatoos, particularly lesser sulphur-crested cockatoos, make popular pets. They talk, laugh, whistle and chew all the furniture and plants in sight. Keep only one pair in an aviary of welded wire mesh or diamond mesh wire, as they are very bad wire-biters. They are also noisy.

Description: *Male* – White. Cheeks: yellow. Crest: white and yellow. Undersides: The feathers are white, but become yellow where they enter the skin. Tail and undersides of the wings: white with a yellow sheen. Eye ring: bare and creamy white. Beak: dark grey. Legs: dark grey. Iris: dark brown. *Female* – As for the male, but the iris is red-brown. Size: 33 cm.

Diet: Parrot seed, lots of fruit and vegetables, dog cakes, peanut butter, meat and bone meal, bread, bird grit, a min-

43 Jenday conure   **44** Lesser sulphur-crested cockatoo   **45** Madagascar lovebird

eral mixture and also pumpkin pips and extra nuts, dates or raisins as snacks. Bread soaked in water or milk and mixed with mashed hard-boiled egg must be added when there are chicks. They must also get plenty of branches, preferably fresh and green, or sugar-cane, to chew on because they have a strong chewing instinct which must be satisfied.

Breeding habits: They breed in a large, deep box. The opening of the box must be reinforced with tinplate, or they will chew it to pieces. An old 50-litre drum is also suitable if one end is cut open halfway. There must be a ladder on the inside of the box, as well as wood shavings. The female lays up to three eggs and incubation lasts about 24 days. Both sexes brood; the male during the day. The chicks emerge from the nest about 10 weeks after they have been hatched.

MADAGASCAR OR GREY-HEADED LOVEBIRD (*Agapornis cana cana*) PHOTO 45
Origin: Madagascar.

Although they are not bred in South Africa on a large scale, they do have their devotees among bird lovers. During the breeding season the female will defend her nest fiercely. It is safest to supply a breeding pair with their own aviary, unless the aviary is very large.

Description: *Male* – Head, neck and breast: grey. Upper parts: dark green. Undersides: light green. Tail: green and black. Beak: horn-coloured. Legs: grey. *Female* – Head, neck and breast: not grey, but green like the rest of the body. For the rest like the male. Size: 14 cm.

Diet: A seed mix suitable for lovebirds, dog pellets, greenstuff, a mineral mixture, shell grit and coarse grit. When there are chicks, this diet must be supplemented with bread soaked in milk or water, as well as mashed hard-boiled egg.

Breeding habits: They will occupy a cockatiel, finch or budgie nest or some other hollow object and build a nest in it using straw, grass, twigs and bark. As is the case with some other lovebirds, the female shoves the nesting material under her wings or into the feathers on her back and then flies to the nest with it. She drops a good deal of the material along the way, but nevertheless builds a large nest which she then enlarges further even after the eggs have been laid. The aviculturalist must therefore ensure that there is always enough nesting material for her.

Three or four eggs are laid and only the female broods, although the male often sits next to her. Incubation lasts 22 days. Both parents feed the chicks, who leave the nest after about 42 days.

MEALY ROSELLA (*Platycercus adscitus palliceps*)
PHOTO 46
Origin: Australia.

This popular rosella is hardy, breeds well and is therefore suitable for beginners. Their voices do not bother the neighbours, but they are aggressive and must be kept in an aviary by themselves when they brood.

Description: *Male* – Cheeks: white. Throat: blue. Head and neck: yellow. Back: yellow and black. Wings: blue. Thighs: blue. Breast: white and grey-blue. Tail: blue. Underside of tail: red. *Female* – As for the male, but her colours are duller. Size: 30 cm.

Diet: A seed mix suitable for parakeets, dog pellets, vegetables, greenstuff, fruit, peanut butter, a mineral mixture, shell grit and coarse grit. When there are chicks, bread soaked in milk, and hard-boiled egg, must be added.

Breeding habits: They breed readily. Four to six eggs are laid in a wooden box containing sawdust. Only the female broods. Ensure that the box is large enough to accommodate the long tail. There are no particular problems with rearing the chicks. Rosellas readily interbreed with Australian parakeets. Make sure that you buy purebred birds.

MOUSTACHED OR BANDED PARAKEET (*Psittacula alexandri fasciata*) PHOTO 47
Origin: India, southern China, Vietnam, Java and Thailand.

They are relatively rare. They sometimes bite wire and should therefore preferably be kept in aviaries of welded wire mesh. Keep only one pair of moustached parakeets per aviary. They cannot share an aviary even with doves. They screech loudly and can cause problems with the neighbours. Young birds can be tamed and will even learn a few words. There are many subspecies which differ slightly from one another.

Description: *Male* – Beak: red. Head: blue-grey. A black band connects the eyes and the bird has a black moustache beneath the beak. Neck: light green. Upper parts: green. Breast: brown-red with a purple sheen. *Female* – Beak: black-grey. For the rest like the male, except that her colours are a little duller. Size: 33 cm.

Diet: A seed mix suitable for parrots, dog pellets, fruit, vegetables, peanut butter, a mineral mixture, shell grit and coarse grit. When there are chicks, bread soaked in milk, and hard-boiled egg, must be supplied as well.

Breeding habits: They do not breed readily, but when they do breed, they use a large, deep parrot nest. The nest must be big enough to leave room for their tails, and the opening must be reinforced with tinplate. Wood shavings or sawdust must be placed in the bottom of the nest to prevent the eggs from rolling around.

Three or four eggs are laid. The incubation period is 28 days. Only the female broods. The chicks stay in the nest for about 50 days.

NYASSA LOVEBIRD (*Agapornis personata lilianae*)
Origin: Zambia, Zimbabwe and Malawi.

These are among the smallest of the lovebirds and look a great deal like Fischer's lovebirds. Buyers must beware not to buy interbred birds. There is a lutino mutation (yellow with a red eye) and a few other mutations.

Description: *Male* – They look a great deal like Fischers, apart from the following differences: The Nyassa is smaller

46 Mealy rosella   **47** Moustached or banded parakeet   **48** Peach-fronted conure

than the Fischer and has less yellow on the shoulders. However, the most noticeable difference is that the Fischer has blue feathers on the rump and underneath the wings, while the Nyassa is green there as well. *Female* – As for the male. Size: 13,5 cm.

Diet: A seed mix suitable for lovebirds, greenstuff and a little fruit such as apple, dog meal or poultry meal, a mineral mixture, shell grit and coarse grit. When there are chicks, they must also get bread soaked in water or milk, and mashed hard-boiled egg.

Breeding habits: They are colony breeders and will fill a wooden box with lots of nesting material which the female brings to the nest stuck into the feathers of her body. The aviculturalist must supply ample nesting material so that she can fill the nest further while she broods. Three or four eggs are laid; the chicks emerge after about 22 days and leave the nest after about 43 days.

PEACH-FRONTED CONURE (*Aratinga aurea*)
PHOTO 48
Origin: Brazil, Bolivia and Paraguay.
This species is often incorrectly called the orange-fronted or golden-crowned conure in South Africa. Conures normally have bare patches around the eyes, but the peach-fronted conure is an exception. There are various subspecies which differ slightly from one another. They become very tame and if one is kept in a cage by itself, it will mimic tunes and words. They are fairly hardy as far as cold is concerned, and breed reasonably well. They do not screech too loudly or make too much noise.
Description: *Male* – Orange to yellow patch from the nose to the crown of the head, followed by blue on the crown. Yellow feathers on the orbital ring. Wings: green and blue with black tips. Tail: green with a blue tip. Undersides: yellow-green. Upper parts: olive green. *Female* – As for the male, but her colours are slightly duller. Size: 26 cm.
Diet: A seed mix suitable for parakeets, dog pellets, a good deal of fruit and vegetables, as well as a mineral mixture,

shell grit and coarse grit. When there are chicks, bread soaked in milk or water, and mashed hard-boiled egg, must be added.

Breeding habits: They build a nest in a wooden box such as a cockatiel nest or a smallish parrot nest. There must be wood shavings or sawdust in the bottom to prevent the eggs from rolling around. Incubation lasts 26 days and the chicks remain in the nest for about 50 days. The female sometimes lays two sets of eggs in one season. It is better to keep only one pair in a breeding aviary, perhaps with some quail or other birds which are not in direct competition with them. During the breeding season the male can become aggressive towards other birds and may even kill them.

PLUM-HEADED PARAKEET (*Psittacula cyanocephala cyanocephala*)   PHOTO 49
Origin: Sri Lanka.
This pretty parakeet has a beautiful, melodic voice. It is mild-mannered towards and tolerant of other birds.
Description: *Male* – Head: plum-coloured with a black band around the edge. Body: yellowish green. Wings and tail: dark green with yellow and blue feathers. Shoulder: plum-coloured. Beak: yellow and black. Young males look like females. The heads of the young males only change colour after about 12-18 months. *Female* – Head: grey. Lacks plum-coloured shoulder. Size: 30 cm.
  There is a similar species, the blossom-headed parakeet, which is slightly smaller and has a rose-red head. Both sexes have red shoulders. They originate from Indo-China.
Diet: A seed mix suitable for parakeets, lots of fruit and vegetables, dog pellets, a mineral mixture, shell grit and coarse grit. When there are chicks, grass seeds, bread soaked in water or milk, and mashed hard-boiled egg must be added.
Breeding habits: Plum-headed parakeets display a beautiful courtship ritual which can last for months. They prefer to make their nest in a hole in the ground, but will also use a

49 Plum-headed parakeet   **50** Princess of Wales   **51** Rosy-faced or peach-faced lovebird

box or hollow tree trunk. Place sawdust in the bottom of the wooden nest and suspend it in such a way that the birds can sit on top of the box. The female lays four to six eggs and hatches them by herself. She does not leave the nest before the chicks are about 10 days old. During the entire brooding period and the early stages of raising the chicks, the male has to feed the female and the chicks.

PRINCESS OF WALES   (*Polytelis alexandrae*)

PHOTO 50

Origin: Australia.

This lovely parakeet with its delicate colours is not noisy and can be kept in an urban environment. They can also be kept in an aviary constructed from plain chicken wire. They are among the more expensive parakeets. They can share an aviary with other birds, but not their own kind.

Description: *Male* – Head and neck: light blue. Lower neck and upper part of back: olive green. Lower back and rump: blue. Tail: olive green, blue-green, greenish yellow, grey and pink. Throat: Pink. Wings: yellow and blue. Breast and belly: blue-grey with a green and yellow sheen. Thighs: pink turning to blue. Beak: coral. Iris: orange. *Female* – As for the male, but the colours are paler. Size: 45 cm.

Diet: Parakeet seed, greenstuff such as vegetables and fruit, dog pellets, peanut butter and soaked bread, shell grit and minerals. When there are chicks, mashed hard-boiled egg must be added to the bread.

Breeding habits: They display an interesting courting ritual. They need a deep nest with wood shavings on the bottom. The female lays three or four eggs and only she broods. Incubation lasts 20 days and the male feeds her during this time. The chicks leave the nest after five weeks and can breed when they are one year to 18 months old.

QUAKER OR GREY-BREASTED PARAKEET

(*Myiopsitta monachus monachus*)

Origin: South America.

Quaker parakeets belong to a group of parrot-like birds who do not, like other parrots, breed in a hole in a tree or in a wooden nest. They build giant nests from branches and sticks in a fork in a tree or on a platform. They screech and make a noise the whole day long and are therefore not always suited to an urban garden. However, they are lively and amusing and do therefore have their adherents among aviculturalists. They will often tolerate other quakers in the same aviary as themselves. Quakers breed regularly and are hardy as far as cold is concerned, so they are a good choice for beginners. There are various subspecies that differ only slightly from each other.

Description: *Male* – Green with a blueish sheen. Undersides: yellowish green. Wings: green with blue. Forehead, face, throat and breast: grey. Beak: horn-coloured. Legs: yellow-grey. *Female* – As for the male. Size: 29 cm. Surgical sexing is recommended.

Diet: Mixed seed suitable for parakeets, as well as green-stuff, dog pellets and fruit as well as a mineral mixture, shell grit and coarse grit. When there are chicks, add bread soaked in water or milk, as well as mashed hard-boiled egg.

Breeding habits: There must be a spot in the aviary where they can build their large nest. A forked tree trunk with many branches is suitable. If this is not available, a platform must be erected for them. This can be done by stretching chicken wire horizontally, or fixing a few planks side by side in a sheltered spot. They may even build their nest on top of a cockatiel nest. The more space there is, the larger the nest will be. Sometimes they will even build two compartments – one for breeding and the other for sleeping. Naturally the aviculturalist must make provision for this nest-building by supplying large quantities of willow or fruit tree branches or the branches of non-poisonous shrubs. The branches should preferably be soft and pliable, i.e. fresh and green. Grass and teff will also be used and stuffed in amongst the branches.

When there is more than one breeding pair in an aviary, the different pairs will often build one nest together. If the aviculturalist does not make provision for a sturdy platform for such a nest, the whole lot can collapse and fall to the ground. This means that all the chicks will die and the eggs will break and that you will sustain unnecessary losses.

As soon as there are eggs, the parents can be let out of the aviary to fly about freely, as they will always return. However, the problem is that neighbours, cats, hawks and children may catch them. It is therefore not recommended.

RED-RUMPED OR RED-BACKED PARAKEET (*Psephotus haematonotus*)
Origin: Australia.

Red-rumped parakeets are an excellent choice for a beginner. They have beautiful melodic voices, are mild-mannered, do not chew wire and breed well. It is easy to distinguish between males and females. During the breeding season they may sometimes attack other small parrots or parakeets, but they can be kept together with finches and quail. Do not keep more than one pair of red-rumped parakeets per aviary.

Description: *Male* – Rump: red. Lower breast and belly: yellow. Back: green with a brown sheen. Head: bright green with a turquoise sheen. Wings: blue-green with a yellow patch. Some wing feathers are blue on the side. Tail: upper part blue-green with white tips; underparts whitish and dark grey. Beak: dark horn-coloured. A yellow mutation is bred. *Female* – Her rump is green instead of red. She can easily be distinguished from the male. The rest of her colours are paler than those of the male. Size: 27 cm.

Diet: A seed mix suitable for parakeets, fruit and vegetables and a mineral mixture, also shell grit, coarse grit and dog or poultry meal. When there are chicks, bread soaked in water or milk, as well as mashed hard-boiled egg, must be supplied.

Breeding habits: Although they can begin breeding at 12 months, good results can only be expected at about two years. They breed in a wooden box which is large enough to accommodate their long tails. A cockatiel nest will normally suffice. Place sawdust in the bottom of the nest. The female will chew it and lay her three to five eggs in it. She broods for three weeks. During this time the male will keep watch near the nest. Both parents raise the chicks. A few weeks after they have left the nest, the chicks must be removed, because the male may kill them as soon as the female begins brooding again.

ROSY-FACED OR PEACH-FACED LOVE-BIRD (*Agapornis roseicollis*) PHOTO 51
Origin: From southern Angola through Namibia to the Orange River.

Rosy-faced lovebirds are not colony breeders like some of the other lovebirds. They kill one another if more than one pair is kept in the same aviary. They are the largest of the lovebirds. They are hardy, breed very well and are suitable for beginners.

Description: *Male* – Face and throat: rose-red.

Underparts: yellowish green. Back of the head and neck: yellowish green. Back and wings: olive green. Rump and upper parts of the tail: blue. Rest of the tail: olive green. *Female* – As for the male. Her head is smaller, her beak smaller and the rose-red colour on the head and throat sometimes paler. Size: 15 cm. There are a number of mutations such as pastel blue, pied and others.

Diet: A seed mix suitable for lovebirds, greenstuff, dog pellets and a mineral mixture, shell grit and coarse grit. When there are chicks, bread soaked in milk or water, and mashed hard-boiled egg, must be given as well.

Breeding habits: They breed in a wooden box in which they make a nest using teff, oats, grass and other available material. The aviculturalist must provide for these needs. The female pushes the nesting material into her feathers and carries it to the nest. Place a handful of nesting material in the nest. If the female merely needs to round off her nest instead of having to fill an empty box, it saves her many trips. Three or four eggs are laid and the chicks are fed by both the male and the female. They interbreed with other lovebirds and must not be kept in the same aviary as other species.

SCARLET MACAW (*Ara macao*) PHOTO 52
Origin: South America.

Scarlet macaws are possibly the best known of the macaws, as they are often pictured on travel brochures. However, they are presently very rare in the wild because so many of

52 Scarlet macaw

them have been captured. (Photo 52 was taken in a remote part of the Amazon where they still survive.) There are many of them in the aviaries of bird lovers. They need to have a very large aviary if you want them to fly. The aviary must be constructed from diamond mesh wire to keep them inside. They often screech and make a noise.

Description: *Male* – Head, top part of the back, belly and throat: red. Rump and wingtips: blue. Rest of the wings: yellow and green. Upper mandible: yellow. Lower mandible: black. Face: bare and white. *Female* – As for the male. Size: 85 cm. Surgical sexing is essential.

Diet: As for the Caninde macaw.

Breeding habits: As for the Caninde macaw.

SENEGAL PARROT (*Poicephalus senegalus mesotypus*) PHOTO 53

Origin: Senegal and from Gambia to Guinea.

These are dainty parrots from Africa. They can be kept in an aviary constructed from plain chicken wire as long as the wire is not rusted. However, it is safer to keep them in an aviary constructed from welded wire mesh, as they are clever enough to discover a weak spot in a plain chicken wire aviary, bite until it gives way, and escape. Young Senegals tame well.

There are a number of subspecies which differ slightly from one another, particularly as regards their colouring, e.g. the belly of a well-known subspecies is yellow instead of orange.

Description: *Male* – Head: grey-green. Back, wings and tail: olive green. Throat: yellow. Breast: green. Belly: orange. Underparts of tail: orange. Thighs: green. Eyes: yellow. Beak: dark grey. *Female* – As for the male, but her colours are often duller, particularly underneath the belly. However, this is not a sure sign, because great variation occurs among males as regards the belly's colour. Some males may display less orange on the belly than others. Size: 23 cm. Surgical sexing is recommended.

Diet: A seed mix suitable for parrots, i.e. it must contain peanuts. Also fruit, vegetables such as green mealies, peanut butter, dog pellets, a mineral mixture, shell grit and coarse grit. When there are chicks, they must also get bread soaked in milk or water, and mashed hard-boiled egg.

Breeding habits: As is the case with most true parrots, it is difficult to persuade them to breed. They breed in a cockatiel or parrot nest suspended high above the ground. The nest must contain sawdust. Two or three eggs are laid. The male and female take turns to stay with the eggs and later with the chicks. Although more than one pair of non-breeding birds can be kept to an aviary, it is preferable to separate a breeding pair as they will kill one another.

STANLEY'S PARAKEET (*Platycercus icterotis icterotis*)

Origin: South-western Australia.

Stanleys are among the smaller rosellas. They breed well, are hardy and therefore a suitable choice for beginners.

53 Senegal parrot

Their voices cause no disturbance and they can be kept in an aviary constructed from plain chicken wire.

Description: *Male* – Head, neck, throat and breast: blood red. Cheeks: yellow. Wings: blue. Thighs: yellow. Rump: golden green. Shoulders: blue. Wings: black and blue. Tail: green and blue. Back: black and green. *Female* – Her colours are duller and she is smaller than the male. Size: 25 cm.

Diet: A seed mix suitable for parakeets, greenstuff, vegetables and fruit, a mineral mixture, peanut butter, dog pellets, shell grit and coarse grit. When there are chicks, bread soaked in milk or water, as well as mashed hard-boiled egg, must be added.

Breeding habits: They breed in a wooden box containing a thick layer of wood shavings. Give them a choice of more than one nest. Suspend the nests and keep only one breeding pair per aviary. The female lays up to six eggs on which she alone broods. Do not fuss about the nest too much, because the birds could abandon the chicks or the nest.

SUN OR YELLOW CONURE (*Aratinga solstitialis*) PHOTO 54

Origin: Guiana, Venezuela and north-eastern Brazil.

These beautiful loudmouths become tame and make good pets as long as you can tame them when they are still young. They can be kept in aviaries constructed from plain chicken wire, but do not keep more than one pair per aviary. Also do not release other parakeets into the aviary.

Description: *Male* – Head, neck and throat: golden yellow. Forehead and cheeks: orange. Belly, rump, thighs and lower back: orange. Underside of tail: green and yellow. Shoulders: yellow. Wings: yellow and green. Beak: grey. Orbital ring: dark-coloured, small and bare. *Female* – As for the male. Size: 30 cm. Surgical sexing is recommended.

Diet: A seed mix suitable for parakeets, greenstuff and fruit, a mineral mixture, shell grit and coarse grit. Also provide dog meal or dog pellets. When there are chicks, bread

54 Sun conure

soaked in milk or water, and mashed hard-boiled egg, must also be provided.

Breeding habits: It is fairly difficult to get them to breed. When they do breed, they will use a cockatiel nest in which wood shavings have been placed. The female lays three to five eggs and only she broods. The chicks leave the nest after about two months.

SWAINSON'S BLUE MOUNTAIN LORIKEET OR RAINBOW LORIKEET (*Trichoglossus haematodus*) PHOTO 55

Origin: Australia, Timor and other islands north of Australia.

It is a pleasure to keep these lovely brush-tongues. Their colours outshine those of the rainbow and they have a playful nature like a puppy's. Even breeding birds become so tame that they will play with their owner's hand. They like to bath and it is essential to provide them with water for bathing at all times, as this helps to keep them clean despite their messy diet of ProNutro.

Breeding pairs must be kept by themselves in an aviary as they will kill other breeding pairs. They can be kept in an aviary constructed of plain chicken wire. They breed regularly. There are more than 20 subspecies which differ from one another only slightly.

These subspecies occur on the islands northwest of Australia where they have developed slightly differently from the other rainbow lorikeets because of their isolation from the other species, and differences in the available food. They are hardy as far as cold is concerned and a suitable choice for beginners.

Description: *Male* – Head: purple with a light green collar. Wings, back, rump and tail: dark green. Breast: red with orange. Lower breast and belly: purple. Thighs: green. Underside of tail: olive green with yellow. Underside of wings: red at the shoulders and for the rest black and yellow. Beak: orange. *Female* – as for the male, but the red on her breast, in particular, is often less conspicuous and less widespread. She is also built slightly more daintily. Size: 26 cm. Surgical sexing is virtually essential to obtain a true breeding pair.

Diet: ProNutro mixed well with water and honey or syrup constitutes their staple food. Peanut butter, fruit, bread soaked in milk and a mixture of sunflower, oat, sorghum and millet seeds must be added. A seed mix for parakeets is suitable. Apart from the seed, the rest of the food must be provided fresh daily. From this variety they will choose for themselves what they want. Their choice varies, depending on whether there are chicks or not. While they are raising chicks, they eat much more of the bread with milk, but in winter they will eat more seed.

Breeding habits: They make a nest in a cockatiel nest. Place a good deal of wood shavings (or bran) in the bottom of the nest.

As soon as the chicks have hatched, these shavings must be replaced weekly with clean shavings, as the chicks have very watery droppings and quickly foul the nest. A special nest with charcoal is described on p. 19.

Two eggs are laid and the parents normally raise both chicks successfully. Rainbow lorikeets can breed at 18 months or two years of age.

As is the case with all birds, they must first learn how to raise the chicks and a young pair may fail once or twice before they get going.

55 Swainson's Blue Mountain lorikeet or rainbow lorikeet

YELLOW-FRONTED AMAZON PARROT

(*Amazona ochrocephala ochrocephala*) (PHOTO 56 is of a subspecies, a wild parrot which eats bananas in the Amazon.)

Origin: From Mexico down to the Amazon region and in eastern Peru.

They are fairly common and popular as talkers. There are a number of subspecies, some with red on the wings and others with a greater or lesser distribution of yellow over the face. They are wire-biters and must be kept in aviaries constructed from welded wire mesh. If it is the intention to breed with them, it is better to use birds from the wild, and not pets. Surgical sexing is essential.

Description: *Male* – Body: grass green. Forehead: yellow. In some subspecies the yellow spreads further than only the forehead. Wings: green with red on the shoulders and wingtips. Eyes: red. Orbital ring: white and bare. Beak: black with a reddish spot on either side. *Female* – As for the male. Size: 35 cm.

Diet: A seed mixture suitable for parrots, greenstuff, dog cakes, a great deal of fruit, nuts, a mineral mixture, shell grit and coarse grit. When there are chicks, mashed hard-boiled egg and bread soaked in milk or water must be added.

Breeding habits: It has always been thought that it is impossible to breed these parrots in captivity. Because the parrots were kept mainly as pets, few people tried to breed them. A tame parrot does not easily become a breeding

56 Yellow-fronted Amazon parrot

parrot because it often rejects its own kind and relates better to humans.

Furthermore it was virtually impossible to determine their sex and bring together a true pair. With modern surgical sexing, however, it is possible to bring together a true pair. Unless the birds are too tame, breeding results can be expected in an ordinary parrot nest. Of course the chicks become very tame.

10

Finches and waxbills

Finches are most charming birds. Because they are seed eaters, they are known as 'hardbills'. Birds which live mostly on nectar, insects or fruit are known as 'softbills'. What aviculturalists call 'finches' is not ornithologically correct. True finches are only a small group of birds but, as this book is for the layman, popular nomenclature, as used by aviculturalists, is employed.

There are certain advantages to finches. Because they are small, they do not require as much space as parrots. A number of pairs of the same species can be kept in the same aviary, unlike parrots, where normally only one pair of the same species occupies an aviary. Furthermore a large variety of finches can live together. In contrast to parrot-like birds they do not normally destroy plants and the aviary can therefore be decorated with shrubs. They are not as noisy as, nor do they screech like, some members of the parrot family. This makes them a good choice for the city dweller.

Finches mature more quickly than members of the parrot family. At the age of eight months many of them can breed, whereas an aviculturalist must sometimes wait for years before a parrot reaches maturity. Most finches breed more than once a year, or at least attempt to. When an attempt at breeding fails, the breeder of finches, unlike a parrot breeder, does not have to wait very long before the nest is once more full of eggs. Where there are eggs, there is hope – and where there is hope, there is interest.

Finches seldom become as tame as the parrot types and, with a very few exceptions, cannot become pets. The feeding of some finches such as waxbills can cause problems, particularly if they require a great many insects. The birds generally known as 'finches' can be divided into various groups, e.g. waxbills, mannikins, sparrows and cardinals.

Finches

Finches follow a fairly simple diet in that they are able to breed and raise chicks on a diet of seed, greenstuff, a mineral mixture, shell grit and coarse grit. However, in nature finches usually take in a great many insects while they are raising chicks, but they are able to raise chicks on a substitute diet. Apart from the seed mix, brown bread soaked in milk, mashed hard-boiled egg, commercially available rearing mix and seed sprouts are adequate supplements during the breeding season. Of course live food is always welcome, but usually not essential.

The Australian finches such as the Gouldians, diamond sparrows, Parsons, Bichenos and long-tailed grass finches are among the most popular finches. It is strange that we in South Africa fare so relatively poorly with the Australian finches. After all, we have the same climate as Australia, yet we cannot breed them in large enough numbers to supply even our own needs. An aviculturalist specialising in Australian finches and able to breed them on a large scale would secure an excellent market for himself in South Africa as well as abroad.

Throughout the year finches like sleeping in sheltered calabashes or boxes. Extra nests, used only for sleeping purposes, must therefore always be available. If they are forced to sleep outside, they may die of cold.

Waxbills

Waxbills are chirpy birds which provide much pleasure in any aviary. Most of the waxbills available to us come from Africa. Among them are the Cordon Bleus, blue-capped Cordon Bleus, orange-cheeked and red-eared waxbills and Peter's twinspot. The blue waxbill is an example of a South African species, while strawberry finches (also waxbills) hail from India.

Most waxbills have sweet voices, are colourful and should do well in South Africa in the hands of an aviculturalist who specialises in them. This is because they need a good deal of live food in order to breed and raise their chicks. If you wish to start a waxbill avicultural operation, you must therefore pay attention to breeding mealworms and be assured of a plentiful supply of termite or ant nests in the vicinity. Dog meal or pellets can go a long way towards supplementing live food and all efforts must be made to teach the waxbills to eat these. The nesting facilities we provide the waxbills with in aviaries also depart from their natural needs to such an extent that they refuse to breed. See p. 21 for the nesting requirements of waxbills.

Mannikins

Mannikins look like finches, but have shorter, stouter and stronger bills than those of true finches. Among them there are the Bengalese finch, silverbill and Java sparrow. In general they breed well and do not need live food. They are not as colourful as other finches, but are hardy and a good choice for beginners. Many mannikin species are kept as caged birds.

Cardinals

Cardinals can be regarded as a transitional phase between hardbills and softbills. They do eat seed, but require plenty of fruit and a certain quantity of live food in order to breed.

Cardinals are beautiful birds from the Americas. They are colourful; some are red all over. They are large, often aggressive, strong and hardy. It is not unusual to see the Virginia cardinal, which hails from North America, breeding in an open nest in the snow.

Because they are highly active, they must be accommodated in large aviaries and definitely not in cages.

Individual descriptions

AFRICAN SILVERBILL   (*Euodice cantans*)
Origin: Western and central Africa.
Although its colouring is rather dull, this mannikin is a real stalwart in any aviculturalist's aviary. Not only do silverbills breed well, but they are also first-class incubators for the eggs of other finches.

They are good foster mothers for strange chicks such as Cordon Bleus, red-eared waxbills and star finches, which are often too restless to breed themselves. Silverbills are a good choice for a beginner.
Description: *Male* – Back: light brown. Breast and undersides: cream. Wings: dark brown. Rump and tail: almost black. The male sings to the female. *Female* – As for the male. Her bill is slightly smaller than that of the male and she does not sing to him. Size: 14 cm.
Diet: A simple diet of finch seed, greenstuff, a mineral mixture, shell grit and coarse grit is suitable. When there are chicks, brown bread soaked in milk, and hard-boiled egg, must be given in addition.
Breeding habits: Silverbills build their nests in finch or budgie nests, tins or other sheltered hollows and need plenty of teff or grass, wool, cotton, feathers and bits of fabric for this.

The aviculturalist can save them a great deal of trouble by placing a handful of teff or grass in the nest and making a hollow in this, so that the birds merely need to round off the nest.

The eggs hatch within 12 days and the chicks leave the nest after three weeks. It is not unusual for a pair to raise up to 20 chicks in a season.

This can severely exhaust the female. Give the female some rest during the winter months by removing the male.

A nest which is used so often, needs to be examined regularly. Remove the nesting material if it is wet or infested with insects and clean the box or tin when the chicks have been removed so that the parents can build a new nest for the next set of eggs.

Silverbills interbreed with spice finches, zebra finches and pin-tailed nonpareils.

BENGALESE OR SOCIETY FINCH   (*Lonchura domestica*)
Origin: These birds do not occur in nature, but were developed in the Far East by means of a whole range of crossbreeding.

This happened so long ago that the actual original races are unknown, although bird experts like to speculate about the precise parentage of the Bengalese finch.

The Bengalese finch is a mannikin with a short, stout bill. Bengalese finches like bathing. Furthermore they are such outstanding foster parents for the chicks of other finches that aviculturalists keep them for this purpose.
Description: There are various colours and colour combinations, e.g. white, cinnamon and brown. Silver finches have a mixture of brown and white pigment in their feathers. The colours are spread over the finch in an infinite variety of patterns and no two finches look alike. Some sport a crest. Solid colours, e.g. all brown or all cinnamon, are sometimes called 'selfs'.

Pure white is regressive with regard to brown. If you continuously breed with pure white Bengalese, the birds later show problems such as blindness and infertility. White Bengalese finches must occasionally be crossed with light cinnamon or white-and-cinnamon finches.

The sex of a bird cannot be determined by appearance, only by behaviour. The male puffs himself up when he sings. Size: 13 cm.
Diet: Finch seed, greenstuff, a mineral mixture, shell grit and coarse grit. Sprouted seeds and brown bread soaked in milk are essential supplements when chicks are being raised. When they are expected to raise waxbills' chicks, they must be given live food, or the chicks may die.
Breeding habits: Bengalese finches begin breeding at the age of eight months. Give them a finch nest in the form of a wooden box, calabash or tin containing teff or grass. They appreciate pillow feathers with which to line their nest. As is the case with all finches, feathers, wool, cotton fluff and pieces of fabric are welcome when they build their nest.

Six to eight eggs are laid and both parents brood during the incubation period of 14 days. Both parents feed the chicks until they leave the nest at 21 days, whereafter they are fed outside the nest.

Bengalese finches can even be kept in canary breeding cages.

They are colony breeders and often help one another to build nests and even hatch the eggs. Sometimes three or four females lay their eggs in one nest, hatch them together and raise the chicks together.

For this reason they should not be kept in an aviary together with rare and expensive finches. It is, however, precisely these characteristics that make them such excellent foster parents for the discarded chicks of other finches and why they so readily hatch other finches' eggs.

All serious finch aviculturalists should therefore keep a number of Bengalese finch pairs to serve as foster parents.

Bengalese finches as foster parents: Some finches, such as star finches, are sometimes too restless to hatch their eggs in a busy aviary. Place such eggs in the nest of a Bengalese finch together with the Bengalese's eggs – provided that the eggs are roughly equally close to hatching. If the eggs of the strange finch are not as close to hatching as those of the Bengalese, it is best to remove the Bengalese's eggs. If the Bengalese's chicks appear first, she will stop brooding. The remaining eggs then become cold and the embryos will die.

Strange baby finches can also surreptitiously be placed in the nest of a Bengalese finch. The parents will then raise them together with their own chicks. Older strange chicks may perhaps be discarded, particularly if they have strange colours, such as green parrot finches.

When stuck with a fairly grown discarded finch, e.g. one already covered in feathers, and the Bengalese finches refuse to feed it, you can place the finch on the ground in an aviary with Bengalese finches.

With luck a dutiful foster parent may arrive to feed the discarded chick. If this does not happen, hand-rearing is the only alternative.

Bengalese finches are very often used to raise Australian finches. They are not as successful in the case of waxbills, probably because they eat too little live food to provide for the needs of the waxbill chicks. The waxbill chicks usually die if their own parents cannot feed them.

Not all Bengalese finches make good foster parents. The serious finch breeder will determine beforehand which of them are good foster parents and ring them so that they can be identified when their services are needed.

BICHENO OR OWL FINCH (*Poephila bichenovi*)
PHOTO 57

Origin: Australia.
Bicheno finches are the smallest of the Australian finches. They are suitable for a collection as they are mild-mannered. However, they will defend their nest vigorously. They are not hardy and can therefore not be kept in fairly cold regions unless the aviary is heated. Like most other finches, they like sleeping in boxes or nests and these must be available the whole year round. The male will often sleep outside and then you may lose him during a cold night.

Description: *Male* – Body: grey and white with a black band across the breast and around the face. Wings: dark grey with white dots. Tail: black. Bill: silver. Legs: grey. *Female* – As for the male. Sometimes the breast is paler than that of the male. Size: 10 cm. Sexing on the grounds of appearance is extremely inaccurate. The male courts the female by dancing for her. Surgical sexing is recommended. There is a species with a white rump which originates from the more tropical parts of Australia.

Diet: A seed mix suitable for finches, a mineral mixture, greenstuff, poultry rearing meal or similar supplement, shell grit and coarse grit. When there are chicks, sprouted

57 Bicheno finch

seeds, mashed hard-boiled eggs and/or rearing mix must be given additionally.

Breeding habits: They build a nest of soft material in a finch or budgie nest or calabash. Soft teff hay, carrot tops, kikuyu grass and pillow feathers are suitable for this purpose. Four to six eggs are laid and both parents brood. The chicks hatch within 12 days and are fed by both parents. They leave the nest after 20-25 days, but must still be fed for some time.

CUT-THROAT FINCH (*Amadina fasciata*)
Origin: Africa.
There are two types of cut-throat finches. The one hails from Ethiopia and East Africa and the other from other regions of Africa, including South Africa. The colours of the former are brighter and the red stripe is broader, so they look more attractive. These finches are hardy and suitable for colder regions. They are a suitable choice for beginners.

Description: *Male* – The male has a conspicuous red stripe across the throat which is lacking in the female. Breast: creamy brown. Belly: brown with white dots. Back and wings: brown. Head: white and brown bars. Bill: cream. Legs: cream. *Female* – As for the male, apart from the red band across the throat. Size: 13 cm. The male tries to sing to the female in a barely audible voice and puffs up the feathers of his throat.

Diet: A seed mix suitable for finches, a mineral mixture, shell grit and greenstuff or other supplements. When there are chicks, they must get brown bread soaked in milk, sprouted grass seeds, mashed hard-boiled egg and/or rearing mix.

Breeding habits: They breed well in a finch nest which they round off with grass or teff. The female lays four to six eggs and the parents take turns to brood. The chicks emerge after 12 days. Do not peer into the nest too often while they are brooding, because they may abandon the eggs.

CORDON BLEU (*Uraeginthus bengalus*) PHOTO 58
Origin: Central America.
Because this bird is a waxbill, it fares best in an aviary which is thickly planted and attracts plenty of insects. Because they like scratching on the ground looking for insects, an

58 Cordon Bleu   **59** Diamond sparrow   **60** Gouldian finch (yellow-headed)

aviary with a soil floor is desirable; if not, fresh sods of top-soil must be added to the aviary every week.

Description: *Male* – Back, wings, top of the head and breast: soft brown. Rest of the body: sky blue. A red stripe extends across the cheek. *Female* – As for the male. She lacks the red stripe across the cheek. Size: 13 cm.

Diet: As many insects as possible. Chopped mealworms, termites and ant eggs must be provided at least three times a week (preferably more often). Also finch seed, a mineral mixture, greenstuff, shell grit and coarse grit. Try to persuade them to eat at least the protein part of dog meal. When there are chicks, they must get even more live food, as well as bread soaked in milk, mashed hard-boiled egg on its own or mixed with rearing mix, and/or moistened dog meal.

Breeding habits: Cordon Bleus will breed reasonably, provided they get enough insects in their diet. They prefer to build a nest of grass in a thick shrub. If this is not possible, they will move into a budgie or finch nest filled with grass. Provide soft grass or teff hay, whole carrot tops, long kikuyu grass and pillow feathers.

Birds who interfere with the nests of their neighbours, such as zebra and Bengalese finches, must be kept away from Cordon Bleus (see p. 30).

Both sexes help to build the nest, but only the female broods.

It takes 12-13 days for the eggs to hatch and the chicks leave the nest after another 15 days. The chicks look like the female until the red patch on the cheek, which distinguishes the male, appears at about five months.

DIAMOND SPARROW (*Staganoplaura guttata*)
PHOTO 59

Origin: Australia.

Diamond sparrows are extremely popular, fairly hardy as far as cold is concerned, and breed fairly readily. Diamond sparrows need plenty of flying space, or they may become too fat.

Description: *Male* – Head: grey. Throat: white. Back: grey. Flanks: black with white spots. A black band extends across the breast. Rump: blood red. Undersides: white. Legs: grey. Bill: dark red. Eye ring: red. *Female* – As for the male. Sometimes the bill is a lighter red and the ring around the eye slightly paler. Size: 13 cm. The male sings with slightly more variation than the female, who merely chirps.

It is very difficult to identify a true pair on the grounds of appearance only, and surgical sexing is recommended. There is a cinnamon-coloured mutation.

Diet: Finch seed, greenstuff or other supplements, a mineral mixture, shell grit and coarse grit. Try to persuade them to eat at least a part of dog meal, laying meal or poultry growth meal.

When there are chicks, they must also get brown bread soaked in milk or water and mixed with grated hard-boiled egg. Rearing mix is also suitable, as are the contents of mealworms.

Breeding habits: The male courts the female by carrying a piece of grass to her and shaking it to and fro in front of her while jumping about. She normally looks bored, but this does not mean that she has not accepted him.

They breed in finch or budgie nests in which they build a nest from grass, teff and feathers. The female can lay up to six eggs.

Both parents hatch the eggs and they begin brooding as soon as the first egg has been laid. This means that the chicks hatch consecutively within a few days. The chicks leave the nest after 22-24 days, but sleep with their parents at night.

Diamond sparrows normally raise the chicks themselves, but if they refuse to do so, Bengalese finches may help. Do not give a Bengalese finch more than three chicks, because diamond sparrow immatures eat a great deal and the foster mother will not be able to cope with the feeding.

If a pair of diamond sparrows refuses to breed, they are probably of the same sex.

GOULDIAN FINCH (*Poephila gouldiae gouldiae*)

PHOTO 60

Origin: North Australia.

As far as colour is concerned, the Gouldian finch must surely be the king of all the finches. In comparison to other finches they are very restful, even passive. Fortunately they breed very well – and this is their saving grace, because they also die very easily! Because they are so beautiful, they are extremely popular and there is a good market for them.

In an effort to keep their Gouldians alive, some aviculturalists build expensive aviaries in which the temperature is thermostatically controlled and even the moisture content is kept at a so-called ideal level. Unfortunately such expense does not always lead to success. Birds which are cosseted in this way usually have very little resistance to mild stress situations.

Other aviculturalists build expensive brick or glass rooms instead of open aviaries. Some aviculturalists even cover their birds with a tarpaulin every night or try all kinds of additives to the food – yet the Gouldians drop like flies from time to time. Still, there are aviculturalists who achieve success with the birds.

As Gouldians are sensitive to temperature changes, it helps to keep them at a temperature which varies only between 55-70 °F. Deaths occur particularly when Gouldians are sold and transported to a new aviary. Up to 75% of the bought birds can succumb within the first 10 days. During the process of capture they must therefore be chased about as little as possible. Furthermore they must be transported in a semi-dark travel box with as few other birds as possible and released into their new aviary as early as possible in the day so that they can make themselves at home before it gets dark.

The aviary must be clean, quiet and sheltered, without aggressive birds disturbing the mild-mannered Gouldians. For the first few days you can stand translucent fibreglass sheets upright around the aviary so that the birds are not frightened unnecessarily, until they become used to the new environment.

Food and water must be clearly visible and be available at various spots, particularly if the aviary is large. The food must be the same as that to which the Gouldians were accustomed. An intensive five-day treatment with a multi-vitamin mixture will also help the newcomers to survive. The water in particular must be crystal clear. Birds exposed to stressful situations such as a new aviary sometimes develop scour. If the food and water become contaminated, the disease can spread throughout the aviary like wildfire. Remove Gouldians which appear ill so that they will not infect the others, and keep the food and water absolutely clean. Try as far as possible to create the same circumstances as those maintained at the successful aviculturalist's operation.

Sudden cold snaps cause Gouldians to die in droves. In regions of the country where winters are cold, the aviculturalist must make provision for proper protection in the shape of a room in which the birds can be kept at night and on cold days. If not, the places where they sleep must be heated by means of light bulbs or infra-red lamps (see p. 13 for the heating of aviaries).

Gouldians also have a low resistance to diseases. A concentration of germs which do not harm other birds will cause Gouldians to die.

Strict hygiene is therefore of the utmost importance, particularly near the food and water bowls. Be on your guard against coccidiosis.

Description: Three types of Gouldians are commonly bred: red-headed, black-headed and yellow-headed Gouldians. There is also a white-breasted mutation which appears rather pale next to the natural colours. Apart from the heads, the other colours are the same. *Male* – Neck, back and wings: green. Breast: bright purple. Lower breast and belly: dark yellow. Back of head and rump: light purple. Face and head: red or yellow with a black edge, or black. Bill: cream. Legs: flesh-coloured. *Female* – As for the male, but her breast is a paler purple. Size: 13 cm. It is easy to distinguish between the sexes, except in the case of young birds, where both sexes look like the female.

Diet: Plain finch seed mixes, greenstuff or similar supplements, a mineral mixture, shell grit and coarse grit. Japanese millet as well as mixed grass seeds which can be bought from grass farmers form an important and essential supplement to the Gouldians' diet.

Just ensure that the grass seeds have not been fumigated or treated for insects. When there are chicks, bread soaked in milk and mixed with hard-boiled egg must be added. Rearing mix and sprouted seeds are also good additions.

Breeding habits: Gouldians begin breeding in January and the breeding season lasts until October. Young birds are marketed in November, December and January, when they change colour for the first time.

The male courts the female by jumping up and down while trilling to her. If she likes him, her tail trembles. They breed in finch nests containing grass, teff or soft green leaves such as carrot tops, as well as pillow feathers. Special Gouldian nests made of wood are commercially available. This is an L-shaped finch nest with a sliding top. Place a handful of nesting material in the box to save the pair some time, so that they merely need to finish off the nest to their own taste.

Gouldians lay about six eggs and both parents sit on the nest. The chicks hatch within 16 days. They have fluorescent spots on the sides of their bills so that the parents can see the chicks in the dark nest in order to feed them.

Young Gouldians are grey and assume their colours only at the age of one year. They die easily while moulting and taking on the adult colours. Ensure that soft food is available until the completion of the moulting.

Prevent them from breeding before they are one year old. A pair becomes extremely attached to one another. If they are separated in winter, they must be ringed so that the same pair can get together again.

GREATER HILL MYNAH   (*Gracula religiosa*)
Origin: Indonesia.

A small mynah from India could be mistaken for the real talker, but does not have the same gift of the gab as the larger mynah from Indonesia.

This mynah is very popular because it becomes so tame and learns to talk and whistle even better than a parrot. When a mynah is kept as a pet, it must have a very large cage.

This must be cleaned regularly as they mess large quantities of wet droppings on the floor. A pet mynah must be removed from the cage regularly and be allowed to climb about or even to fly freely. A tame mynah will always return to its owner's shoulder when called.

Mynahs can also be kept in an aviary outside, but in such a case will never learn to talk well. If they must share an aviary with other birds, the other birds must be big and strong. Mynahs will habitually kill small birds and eat them. They will even eat their own chicks.

It is this characteristic which causes bird experts so much worry about the imported mynah which is entering South Africa at present.

They are spreading slowly but surely throughout the country. Some bird experts feel that they may displace our indigenous species. It is therefore irresponsible to release a mynah to swell the feral population.

In their natural state mynahs live in wooded regions where they are always assured of shade. It is wrong to hang a mynah's cage outside in the sun without providing the bird with adequate shelter. Many mynahs die of heat exhaustion because their owners do not know any better. They must therefore always be able to retreat from the sun to available shelter.

Description: *Male* – Black with a green sheen on the back. Bright yellow folds of featherless skin behind the eyes and ears, even reaching behind the head. Legs: yellow-orange. *Female* – As for the male, but with a more slender build. Size: 22 cm.

Diet: Lots of fruit and vegetables, raw chopped or minced meat and wet or dried dog meal or dog pellets.

Breeding habits: If you plan to breed with them, a pair must be kept alone in an aviary. They will build a nest from grass, twigs and teff in an open basket or even an enclosed parakeet nest.

GREEN AVADAVAT   (*Amandava formosa*)
Origin: India.

The pretty green avadavat is rare and expensive, and not for beginners, but it is an interesting challenge for the knowledgeable aviculturalist.

Description: *Male* – Back and wings: olive green. Rump: brown-yellow. Tail: black. Undersides: various shades of yellow. Flanks and thighs: black and white stripes. Face and throat: dull green-yellow. Bill: deep red. *Female* – The same, but all the colours are duller. Size: 11 cm.

Diet: Finch seed, sprouted seeds, greenstuff, mineral mix-

ture and as much live food and dog meal or dog pellets as possible, as well as shell grit and coarse grit.

Breeding habits: These birds will breed only if they are provided with plenty of insects. They also require a good deal of space. The chicks in particular must get lots of mealworms, ant eggs and termite larvae to survive. They breed in a wooden finch nest, a dense shrub, a calabash or any other suitable sheltered spot. They need a great deal of nesting material such as carrot tops, teff hay and pillow feathers. See p. 21 for more information about nests for waxbills.

JAVA SPARROW   (*Padda oryzivora*)
Origin: Indonesia.

Java sparrows are sometimes kept in a cage, where their feathers soon become tatty. It is better to keep them outside in an aviary.

Because they are bigger, stronger birds, they should rather not be mixed with smaller finch species. They can share an aviary with cardinals, diamond doves, quail, budgies and long-tailed parakeets. They are hardy and a suitable choice for beginners.

Description: *Male* – The original Java sparrow from the wild has a dove-grey colour. Head: black. Tail: black. Cheek: a large white patch. Undersides: white. Bill: large, stout and pink with a white edge. Legs: flesh-coloured. *Female* – As for the male. Her bill is smaller. Size: 14 cm. The male sings, but the female does not.

The white Java sparrow, a mutation which was bred originally by the Japanese, is completely white, with pink in the bill, the ring around the eye and the legs. Young white Java sparrows often have a lot of grey in their feathers, but this becomes white later on.

There is also a pied mutation. In the case of the pieds the colour patterns differ a great deal from one bird to the next.

Diet: Plain finch seed mixed with a little sunflower seed is suitable. Because they are so large, they can handle larger seeds. Also feed them plenty of fruit, greenstuff, vegetables, a mineral mixture, shell grit and coarse grit. When there are chicks, they must get bread soaked in milk, and hard-boiled egg.

Breeding habits: Java sparrows bred in aviaries make excellent breeding birds, but their nests must be at least one metre away from the nests of other birds, because they vigorously defend them against intruders.

A finch or parakeet nest is suitable. Dry grass, feathers, wool, cotton or small pieces of fabric must be provided for lining the nest. Incubation lasts about 13-14 days and the chicks leave the nest after three weeks.

LONG-TAILED GRASS FINCH   (*Poephila acuticauda*)   PHOTO 61
Origin: North-western Australia.

There are two types of long-tailed grass finch, namely the long-tailed grass finch with the yellow bill, and the Heck's grass finch with the red bill. A long-tailed grass finch with

61   Long-tailed grass finch (left) and Heck's grass finch (right)

an orange bill is a cross between these two. Unfortunately the South African long-tailed grass finches are severely hybridised and it is difficult to get hold of a pure bird. The two types must always be accommodated separately. Both types are somewhat sensitive to the cold as they originally hail from the warm, bushveld-like north-western Australia.

Description: *Male* – Head: silver-grey. Body and wings: grey-brown. Undersides: paler grey-brown. The bird's pitch-black bib is characteristic. There is also a conspicuous stripe across the eye. Thighs: black and white, but not in the form of bars. Tail: long, thin and black. Bill: red, yellow or orange, as explained above. The male puffs up his bib and sings and dances for the female. *Female* – As for the male, but her bib is often smaller. Surgical sexing is recommended. Size: 16 cm.

Diet: Mixed finch seed, greenstuff or other supplements such as poultry growth meal, a mineral mixture, shell grit and coarse grit. When there are chicks, brown bread soaked in milk, hard-boiled egg and/or rearing mix must be added.

Breeding habits: The male prefers to pick his own mate and will therefore not necessarily pair off with the female assigned to him. Keep a colony of the birds so that there is a choice of mates. They often mate for life, and then breed well.

Should a male and female be separated in winter, they must be ringed so that the true pairs can get together again. Do not allow them to breed before they are a year old.

Finch or budgie nests must be suspended in sheltered spots. Place a handful of teff or grass in the nest. Provide plenty of extra teff or grass and other soft material so that the birds have no need to fight over it. Sometimes they will build a nest on top of a canary nest.

The female lays about four eggs. The male helps to hatch them. Incubation lasts 17 days. Do not peer into the nest too often.

MASKED GRASS FINCH   (*Poephila personata*)
Origin: Australia.

They can sometimes cause problems in an aviary because they often utter an alarm call and frighten the other finches. They breed well, however.

Description: *Male* – Bill: noticeably large, stout and yellow. Face: black. Head and back: brown. Breast and belly: white. Thighs: black. Tail: white and black. Legs: flesh-coloured. *Female* – As for the male. Her colour is slightly duller and her bill smaller than that of the male. Size: 17 cm. It is difficult to distinguish between the sexes.

Diet: Finch seed, greenstuff or other similar supplements such as poultry growth meal, a mineral mixture, shell grit and coarse grit. When there are chicks, the diet must be supplemented with bread soaked in milk, hard-boiled egg, sprouted grass seeds and/or rearing mix.

Breeding habits: Their nests must be far away from those of other birds because they chase away everything that comes near. The nest is built in a budgie or finch nest or calabash. They use teff, grass, feathers and other soft material for their nest. They usually raise their chicks themselves.

ORANGE-CHEEKED WAXBILL   (*Estrilda melpoda melpoda*)   PHOTO 62
Origin: West Africa.

These are bright, chirpy birds which are very popular. They are peaceable towards other birds and suitable for a mixed aviary.

Description: *Male* – Upper parts: dark grey. Underparts: light grey with an orange sheen. Underparts of tail: grey-black. Cheeks: orange to above the eye. Bill: red-orange. Rump: red. *Female* – Her bill, cheeks and breast are paler than those of the male. Size: 11 cm. The male courts her by dancing before her with his tail spread out.

Diet: As is the case with all waxbills, live food is important. However, they are not so greatly dependent on this as other waxbills and will breed on a diet of finch seed, greenstuff or similar supplements, a mineral mixture, shell grit and

62   Orange-cheeked waxbill

coarse grit. When there are chicks, rearing mix, hard-boiled egg and brown bread soaked in milk must be given in addition.

Try to persuade them to eat dog meal and complement the diet with live food about three times a week.

Breeding habits: They will occupy a budgie or finch nest or tin can and build a pretty vaulted nest of grass or teff in it. Sometimes they will also build a nest of grass on the ground or in a shrub.

The nest must be sheltered because the parents leave the nest as soon as other birds come too close (see p. 21 for waxbill nests).

Both parents sit on the eggs and the chicks emerge after 11-12 days. They leave the nest after another 14 days.

If the parents kick the chicks out of the nest, the problem can be solved by removing the male as soon as the chicks hatch.

If you do it before hatching, the female often stops brooding. If this happens, Bengalese finches or silverbills can hatch the eggs and raise the chicks.

63 Parson finch

PARSON FINCH (*Poephila cincta cincta*) PHOTO 63
Origin: Australia.
Description: *Male* – Parsons look a lot like grass finches, excepting that the tail is short, the bill black and the legs red. As in the case of the grass finch, the parson sports a black bib. *Female* – As for the male. The bib is often smaller, but sexing only on the grounds of appearance is inaccurate. Size: 14 cm. Young males often look like females. When mating the male dances before the female and puffs up his bib.
Diet: Finch seed, dog meal or poultry growth meal, greenstuff, a mineral mixture, shell grit and coarse grit. When there are chicks, mashed hard-boiled egg, bread soaked in milk and/or rearing mix must be provided.
Breeding habits: They may breed better than the other grass finches – if a pair refuses to breed, they are probably of the same sex.

They make a grass or teff nest in a finch box, or sometimes in an open basket or canary nest. Both parents sit on the four to six eggs and both feed the chicks.

PEKIN ROBIN (*Leiothrix lutea*)
Origin: China.
A pretty, hardy bird which can be kept where winters are cold. They are popular and very lively and become quite tame. Pekin robins sing well and are sometimes kept as caged birds.

Pekin robins are aggressive towards their own kind and will even kill one another. Do not keep more than one pair in an aviary. They also steal smaller finch's eggs and eat these. Rather mix them with larger birds that can defend their nests.
Description: *Male* – Brownish green. Wings: brown with red feathers near the tips. Eye: black. Eye ring: cream. An oval white stripe which extends from the ear to the nose is

characteristic. Bill: red. Breast: yellowish to orange. Legs: cream. *Female* – As for the male, but somewhat duller. Size: 15 cm. Young males look like females. The male sings very prettily, while the female calls monotonously.
Diet: Although Pekin robins are insectivorous, they learn to eat a finch seed mix.

Fruit, greenstuff, peanut butter and mealworms or dog meal must also be added, as well as shell grit, a mineral mixture and coarse grit. Feed them ant eggs or termites twice or three times a week.
Breeding habits: They use a finch or budgie nest in which to build their own.

Place teff, grass or moss in the box so that they merely need to finish off the nest. They do this with twigs, bark or other nesting material.

Nests must be suspended high above the ground and be private. Hide them behind branches or plants. The three to five eggs hatch after 13 days.

The chicks leave the nest after 12 days, but depend on their parents for a long time.

PETER'S OR RED-THROATED TWINSPOT (*Hypargos niveoguttatus*)
Origin: East Africa.
This pretty dark red bird comes from warm regions and is therefore sensitive as far as cold is concerned. They do not fare well in regions where frost occurs, unless they are covered during winter, or the aviary is heated. They mix well with other species and like to scratch about on the ground for insects.

An aviary with a soil floor planted with grass and containing plenty of plants is therefore preferable. If not, a few sods of soil must be placed in the aviary every week.
Description: *Male* – Face and throat: dark red. Flanks:

64 Pin-tailed nonpareil

nearly black with white dots. Wings: brown. Back: light brown. Rump: red. Tail: red. Bill: grey. Head and neck: grey. *Female* – Face and throat: straw-coloured. For the rest like the male, but her colours are duller. Size: 12 cm. The male courts the female by picking up a blade of grass or feather and dancing for her with outspread wings and a stretched out neck.

A bird coloured pink instead of red occurs on the east coast of southern Africa. As these birds occur in South Africa, you probably need to obtain a permit in order to keep them.

Diet: They need plenty of insects. Chopped mealworms (raw or cooked), termite larvae and ant eggs must be supplied together with finch seed, mineral mixture, greenstuff and shell grit.

They also eat fruit such as oranges and pawpaws once they have learnt to do so. Live food must be provided at least three times a week. When there are chicks, more live food must be provided. Supplement the diet with hard-boiled egg, bread soaked in milk, and sprouted seed. Try to persuade them to eat dry dog meal, even if it's only the protein part.

Breeding habits: They need grass, teff, feathers and other soft material with which to build their nest. They do this in a shrub fairly close to the ground. They will also use a calabash or a finch or budgie nest in which to build their own (see p. 21 for waxbill nests).

The chicks hatch within 13 days and fly after about three weeks.

When Bengalese finches are used to raise the chicks, they usually die, probably because the Bengalese finches do not eat enough live food.

PIN-TAILED NONPAREIL (*Erythrura prasina*)
PHOTO 64

Origin: India and Indonesia.

The orange on the belly fades in captivity. These birds are rare in South Africa and not very easy to handle. They can live in an aviary together with other finches, particularly zebra finches and grass finches. Fatalities are high.

Description: *Male* – Face and throat: blue. Head and back: green. Rump and tail: red. Breast and belly: orange-red. Bill: dark grey. *Female* – As for the male, but her colours are slightly duller. Young males look like females. Size: 11 cm.

Diet: In their natural state they are rice eaters. If they live with other finches, they will follow the example of the other finches and eat with them. Make sure that, apart from the usual finch seed, greenstuff, mineral mixture and shell grit, there are plenty of canary seeds for them, as well as shelled oat seeds. Because they do not breed or survive all that well, it is important for the aviculturalist to give them mealworms, termite and ant eggs. When there are chicks, they still need live food, as well as sprouted seeds, bread soaked in milk, and mashed hard-boiled egg.

Breeding habits: They like to build a grass nest in a thick shrub or tufts of grass and can therefore be treated like waxbills. Sometimes they will move into an artificial finch nest, e.g. a budgie nest. Incubation lasts about two weeks. The two or three chicks emerge from the nest at about three weeks and can get along without their parents after ten days.

RED-CRESTED CARDINAL (*Paroaria cucullata*)
PHOTO 65

Origin: South America.

The red-crested cardinal is a showy, strong and lively bird. They can be aggressive and it is best to keep one pair on their own, or with other large, strong birds. They become very tame. The colours do not fade in captivity.

Description: *Male* – Face, crest, throat and breast: red-orange. Head: white and grey. Back, wings and tail: grey. Lower breast and undersides: white. Legs: grey. Bill: horn-coloured. *Female* – As for the male, but slightly smaller and

65 Red-crested cardinal

more slender. The red on her head is paler. Size: 20 cm. The male sings during the breeding season.

Diet: Cardinals are halfway between seed-eaters and insect-eaters. Fruit and live food are therefore essential, together with their seed mix. Finch seed mixed with sunflower seed will do. They love mealworms, grasshoppers, worms, crickets and termites about twice or three times a week. Also feed them greenstuff, a mineral mixture, shell grit and coarse grit. It is important to persuade them to eat wet or dry dog meal or dog pellets. Dog food has a high protein and mineral content and compensates, to a degree, for a diet lacking in insects. Peanut butter is an excellent addition to their diet. They may not eat it straight away, but persevere in presenting it until they have learnt to eat it. When there are chicks, the amount of insects must be increased and they must also be given hard-boiled egg.

Breeding habits: They build an open nest in a shrub. Give them a number of baskets or straw plates in a sheltered spot so that they can rather breed under a roof, or else they will sit in the open and the rain. They prefer building their nest close to the ground – about a metre above the ground. They use twigs, leaves and grass to build an untidy nest on top of the basket.

Both parents sit on the four to six eggs and both parents feed the chicks. Without live food the chicks will probably die.

RED-EARED WAXBILL (*Estrilda troglodytes*)
PHOTO 66

Origin: Africa.

This tiny waxbill is very lively, and its tail is never still. It is sensitive to the cold and where the temperature sometimes drops below freezing, the aviary must be heated to prevent losses (see p. 13 for the heating of the aviary).

Description: *Male* – Reddish brown. Bill: red. Head: A red stripe extends from the bill, around the eye to the back of the head. The reddish colour becomes stronger during the breeding season. The male courts the female by dancing before her with a blade of grass in his bill. *Female* – As

for the male. Her colour may be slightly duller, but it is very difficult to determine a true pair on the grounds of appearance only. Size: 10 cm.

Diet: Because these are waxbills, they are dependent on insects, but not to the same degree as some other birds. They will breed on a high-protein diet. Give them finch seed, a mineral mixture, shell grit and greenstuff. Try to persuade them to eat at least the protein part of dog meal. Live termite larvae twice a week, as well as ant eggs, will help a great deal.

Hard-boiled egg, brown bread soaked in milk, chopped mealworms and sprouted seeds must be added when there are chicks.

Breeding habits: They will accept a wooden box and build a nest of grass in it. The nest has a spout-shaped projection and often an extra hollow in which the male stays. The nest is lined with hair, wool, feathers or other soft material; the aviculturalist must provide enough of these nesting materials.

More than one wooden box must be available so that they can have a choice. These must also be placed in sheltered places away from the nests of larger birds. If they refuse to accept a wooden box, provide them with nests as discussed on p. 21.

Three eggs are normally laid. Both parents hatch the chicks. The chicks appear after 11-12 days. Two weeks later they leave the nest.

Red-eared waxbills interbreed with orange-cheeked waxbills.

Good mating pairs must be marked if they are to be separated in winter so that the correct male can later be returned to the correct female.

RED-HEADED AURORAS (*Pytilia hypogrammica*)
PHOTO 67

Origin: Africa.

These birds are extremely rare and do not breed very well in captivity. It is a challenge to persuade them to breed. They like to scratch on the ground.

66   Red-eared waxbill

67   Red-headed auroras

68 Red-headed parrot finch

Description: *Male* – Head: red. Tail: red. Wings: grey and red. Rest of body: grey. *Female* – Her head is grey instead of red. For the rest like the male. Size: 15 cm.

Diet: Plenty of live food, canary seed, grass seed, finch seed mix, greenstuff, shell grit and a mineral mixture. Place fresh sods of soil on the floor of the aviary every week so that they can scratch in these.

Breeding habits: They build a nest of soft nesting material in a sheltered shrub, wooden box, on top of a canary nest, in a calabash or a clump of grass. They are shy birds and there should be space for them to build their nest in a sheltered environment. Aggressive birds or those which may interfere with the nest, such as zebra finches, should not be kept in the same aviary. The chicks need a great deal of live food in order to survive.

RED-HEADED PARROT FINCH (*Erythrura psitticea*) PHOTO 68

Origin: New Caledonia and a few other small islands near Australia.

Red-headed parrot finches are much sought after, rare and expensive. Unlike some other finch species, they retain their colour well in captivity. They are not very hardy and newly imported birds must be acclimatised to their new environment with care. There is a ready market for the aviculturalist who decides to dedicate himself exclusively to the breeding of parrot finches.

Description: *Male* – Body: dark green. Head, face and throat: bright red. Tail: red. Legs: flesh-coloured. *Female* – As for the male, but her colours are slightly duller. Size: 13 cm. Selecting a pair merely on the basis of appearance is not a reliable procedure.

Diet: Finch seed, greenstuff or similar supplement, a mineral mixture, sprouted seeds, shell grit and coarse grit. As they catch insects in nature, you must try and persuade them to eat dog meal, or parts of dog meal mixes. A large aviary with many plants which attract plenty of insects will also help. Feed them mealworms, termites or ant eggs about three times a week.

Breeding habits: The female readily lays eggs in a finch or budgie box filled with grass or teff. Live termites a few times a week will increase the chances of successful breeding. Give them rearing mix and hard-boiled eggs when they are raising chicks.

If they get the correct food, they can raise three sets of chicks a year. Their breeding habits are similar to those of the blue-headed parrot finch. Keep some Bengalese finches ready to help out, if necessary.

SPICE OR NUTMEG FINCH (*Lonchura punctulata*)

Origin: India.

A popular mannikin which is freely imported, they are hardy as far as the cold is concerned and they have simple dietary requirements. They are therefore the ideal choice for the beginner, even though they do not always breed copiously.

Description: *Male* – Head, upper parts and tail: dark brown. Underside: Each white feather is edged with brown so that the bird appears speckled. Bill: grey. Legs: brown-grey. Eyes: black. *Female* – As for the male. Size: 13 cm. Sexing on the grounds of appearance is inaccurate. Try to distinguish the male by the song it sings. If possible, buy several pairs so that they can choose their own mates.

Diet: Finch seed, greenstuff, a mineral mixture, shell grit and coarse grit. Supply sprouted seeds and brown bread soaked in milk when they are raising chicks. As is the case with all finch species, they love live food, and chopped mealworms are welcome. However, live food is not essential for their survival.

Breeding habits: They do not breed freely in captivity because they leave the nest at the smallest disturbance. Place a finch nest or calabash in a sheltered spot such as a shrub. A pair will then make their own nest in this, using teff, grass and feathers.

The incubation period is 13 days. If they do not raise their chicks themselves, Bengalese finches can take over.

STAR FINCH (*Bathilda ruficauda*)

Origin: Northern Australia.

Star finches do not sleep in their nests at night and must be protected from the rain and cold. They love bathing.

Description: *Male* – Back: olive green. Face and breast: olive green with white spots. Cheeks, forehead and beak: red. Tail: brick red. Underparts: yellow-green. Legs: flesh-coloured. *Female* – As for the male, but with less red on the face. Size: 13 cm. Young males look like females.

Diet: Finch seed, greenstuff or similar supplement, a mineral mixture, shell grit and coarse grit. When there are chicks, bread soaked in water or milk, grated hard-boiled egg and/or rearing mix must be added.

Breeding habits: They should not be allowed to breed before they are 18 months to two years old. Should they mate before this time, Bengalese finches can be utilised to hatch the eggs.

Star finches build a nest in a shrub, clump of grass, finch or budgie nest or tin loosely lined with grass or teff and rounded off with feathers, wool, cotton or other soft material.

The female lays three or four eggs and both parents brood. The chicks appear after 12-14 days and the parents normally look after them well. The chicks leave the nest after about three weeks. They do not need live food, but bread soaked in milk, and hard-boiled egg, must be added to the basic diet when there are chicks.

The parents may mate for life and sometimes refuse to mate with new partners. When a true pair is separated, they must be ringed to ensure that they may later be brought together again.

STRAWBERRY FINCH (*Amandava amandava punicea*) PHOTO 69

Origin: Indonesia and Thailand.

Strawberry finches are among the most popular waxbills. They are extremely rare because they are protected in their countries of origin and are no longer freely captured and exported. They go through two colour phases. In winter the male loses its colour and looks like the female. In captivity they lose their colour permanently and become dark brown or nearly black.

This may possibly be due to too few insects in the diet as well as other unknown factors that differ in nature from life in an aviary.

Description: *Male* – Summer and autumn: dark red with white spots on the wings and breast. Bill: red. Legs: red. Winter: straw-coloured, but the white spots still show. *Female* – Belly and back: straw-coloured. Wings and tail: brown. Bill: red. No spots as for the male. Size: 11 cm.

Diet: Live food is of the utmost importance if breeding results are expected. Keep them in a well-planted aviary which attracts insects. Give them chopped mealworms, ant eggs and termites. The insects must be presented at least three or four times per week. Try to persuade them to eat at least the protein part of dog meal. Also feed them seed sprouts, finch seed, greenstuff, a mineral mixture, shell grit and coarse grit.

Breeding habits: They build a nest in a shrub, in tufts of grass or in wooden nests or other sheltered hollows. To do this they need nesting material such as carrot tops, teff hay

and pillow feathers. See p. 21 for information about nests for waxbills. Strawberry finches do not readily breed in captivity because they do not get enough live food. Sometimes they hatch the chicks, but kick them out of the nest, mate and lay a new set of eggs. This may sometimes be prevented by removing the males as soon as the chicks have hatched, or by allowing the eggs to hatch beneath a Bengalese finch or silverbill.

Give them as much live food, hard-boiled egg and rearing mix as possible, and try moistened dog meal or dog pellets.

The aviculturalist who is fortunate enough to own strawberry finches should do everything in his power to persuade them to breed, as our source of birds from the wild has dried up, and you are always assured of a market.

THREE-COLOURED PARROT FINCH
(*Erythrura trichroa*) PHOTO 70

Origin: New Guinea.

Three-coloured parrot finches are hardy, withstand the cold well and sing beautifully. They do well in an aviary with other birds, but it is better to keep only one pair of their own kind in an aviary. They retain their colours well in captivity.

Description: *Male* – Head: blue. Body: green. Rump and tail: red. *Female* – As for the male. Sometimes the blue on her head does not extend as far back as in the case of the male, and the green may be slightly paler. Size: 13 cm.

Diet: Finch seed, greenstuff, a mineral mixture, shell grit and coarse grit. They will breed better if they get insects to eat three times a week. Cooked and chopped mealworms, termites or ant eggs are welcome as well as an aviary with many plants that attract insects. Try to teach them to eat dog meal, even if only the protein part, to compensate for the low insect portion in the diet. When there are chicks, bread soaked in water or milk, and grated hard-boiled egg, must be given in addition.

Breeding habits: They will finish off a nest in a budgie or finch nest filled with teff or grass. While mating a male will treat the female so roughly and chase her about so persistently that she gets no chance to eat, becomes totally exhausted and may even die.

When you encounter a female on the ground, exhausted and with a head pecked bare of feathers, the male must be

69 Strawberry finch

70 Three-coloured parrot finch

71 Virginian or scarlet cardinal

removed for a few days so that she can recover. The male can then be left with her for one or two hours per day until the eggs have been laid.

In a large aviary with ample place for the female to hide, this problem does not occur.

Sometimes the male ejects the chicks from the nest because he wants to mate again. Rather place him in another aviary as soon as the chicks have hatched. The female will raise the chicks on her own, or otherwise the Bengalese finches may be required to help.

Three-coloured parrot finches breed fairly well and the chicks mature perfectly adequately on rearing mix and hard-boiled egg given together with the basic food.

VIRGINIAN OR SCARLET CARDINAL
(*Richmondena cardinalis*)   PHOTO 71
Origin: United States of America.
These beautiful birds are strong and aggressive and should rather be kept in an aviary by themselves, or with birds large enough to defend themselves, such as parakeets. They become quite tame and are a pleasure to keep.
Description: *Male* – Deep red with black about the bill. A red crest held saucily erect. Bill: orange-red. *Female* – Brown with a little red on the head, crest, bill and wings. Size: 20 cm. Because the sexes are so different, it is easy to pick out a true pair. The red colouring fades to a watery pink in captivity.
Diet and breeding habits: As for the red-crested cardinal, but they lay fewer eggs at a time. It is alleged that soy meal in the diet will prevent the colour from fading.

WHITE-HEADED MANNIKIN OR WHITE-HEADED NUN   (*Lonchura maja*)
Origin: Indonesia.
These birds are hardy, require a simple diet and are therefore a good choice for beginners. They live in peace with other birds.
Description: *Male* – Head: white. Body: brown. Eyes: black. Bill: grey. Legs: grey. *Female* – As for the male, but her head and bill are smaller. Size: 13 cm.
Diet: Finch seed, greenstuff or similar supplement, a mineral mixture, shell grit and coarse grit. As with all finches, they enjoy mealworms. When there are chicks, they must also get brown bread soaked in milk, and grated hard-boiled egg.
Breeding habits: Sometimes they breed with difficulty, but when they do breed, they raise the chicks very well. The four eggs hatch after 12 days and the chicks leave the nest at 25 days. They sometimes interbreed with Bengalese finches.

ZEBRA FINCH   (*Poephila guttata*)
Origin: Australia.
Zebra finches are ideal birds for the beginner. They have a simple diet, are peaceable towards other birds and breed well. However, they are very inquisitive and will fuss about near other birds' nests, pull at the nesting material and try to 'help' with the chicks. This can discourage other finches to such a degree that they give up and abandon their nests.

Zebra finches should therefore rather not be kept with other finches. However, they do well with doves such as diamond doves or mild-mannered psittaciformes such as budgies, cockatiels or grass parakeets, and also with quail and pheasants.
Description: The description is for the original bird from the wild. Many different mutations are available today. *Male* – Upper parts: grey. Undersides: grey-brown and white. Cheeks: bright orange-brown. Flanks: orange-brown with white spots. Throat: black and white bars. Bill: red. Legs: orange. *Female* – She lacks the conspicuous orange-brown cheeks. There are no black and white bars on the throat and no orange-brown with white dots on the flanks. Bill: paler red than that of the male. Size: 13 cm.

Mutation colours: White, cinnamon, pied, Isabella and albino. Aviculturalists often have their own names to describe particular mutations. In the case of some mutations, e.g. the white zebra, the male often lacks the orange-brown cheeks. In such cases sexing can only be done by looking at the colour of the bills. The female's bill is paler than that of the male.

Diet: Finch seed, greenstuff or similar supplements, a mineral mixture, dog meal, shell grit and coarse grit. When there are chicks, bread soaked in milk and grated hard-boiled egg must be added.
Breeding habits: Zebra finches begin breeding at five months. They will breed throughout the year if allowed to do so. This can exhaust the female to such a degree that she may die. During winter the male should be separated from the female for about three months.

Zebras are good at raising their chicks and present few problems. They build a nest in a shrub, a fork in a tree, a tin, finch or budgie nest, calabash or any corner which they regard as a suitable spot.

The aviculturalist must provide plenty of teff or hay, and also wool, feathers, cotton and bits of fabric. Help the birds by stuffing the wooden nest or tin full of teff and making a hollow in it with your fist so that the birds merely need to finish off the nest. Because they breed so continuously, you must watch the nest; if it is wet and soiled, the contents must be removed and replaced by dry grass or teff.

Zebra finches lay five or six eggs. The eggs are laid on consecutive days. Incubation usually starts after two or three eggs have been laid, which means that one or two chicks are late in hatching.

Both parents sit on the eggs and both feed the chicks. If the female dies, the male often raises the chicks by himself. The chicks leave the nest after about 20 days, but are then still fed for a few weeks.

Show canaries

Breeding show canaries offers the modern bird enthusiast a fascinating challenge. A tremendous variety of these birds is available today – long ones and thin ones, short ones and fat ones, pretty ones and funny-looking ones, in many colours and offering intricate or plain song routines.

This was not always so. The original canary was a rather plain olive green bird which originated in Madeira and the Canary Islands. By interbreeding with other birds from the wild, as well as the selection of certain characteristics, a large variety of canaries has been bred. This is why many of the canaries of today look nothing like their forefathers.

Basically there are three types of canaries, namely the singing canaries, those bred for their colour and those bred for their build. At canary shows, which are held country-wide, there are divisions for so many different types of canaries that a breeder wishing to compete in as many of them as possible could keep himself busy for a lifetime.

Breeding show canaries is a specialised business and if you want to concentrate on this operation, you must join a canary club. Only breeders belonging to a club may take part in shows and receive rings for the canaries.

The following are some of the better known types of canaries:

Yorkshire: This is a particularly large type of canary with a length of at least 17 cm. Altogether 22 colours are recognised for show purposes, among them white, yellow, green and cinnamon.

Border (photo 72): A neat little canary no larger than 14 cm. They sing well and are popular as pets. There are 14 recognised colours for this very popular canary type.

Norwich: This is a large canary of about 15-16 cm in length. There are 14 recognised colour variations for this canary as well. Because they breed rather poorly, they are relatively rare and therefore expensive.

Red Factor (photos 73, 74 and 75): Very popular. Red Factor canaries were originally bred from crossings with the red-hooded siskin. They look beautiful in various shades of red, and what's more, they sing, too. The Red Factor canaries occur in such a large variety of colours that there are more than a hundred recognised colour classes.

Colour canaries: They carry no red factor, as is the case with the Red Factor, and their colours include silver, for example. Sixty colour classes are recognised for show purposes.

Gloster: A very small but particularly popular canary no larger than 12 cm. Some have a rounded crest or crown, others do not. If there is a crest, it must be unbroken and stretch right around the head. For show purposes a great deal of trouble is taken to get the crest feathers to lie exactly right. A Gloster with a crest is known as a 'Corona' and one without a crest as a 'Consort'. One must breed both types because a crest bred with a crest has a lethal factor of 25%. This means that 25% of the chicks will probably be dead. (Dark yellow crossed with dark yellow results in a similar lethal factor.)

Lizard: This is a canary with unusual patterns on the back and breast. There are eight colour classes for this type. They are rare and expensive because they breed poorly.

72 Two types of Border canary

73 Red Factor canaries

74 A pale shade of the Red Factor

75 Variegated Red Factor

76 Frilled canary

Frills (photo 76): The feathers of these canaries lie the wrong way round and make 'frills' around the long-legged birds. There are 14 accepted colours for this type.

Roller: This is the champion songster. For show purposes the roller can sing on its own, or in a duet, or three birds may even sing together as a team. A roller must sing well-defined song passages known as 'tours' which are distinct and melodic. There are about 13 'tours' for show purposes. Some of the sounds are described as hollow rolls, schokel, whistles and water tours. Rollers are taught the correct tours by listening to tape recordings.

With such an enormous variety of possible colours, and the fact that some colours are sex-related, while crossing others can result in dead chicks, it is clear that the art of breeding canaries is a highly specialised task. Entire books are devoted to descriptions of colour breeding these birds.

Canary cages

Canaries are kept in open aviaries outside or in a canary room where many small cages are stacked, almost like a block of flats.

Canaries in open aviaries are hardier and fitter than those in a canary room. Yet they must have good protection, as the birds are no longer as hardy as birds in the wild. The European method of housing them, i.e. in a room which can be completely enclosed during winter, with flying space outside the room for sunny days, is particularly suited to canaries. The disadvantage of open aviaries is that you will probably keep a number of pairs in one aviary, which means that no control can be kept over the breeding. If you want to determine which male is to breed with which female, a good number of small cages will be needed. Canaries are very tame, and many canaries have lost their heads in open-air aviaries though the activities of the South African fiscal shrike.

It is a good idea to allow one pair to breed in a double breeding cage. There is a round hole near the bottom in the partition between the two cages – just large enough for a canary to stick its head through it. When the pair's chicks are 21 days old, the chicks are placed in the cage next door. The female then begins to prepare a new nest, while the male will feed the chicks next door through the hole in the partition.

Many fanciers who specialise in breeding canaries seriously build a special canary room. The canary rooms are often as neat, clean and spruce as the operating theatre in a hospital. There are shiny washbasins, neat cupboards for medicines and food, fans and blinds in front of the windows to control the temperature, large glass sliding doors to let in the sunlight, and tiled floors. Here the breeding and living cages are stacked (see photos 77, 78, 79, 80, 81 and 82).

Feeding

Every canary breeder believes in his own feeding method. There are literally hundreds of recipes. Sometimes the mixtures are kept strictly secret. The beginner will make no

77 An example of a canary house of wood, with screens in front of the glass windows. There are louvre windows for additional air conditioning and the tiled floor is easy to clean.

78 This is how canary breeding boxes are stacked in a neat canary room.

79 Show cages for Yorkshire canaries. Show cages are suspended in front of the open door of the canary cage so that the birds can get used to them and enter them voluntarily.

80 The show cage for Gloster canaries

81 A show cage for Red Factor canaries. The greenstuff in the cage is there to tempt the canary from its breeding box.

82 Bathtime, and the special bath is hooked in front of the door of the cage. The door is kept open with a washing peg. Drinking water is placed in a hygienic glass bowl hung outside so that the cage does not become dirty.

mistake if he keeps to the feeding programme set out below, which is followed by some of the most successful canary breeders.

Seed mix: 4 parts canary seed, 1 part Japanese millet, 1 part red millet, 1 part black millet, 1 part white millet. In winter 25% linseed is added.

Greenstuff: Give them greenstuff every day. This can be veld plants such as thistles and chickweed or spinach, parsley, the outer green leaves of a head of lettuce, carrot tops, grated carrots, cucumber, apples and other fruit.

Grit: A bowl of grit must be permanently available. This provides minerals and helps to grind down the seed in the crop.

Soft foods: A rearing mix for canaries (available from pet shops), moistened very well, must be on the daily menu. Give this from the time the chicks have hatched to when they have finished moulting in January or February. After moulting they receive it twice a week. The rearing mix is supplemented with hard-boiled egg (white as well as the yolk) in the proportion of one egg for every four dessert-spoonfuls of dry rearing mix.

Vitamins used for chickens or humans can also be added to the rearing mix, but not more often than once or twice a week. Excessive fat-soluble vitamins cannot be excreted quickly enough, accumulate in the system and are harmful.

To retain the red colour in the case of Red Factors, they must eat carophyll red. Mix it with the soft food. A knife-point in four tablespoons of dry rearing mix is enough. It is particularly important that the canaries get the red colouring matter while their new feathers form and grow.

If canary rearing mix is unobtainable, they can be given a mixture of whole-wheat bread or putu (moistened) and hard-boiled egg plus grated carrot. Egg is such a complete food that it provides for most of the birds' needs. Beware of egg, however: After a few hours it can become contaminated with bacteria, particularly in warm weather. The egg must therefore be consumed quickly or must be removed within a few hours. Also provide the birds with the eggshells – this supplies minerals.

Some canary fanciers give their birds a mixture of Marie biscuits, Complan and hard-boiled eggs. They also dose their birds with a solution of one teaspoon of bicarbonate of soda to two litres of water once a week. Perhaps this does some good – it can certainly do no harm.

Sexing

All that blowing on the vent, looking at the size of the head and other more or less accepted methods of sexing are unreliable. Males sing much better than females, but the only true indication is to watch while the male courts the female.

If you want to buy canaries, it is best to look at the canaries for some time and to observe their behaviour towards one another.

Preparation for the show

Show canaries' cages must be kept scrupulously clean, or the birds will never look good. The bottom is sprinkled with Karbadust and covered with large wood shavings (fine sawdust causes dust which soils the birds).

The perches must be replaced once a week. Used perches can be disinfected and rubbed down with coarse sandpaper before being used again. Insert cuttlefish bones in between the bars of the cage. The canaries use these to sharpen their bills, and they also provide calcium.

The birds must bath daily, if you have the time. This involves suspending all the baths outside the cages in front of the open doors for about two hours. (Use clothespegs to keep the doors open.) If not daily, this must be done twice a week.

All soft food is placed in small bowls fixed to the side of the cage. The bowls are so small that the canaries cannot climb into them and foul themselves.

If everything is clean and right, no further preparation is necessary for the show, apart from using a toothbrush to brush open all feathers which are not properly open. Most canary enthusiasts do not allow their canaries to bath before a show.

However, should it be necessary, for example, to bath a white canary, this is done a week before a show. Bath the canary with baby shampoo in tepid water and then rinse it, also in tepid water. The canary can be dried with a hair dryer. Ensure that only slightly warm air is expelled and hold the drier far away from the bird. Thereafter keep the bird in a fairly warm room without draughts for 24 hours.

Broken tail and wing feathers take two months to grow again. If there is enough time, pull out the broken feathers so that new ones can grow before the show. It takes the small feathers about four weeks to grow.

All that remains is to ensure that the birds become accustomed to their show cages. The various types of canaries are shown in different types of show cages. The cage is suspended in front of the open door of the living cage a few weeks before the show.

A little greenstuff inside the show cage will encourage the canary to enter it. Very soon it will move freely to and fro between the two cages.

Show budgies

A beginner in the world of show budgies should first consult a number of old hands at the game before he/she decides on what an aviary should look like. A large number of suitable aviaries and aviary plans is available. Budgies do not need such large aviaries or so much flying space as birds from the wild.

Budgies can live in anything from a small cage to a huge aviary, but for colour and show breeding it is essential that the mating should be kept under control. It is therefore usual to build a large room for breeding birds wherein a number of small cages are placed, with only one breeding pair per cage.

For the young birds two fairly large, well-protected aviaries are usually built; one for young males and one for young females. These aviaries are well protected because the feathers of a show budgie should not be exposed to the elements. Normally a roof covers the entire length of the aviary.

Long-time show budgie breeders who are serious about it sometimes build aviaries in which the temperature can be controlled between a minimum of 15 °C and a maximum of 30 °C. During the cold winter months the aviaries can be heated by means of asbestos heaters.

In such grand aviaries the relative humidity is kept at 70% by means of a humidifier (the kind used for babies with croup). A hygroscope is usually fixed to the underside of the roof.

When the temperature and humidity of an aviary are controlled in this way, the breeder often prefers to let the birds breed in winter. This is because summer may be too hot in many parts of the country, and better breeding results are obtained in winter.

Beginners with little cash should not be deterred, even if they cannot kick off with such grand aviaries. In the long run the genetic material and the full development of the bird's potential through good feeding and care, as well as training, determine whether it will be a show winner or not. The grandeur of the aviary plays no part, as long as it offers enough protection from the elements.

Young boys and girls with limited funds can achieve good results with only one or two pairs of budgies in a cage in the kitchen. (Just remember that budgies should also get a little sun.)

If the cages are kept scrupulously clean, it is not necessary to treat the birds for internal or external parasites.

Feeding

It is no use investing in good genetic material and then skimping on the feeding. Correct feeding brings out the best in a budgie. An important aspect is to make the feeding programme as simple as possible so that you can keep it up without interruption.

Different breeders will, of course, have their own favourite seed mixes and supplements, but the following

83 The colour is green (blue & yellow). If yellow is bred out, blue remains.

84 This show budgie is close to the ideal for which you should strive.

85 The large black eyes indicate that these budgies are still very young.

86 It is not always necessary to spend a great deal of money building an aviary for show budgies. In this case an old, round concrete dam was converted into a neat budgie aviary.

feeding programme is used by some of the best breeders in the country:

Seed mix: 50% canary seed, 35% white millet and 15% Japanese millet. This can be freely given.

Shell grit: A mixture of sea sand and shell grit must always be available. Sea sand is available from some pet shops. If you use your own sea sand, it must first be boiled (sterilised). An iodine block and also a piece of rock salt must always be available.

Greenstuff: Greenstuff such as spinach is given every second day. If no greenstuff is available, vitamins can be added to the drinking water twice weekly. However, watch out for too many vitamins.

In the case of breeding birds the protein content must be increased. This is done by giving the breeding pairs puppy meal, soya meal or high-protein bread.

Young birds, too, must get high-protein food in the form of whole-wheat bread or biscuits soaked in milk. Once a day give as much of this as the birds can eat within an hour. For the rest the young birds get sprouted oats, Japanese millet or sunflower seed.

The question of seed sprouts sometimes causes confusion among aviculturalists. They allow the seeds to sprout until there is a long green shoot (and the seed often smells bad). This is wrong. The sprout is ready when the husk has burst open and the tip of the new plant sticks out from the husk by about one centimetre.

Some parents do not feed the chicks enough to fill their crops. A chick's crop must visibly bulge with food. If necessary, supplementary food can be given in the evening by injecting ProNutro into the crop. Do this by attaching a rubber bicycle valve tube to the front of a syringe, filling the syringe with a ProNutro and water mixture, inserting the tube into the chick's throat and injecting the ProNutro into the crop. Other soft food, such as canary rearing mix, can be pushed gently into the chick's throat with the back of a

teaspoon. Always work gently and watch out for choking. Give small amounts of food at a time.

Readiness for breeding

If you want to breed, the male and female must be ready for this at the same time. It does no good to set an active male on a female that is not yet ready. A female that is ready to breed will display a brown nose and good, smooth feathers. She is also very lively and gnaws at everything she sees. If both sexes are ready, they will call to each other and sit close together near the wire separating them.

A particularly handsome male can mate with up to three females during the breeding season. Do not allow one pair to produce more than two broods per year.

Record-keeping

If you are really serious about breeding show budgies, it is essential to keep a record of their achievements, mating, etc. One method is to use four books, which contain the following information:

Book A: The ring numbers of the bird and its parents, sex and date when hatched, to whom sold and in which cage placed.

Book B: Full pedigree, i.e. three generations, together with remarks about the birds' achievements, e.g. their breeding successes.

Book C: This is the breeding pair register. In this book details are kept about which birds were mated, the number of eggs laid, the number of fertilised eggs, the number of chicks raised, the ring number and sex of each chick.

87 The ideal show budgie is supposed to look like this. The budgie which occurs in nature looks quite different.

Book D: Show achievements, prizes, catalogues.

Nowadays a computer is often used to store this information.

Show training

Preparations for shows can give as much pleasure as breeding. Two factors need to be given special attention for shows, namely condition and training.

Training should begin when the chicks are still in the nest. They must be removed from the nest from time to time and caressed so that they will grow up tame and become used to handling. The bird must also become used to its show cage so that it will be calm and relaxed in it.

Place young birds in the show cages two by two initially so that they do not feel lonely or frightened. Also supply them with greenstuff in the cage, so that they eventually associate the cage with something pleasant.

While they are in the show cage, they must learn that it is quite normal to be manipulated by hand or by means of the show rod.

Turn them around with the rod or push them around gently with it so that they do not become agitated when a judge does it to them.

Birds must be brought to top condition for a particular show. No budgie can stay in top condition for four or five months. The ideal situation is to bring a budgie to top condition for two shows, about two weeks apart.

Apart from good, balanced feeding, the birds' feathers must receive extra attention for the show. Wet the birds' feathers every day for about a week with a solution of two teaspoons of liquid paraffin to four or five litres of water. The following three days or so the budgies are showered with clean tepid water. The last few days they are not showered, because they will oil themselves.

Dry the birds in the sun (away from draughts) or in front of a heater. They must be showered until quite damp, because the purpose of these showers is, among others, to ensure that the bird's feathers are compact, almost like a cast about its body.

For the last few days the show birds get no greenstuff, because this causes the droppings to soften, which in turn will soil the feathers. If a bird is very dirty, e.g. in the case of

88 A nest for show budgies. The nest is pulled forward to make inspection easier. When it is pushed in, it is closed with a door. Information regarding the parents, chicks and eggs is fixed to the inside of the door.

a white budgie, it is bathed with a shaving brush and baby shampoo.

The last day or two before the show the breeder must ensure that all new feathers are properly open. Brush open closed feathers with a toothbrush. If the feathers of the head are not properly open (a show budgie must be able to erect the feathers on its head like a crest), the head is washed with baby shampoo. The feathers may not be cut, apart from those around the spots on the neck. It is permissible to pluck excess feathers here so that only six good round spots remain.

13

Ornamental waterfowl

Keeping and breeding ornamental waterfowl can be an enjoyable and even profitable activity for bird lovers. On a farm with enough space for large natural dams, a wide variety of waterfowl can be kept. There is often space on a town or city plot for fancy ducks or geese. As long as ducks have a pond, they do not need a great deal more room for movement, because they prefer to spend their time on the water. Geese and swans, however, do like to graze and need more room to move about. Most ducks are not noisy and can be kept in an urban environment, but geese can be noisy.

If waterfowl are required to breed in order to make a profit, it is better for each breeding pair to have their own enclosure with their own pond, even if the pond consists only of half a 200-litre drum. If the birds are kept mainly for pleasure and aesthetic reasons, a large dam with many pairs of birds can be considered. As long as there is enough room for them to flee in case of a fight, one dam with a large number of ducks, geese and swans may even ensure good breeding results. The more space, the better the results.

The most popular exotic waterfowl are surely the colourful mandarin and Carolina tree ducks. They are freely available in South Africa. Others which are available here include the various porchards, Bahama pintail, ringed teal, Philippine duck, ruddy shellduck, greenwing, bronze cap, northern shoveler, tufted porchard, white and black swans and occasionally black-necked swans. There are a few others, but they breed with greater reluctance and are therefore not suitable for the beginner.

The pretty appearance of these waterfowl is deceptive. They are vicious fighters and will happily kill one another. A male swan can peck a Carolina duck to death with the greatest of ease. Birds of the same species can also injure one another to such an extent that they may die. One male will hold another's head under water long enough for it to drown. Even when males are kept together in an enclosure without females, they will fight.

The females, too, can set to with a will. One of my Carolina duck females acted so protectively towards her ducklings that she constantly attacked her mate – to such an extent that I have had to save him from drowning many a time.

However, not all birds display this same aggressive temperament and there are exceptions where ducks of the same species do live together in peace and harmony. Large dams aside (e.g. on a farm), it is preferable for each breeding pair to have its own enclosure and pool, however small.

Most waterfowl require similar treatment: water in which to swim and mate, shelter, food and a sheltered spot on the ground on which to build a nest. The tree ducks are somewhat different as regards their nesting needs.

Mandarin and Carolina ducks

Mandarin ducks (*Aix galericulata*) originally come from the East, while the North Carolina wood duck (*Aix sponsa*) originates from North America. Both species are tree ducks, can fly very well and build their nests in hollows high up in trees. It remains one of the wonders of adaptability that ducklings can fall three to seven metres from a tree without breaking a bone. (A pheasant chick will fall out of a nest a mere metre from the ground and break its legs.)

Mandarin ducklings also have strong spurs on their wings and will climb a tree trunk almost like a bat. Because these ducks can fly so well, it is customary to cut off the front joint of one wing when the ducklings are one or two days old, to keep them from flying away when grown.

Despite the fact that we keep tree ducks in circumstances which differ markedly from their natural state, they adapt very well to captivity.

Mandarin ducks are small. The male is colourful and looks like a little yacht when sailing across the water in a showy display of outspread feathers (see photo 89). He shows off in front of his female and is very cocky towards other males. The showiness is probably its most attractive characteristic. The mandarin female is grey and unobtrusive.

The Carolina male is a little larger, calmer and also has beautiful colours (see photo 90). He does not show off as

89 Mandarin drake and duck

90 Carolina drake

91 Mutations seldom occur among ducks. This pale-coloured mutation of a Carolina pair is something special. As is often the case, mutation colours are more muted and less attractive than the natural colours.

much as the mandarin male. The Carolina female is also grey and unobtrusive.

Because the males are so brightly coloured, they attract predators. Jackals, caracals and raptors are attracted by the male's colourful display and his presence can therefore put the female and the ducklings in danger.

However, nature has made provision for this. Both the Carolina and mandarin males lose their colouring as soon as the female begins to brood.

When the ducklings emerge, the father is as grey as the rest of his family.

Only by March or April, when his offspring begin to display their colours, does the male also begin to take on his.

This can sometimes lead to misunderstandings. A man once bought a pair of mandarins from me. A few months later he telephoned me in high dudgeon. I had sold him useless ducks – the male had lost all his beautiful colouring and was also grey!

Usually more mandarin males than females hatch. This compensates for the fact that more males are caught and eaten in the wild. The surplus of males does, however, pose a problem for aviculturalists. If you have a female, hold on to her!

The ducks can grow to a good age. Bird books do not supply information about their longevity, but I owned a pair who were still breeding every year at the age of 15! Most ducks can begin breeding during the first year, but this first effort is often no more than a trial run, and sometimes nothing happens. If the ducks do not breed during the first year, they must be given another chance to prove whether they can or not.

Pinioning

Most wild ducks can fly very well – not only the mandarins and Carolinas. If they are to live in an enclosure without a roof, the tip of one wing must be removed. This is done when the ducklings are one or two days old. (Once they are older, it is very painful for them if they are pinioned and the ducks bleed badly – so badly that they may die.) Quickly cut off the front joint of one wing with sterilised scissors (boiled in water for 15 minutes). Apply an antibiotic ointment or powder to the wound. The younger the duck, the less pain and bleeding there will be.

When an adult duck must be pinioned, it must be done by a veterinarian. If you are in the country and too far from a vet, yet must pinion an adult duck's wing, ask the dentist to anaesthetise the tip of the wing, bind it well just behind the joint to stop the bleeding, disinfect the spot before you cut it off and afterwards dress the wound with sticking plaster. Watch the wound for possible infection.

If you cut off less than the entire joint, enough feathers will regrow for the duck to be able to fly when reaching maturity, or to knock himself out by flying into the wires of the enclosure. If the birds are pinioned, they can stay in an open enclosure. Unlike parrots and finches, ducks need little shelter, as they are hardy as far as frost and cold are concerned.

Enclosures for ducks

The bottom wire of a duck enclosure must be proof against dogs. Diamond mesh wire is suitable to keep the ducks in and the dogs out. However, it does allow rats in, which may cause damage to the eggs, and small ducklings could crawl through and disappear or get eaten by dogs. Welded wire mesh is therefore better. Some duck farmers build a wall to provide the birds in the duck enclosure with adequate protection.

If the enclosure has a wire roof, cats, owls and crows do not pose a problem. An open enclosure, however, often leads to great disappointment. Rats and mongooses eat the eggs or ducklings, while owls, crows and cats (particularly in the city) will delight in catching the smaller types of ducks.

92 Beautiful waterways with natural vegetation turn this waterfowl farm into a true paradise for its occupants. The electric lamp is lit at night to attract insects. The waterfowl gather beneath the lamp and eat the insects.

Some farmers dream of a farm or smallholding with a large natural dam full of pretty waterfowl. However, they often suffer great disappointment because otters or wildcats catch the birds. The only defence ducks have is to flee by flying away. If they are pinioned to prevent them from flying, waterfowl cannot be returned to their natural environment.

Then they should be protected and the very safest is an aviary with a pond and a wire roof. Second best is an enclosure with a cement dam surrounded by a wall or strong wire.

In large natural dams you often find crabs which catch the small ducklings. One method of giving ducks on a large

93 A neat row of open breeding pens for waterfowl which cannot fly. In the background there are enclosed pens for mandarins and Carolinas. The birds are protected by a high wall around the premises.

open dam a measure of protection is to ensure that there is an island in the dam to which they can flee should something threaten them.

Although ducks are hardy as regards the cold, they must be protected from the burning sun or bitterly cold wind. It is not difficult to provide shelter. Asbestos or plastic sheets, a wall, a grass screen or dense plants and shrubs which deflect the cold winds and provide shade, are adequate.

Because ducks like staying on the dam, the dam itself should preferably be protected against cold winds. Thick clumps of grass such as pampas grass or papyrus provide good shelter from the elements and also provide nesting space for ducks which breed on the ground.

With a little imagination the duck enclosure can be made to look very attractive. A cement dam with rocks on the edge to break the rigidity, a few rockery rocks here and there, dense reeds (e.g. large and small papyrus), one or more trees for shade, and large shrubs will all contribute towards making the environment more pleasant. Forget about flowers and a spring garden – the ducks will graze everything down to ground level.

Ducks cannot share the same aviary as finches. Small finches are very poor fliers when they emerge from the nest and ducks regard them as a delicacy.

In a small aviary with a concrete floor it is a good idea to spread a thick layer of river sand over the concrete. This helps to beat the cold and, more important, it absorbs the droppings and wetness and keeps the aviary neat for weeks. An aviary without sand will begin to smell bad within days and must be scrubbed constantly.

A small aviary of about 1 m × 3 m with a soil floor is impractical. It becomes wet and muddy, stinks and attracts flies. A solution is a thick layer of sand spread over the floor, but even then the soil underneath cannot be scrubbed clean. A concrete floor with a covering of sand is still the most hygienic.

Ponds

Many a duck farmer has scraped a hollow in the ground, lined it with concrete, and a few weeks later found to his dismay that his pond leaks. The simplest way of solving the problem is first to line the hollow in the ground with a layer of plastic material. Fertilizer bags which have been cut open will do the trick.

On top of this layer spread a thick layer of gravel or a mixture of soil, stone and sand and compact it well. Now spread a cement layer consisting of one part cement to three parts sand on top and plaster it smoothly. To make doubly sure that the pond will not leak, paint the cement layer with waterproof paint.

The cement can also be spread directly onto compacted soil, but to ensure that the pond is watertight, more cement than normal must be used. A good mixture is one part cement, two parts sand and three parts fine gravel.

When building a pond for water birds, it is important to

94 To empty and clean the pond with ease, the floor of the enclosure is raised above ground level. The outlet pipe is closed with a rubber stopper.

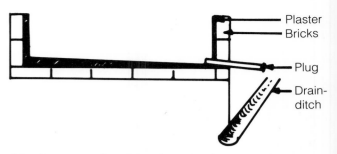

Fig. 19 A cross section of a rectangular dam

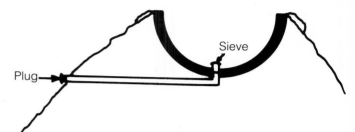

Fig. 20 A cross section of a round or trough-shaped dam

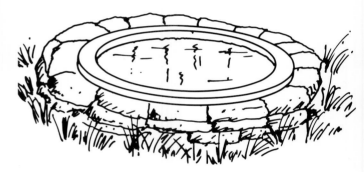

Fig. 21 A pond with a paving surround

plan drainage for the pond beforehand (see figs. 19 and 20). If the ground in the duck enclosure is level, it is better to raise the pond above ground level. Fix the drainage pipe with a mixture of one part cement to one part sand. Pack the mixture around the pipe to a thickness of about 10 cm. Place a sieve over the pipe's inlet to prevent it from becoming blocked.

The outlet can be stopped with a rubber or cork stopper. Rubber stoppers are for sale in various sizes from companies which sell laboratory equipment. A wooden stopper also works fairly well. Alternatively a tap can be fitted to the outlet.

For ducks the pond does not have to be more than 30-40 cm deep. Ensure that the inlet of the drainage pipe is at the very lowest part of the pond. Lay some kind of paving around the pond to ensure that the ducks do not trail mud into the water (see fig. 21).

Asbestos or fibreglass fishponds also make excellent duck ponds.

A halved 200-litre drum works well too, and will last a good few years before rusting through.

Ducks must have water because they normally mate in water, and also transfer essential moisture to the nest by means of their wet feathers.

Botulism

It is very important that small duck ponds be cleaned at least once a week. If not, the ducks could die of botulism within a few hours. Botulism develops when rotting material (such as droppings) soils the water and the ducks then drink the water.

Large dam complexes with automatic pumps which circulate and clean the water can be built. A duck pond can also be built in an existing stream. The water which flows through will keep the pond clean.

Feeding adult ducks

Commercial duck meal, supplemented with plenty of greenstuff such as lucerne, grass, spinach, carrot tops, chopped lettuce, cabbage or peas is all that you need. Duck meal is often unobtainable, but adult ducks do well for years if they are provided with laying meal and greenstuff.

Do not wet the meal, but place the dry meal directly alongside a water bowl. This is very important, because ducks take a beakful of dry meal and then swallow it down with a sip of water. If the water is too far away from the food, they may lose weight and become thin because they are constantly jogging from the food bowl to the water bowl and back.

Do not expect the ducks to drink their swimming water, because this is dirty and full of droppings.

A farmer can also make up his own feeding mixture from what is available on the farm. Use raw mealie meal, boiled potatoes or raw potato peels, putu, porridge or bread as basic food. In order to increase the protein value to the required 20-22%, add fish meal, boiled eggs or fresh or curdled milk. Once or twice a week add vitamin supplements (such as used for chickens) plus a little bone meal or eggshells to provide minerals. Provide plenty of greenstuff with this mixture.

The nest

Ducks start building a nest at about the end of September and brood until about the end of December. Most ducks build a simple nest of grass or twigs which they gather up with their feet. Protection from the rain and hot sun is essential. A neat hut made of grass to cover the nest, a piece of corrugated iron or asbestos sheeting erected as a roof over the nest, or the shade of a dense shrub is quite adequate. They will also use nest boxes if they are provided.

The tree ducks (mandarins and Carolinas) require a box

Fig. 22 A nest for tree ducks

which stands about one or two metres above the ground. There must be a ladder in the form of, e.g. a plank with crosspieces which leads to the opening (see fig. 22).

Note that the opening is to one side and not in the centre. This provides a larger area in which the ducks can hide. Place a thick bunch of grass inside the box. The pair will hollow out and shape the nest themselves. The female lays about 12-15 eggs. When she has finished, she will cover the eggs neatly with down she plucks from her body.

The brooding times of various water birds are as follows:
Mandarins and Carolinas: 31-32 days
Swans: 35-42 days
Geese: 28-32 days
Other ducks: 28-32 days

Hatching the eggs

Ducks normally breed well as long as they have shelter, feel safe in the nest and are not disturbed unnecessarily. If you remove each egg as soon as it is laid, the female will often continue laying. Instead of, e.g. 12 eggs, she will in such a case often lay 30 eggs. In the case of rare and expensive ducks this can be an economic factor. This is why eggs are sometimes removed from a female duck and hatched by some other means.

Bantam hens are excellent in this regard. They hatch strong and healthy ducklings. The hen should only recently have begun to sit before receiving six to eight duck eggs to hatch. A chicken broods for three weeks, but the hen must sit for more than four weeks to hatch the ducklings.

If she has been sitting for some time before she receives the duck eggs, she may not keep it up to the end. Bantams or silkies make excellent mothers for young ducklings. Their placid nature helps to calm wild ducklings as well.

The eggs of wild ducks and geese can also be hatched by means of an incubator. Follow the instructions for the machine as for ordinary duck and goose eggs. The machine usually does not do the job as well as a bantam hen or the female duck herself. The percentage of eggs which hatch is lower and the ducklings often weaker, particularly in the case of the smaller types of incubator. It is important that the humidity in the machine is kept very high and the eggs must be doused well with tepid water twice a day. For the last five or six days the eggs can be dipped in tepid water for a moment when they are being turned. Duck and goose eggshells are very thick and if the shell is too dry, the ducklings cannot hatch.

Rearing ducklings

Although looking after adult ducks and geese is relatively simple, raising wild ducklings is quite a different matter. You always hear the same complaint: The ducklings lived for about four or five days, then all or most of them died.

This is particularly so in the case of mandarins and Carolinas.

There are different ways of raising mandarin and Carolina ducklings. The one which usually has the lowest success rate is the partly natural method, which means that the mother and ducklings are set to run loose in a large enclosure. These ducks all have a wild nature and, particularly if there are ducklings, the mother will restlessly rush up and down alongside the fence. The ducklings will rush after her all the time and never get a chance to eat. Within a few days most of them will have died from hunger and exhaustion. If they get wet because of rain, they will also die. If they fall into the water, it's the same story. If they are cold, they die.

To add to all this, mandarin ducklings are too stupid to know what to eat. In nature they eat live insects which hop about, and frogs which jump and attract their attention. In the enclosure they are now expected to eat food which lies perfectly still! You can understand why they find it difficult to learn what constitutes their real food.

In nature the female hatches about ten ducklings, of which she raises two, but the aviculturalist expects better results than that. This is possible, but then you must lend a hand. Mandarin and Carolina ducklings are wild creatures which cannot be handled as simply and easily as domesticated ducks. Raise them in any of the following ways:

☐ Place the mother and her ducklings in a small enclosure – one metre by one metre is not too small – in which she cannot rush about. The enclosure must have a roof and be sheltered from cold wind and rain by means of sacking or sheeting surrounding the enclosure. This also provides the mother with the seclusion she so desperately seeks when she has ducklings. She cannot look outside and see anything, which helps to calm her down. Make sure that there is a dark hiding place in the enclosure, e.g. a box with its open end turned to the wall. The mother's greatest need during the first few days is for good shelter and darkness in which to hide her ducklings. If the weather turns cold, you can heat the enclosure with an asbestos heater.

☐ Wild ducklings can also be given to a domesticated or Muscovy duck, if such a duck has just hatched ducklings of her own. If the wild ducklings live with the domesticated ones, they learn to eat sooner because the domesticated ducklings will show them how. Keep the domesticated or Muscovy duck in a small enclosure so that the wild ducklings cannot run away. A bantam or silkie hen makes an excellent mother for wild ducklings, although she is unable to oil them and the ducklings will get wet when they swim.

☐ Wild ducklings can also be raised with the help of a brooder. The advantage of a brooder is that the temperature remains constantly warm. The ducklings are raised at the same temperature as chicks. This temperature is about 35-38 °C during the first few days, followed by a gradual lowering of the heat until it reaches room temperature between the second and third week.

It may sound strange, but put the mother duck in the brooder as well. Her presence keeps the ducklings calm so that they do not rush about so much. The mother teaches them to eat and she keeps them warm should there be a power failure. If the mother is present, the initial temperature must be lower, or else she will succumb to the heat. She will show her distress by sitting with her bill open. However, if she is very wild, she may trample some of her ducklings to death. It is often more economical to raise the ducklings in the brooder without their real mother. If the mother's ducklings are removed very early and luck is on your side, the mother will lay another nest full of eggs and brood again. If she has to raise her family by herself, she usually breeds only once a year.

If the ducklings are to remain in the brooder without their real mother, they do not learn to eat, and may die of hunger even in these sheltered circumstances. Place Muscovy or domesticated ducklings in the brooder together with the wild ducklings. The tame Muscovies are unbelievably greedy eaters and soon the wild ducklings will be eating along with them.

To help solve the eating problem further, live mealworms, mealworm beetles, maggots or termites can be sprinkled over the food. The ducklings will begin pecking at the moving insects and in this way learn to eat.

☐ If no domesticated or Muscovy ducklings are available, and the mother rushes about wildly even in a small enclosure, the mandarin ducklings may die despite all your best efforts, because they do not eat. However, there is an infallible method of helping all of them through the first critical seven to ten days, but it takes time and patience. I have helped all of my mandarins and Carolinas through in this way and have not yet lost a single one.

Place the ducklings in a brooder where the temperature is regulated automatically. Mix ProNutro with water into a fairly thin paste and place it in a 10-20-cm³ syringe. Push a piece of rubber tubing of about 6-10 cm in length over the spout of the syringe. A bicycle valve tube works best. Wet the tube with water so that it slips down the duckling's throat with greater ease. Open the duckling's bill and gently insert the tube into its crop. The tube doesn't usually slip easily down the windpipe. As long as the tube moves in and out freely, you can assume with some certainty that it is in the crop. Inject ProNutro until the crop bulges slightly. The crops of small ducklings do not bulge as markedly as those of a small parrot or finch when full. Use your finger to feel whether there is something in the crop.

For the first few days the ducklings are given 1,5-2 ml every two hours. After about four days they are given 3-6 ml every three hours. As they grow, this amount can be increased. In the meantime always place a bowl of food near them. After about a week or ten days most of them eat by themselves.

95 This is how mandarin and Carolina ducklings are force-fed for the first seven to ten days.

Feeding ducklings

If no special meal mixture for ducklings is available, then buy the high-protein meal used for raising turkeys or chickens. Ducklings prefer to eat wet meal, so moisten the meal if you have the time, but then it must be replaced with fresh meal in the morning and evening, otherwise it will ferment, or fungi and bacteria may grow in it. The latter causes scour and the ducklings may die. If the ducklings are to eat dry meal, their drinking water must be placed directly next to the food container so that they can help down the dry meal with a little water.

Give them greenstuff with the basic meal mixture every day. Spinach, parsley, lucerne and chopped cabbage, lettuce or carrot tops are suitable.

All ducks are normally fond of a mixture of mashed hard-boiled egg and chopped lettuce. To encourage the ducklings to eat, this mixture is sprinkled over the dry meal mixture for the first few days. However, the unused egg must be removed after one or at the most two hours, or bacteria will grow in it, which may cause the ducklings to become ill and die if they eat it.

Wet ducklings

An important point when raising ducklings is that they must not get wet. This sounds illogical, but is true. When ducklings emerge from the egg, their down contains no natural oil. They therefore get wet to the skin, catch cold and die.

At an early age the down is oiled to some extent when ducklings crawl under their mother. Her oil is then transferred to them. If they grow up without their natural mother, it may be some weeks before they produce enough oil themselves not to get wet. In their natural state young ducklings can swim for only a short time before they have to get out of the water and in nature rain can cause the ducklings to die.

All ducklings raised artificially must therefore be protected from the wet. However, this is not so easy, because water attracts them like a magnet. If they run around and climb into a drinking trough filled with water, they are wet through in no time and may die. Drinking dishes for ducklings must therefore have a lid with a hole or row of holes large enough for them to be able to stick only their heads through (see fig. 23).

It will do them no harm to begin swimming at only three or four weeks, or when they are well feathered, particularly if they have not been raised by their own mother. If ducklings become sopping wet, they must be rubbed down immediately and warmed.

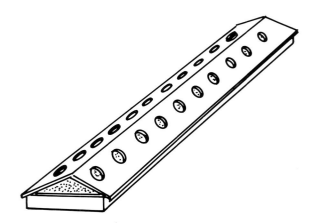

Fig. 23 An example of a drinking trough for ducklings

Swans and geese

Swans and geese need more space than ducks. They also graze more extensively than ducks and provision must be made for this. They are aggressive and, when brooding, they will threaten or attack even their owner. Geese make a hollow under a thick clump of grass or dense shrub and line it with twigs and feathers which the female plucks from herself. Build a roof over the nest, e.g. of long grass, to protect the female from the rain and heat. They will also accept sheltered nest boxes.

Swans build an enormous nest and need plenty of nesting material. Make provision for this by providing heaps of tambookie grass, reeds, elephant grass or whatever is available. Build a suitable roof over the nest (see photo 96). Swans are so rare and expensive that any trouble is justified.

Swans and geese can be left to raise their own chicks, as they do not run away like tree ducks. However, if the weather is continually cold and wet, the very small goslings or cygnets must be brought inside and hand-reared. Fortunately they learn to eat by themselves and require only warmth and dryness in order to survive. When the bad weather clears, they can be returned to their parents, as long as the parents still recognise them.

96 The gigantic nest of a mute swan

Feeding

Swans and geese must get plenty of greenstuff such as grass, lucerne, oats, lettuce leaves, carrot tops, finely chopped carrots, pumpkin and other vegetables. In their natural habitat they eat water plants, the roots of water plants and grass. In addition they eat insects, frogs and snails and provision must be made for this by giving them poultry or dog meal. With this they also get whole maize or a poultry mix consisting of crushed maize and sorghum.

When there are goslings or cygnets, soft food must be provided. This can be porridge, bread, potatoes, putu, hard-boiled egg and/or moistened poultry meal or moistened dog meal. Of course poultry and dog meal and dog pellets have the advantage that they contain a variety of nutrients, are high in proteins and also contain salt, minerals and vitamins.

Gravel must be available, although they will swallow the necessary stones if they find these in their enclosure.

Individual descriptions of swans and geese

BLACK SWAN (*Cygnus atratus*) PHOTO 97
Origin: Australia, Tasmania and New Zealand.
Although they are graceful on the water, they are fairly ponderous on land. They take off with some difficulty. When in the air, their wings make a swooshing sound similar to that of mute swans. They are very active at dusk and will even fly about on moonlit nights. They utter a loud trumpet call and make other sounds as well. This is the national bird of Western Australia and flocks of up to 50 000 swans have been recorded.
Description: *Male* – On water it looks completely black, apart from the red and white beak. However, the under-

parts of the wings are black with a visible white edge which can be seen when it flies. It does not carry its neck as deeply bowed as that of the mute swan. *Female* – As for the male, but smaller. Size: 150 cm.
Breeding habits: Their nesting requirements are discussed on p. 89. The eggs are a pale green. Five or six eggs are the norm, but sometimes the female lays up to 14 eggs at a time. The female broods by night and the male by day. This is the only swan species where both sexes brood. The incubation period is between 34 and 37 days. The parents sometimes carry the cygnets on their backs.

BLACK-NECKED SWAN (*Cygnus melanocoryphus*) PHOTO 98
Origin: Southern tip of South America.
These swans remain on the water most of the time and seldom leave it, except during the breeding season. Although they graze almost exclusively in the water in their natural state, they do adapt well to the food they receive in captivity. On land they are awkward and shy. They have soft and musical voices. Because they are so water-bound, they adapt better to a densely vegetated dam with plenty of shallow water.

97 Black swan

98 Black-necked swan

Description: *Male* – White with a black neck and head. The front of the beak is grey and the back red, with a red knob in front of the nose. The red knob appears only when the swan is fully mature at three or four years, but the black and white feathers appear as early as two years. *Female* – As for the male, but smaller. Size: 100 cm.

Breeding habits: They court by moving around each other and bobbing their heads up and down. They breed from July to November. They like to build their nest in shallow water among reeds using all kinds of plant material; the farmer must make provision for this need when constructing his dam. Three to seven cream-coloured eggs are laid. Incubation lasts 33-36 days. The male looks after the nest while the female broods. She will sometimes sit on the nest for days on end without leaving it to graze. As soon as the cygnets hatch, they are carried to the water on the backs of their parents. The parents' wings protect the cygnets so well that they are almost invisible while enjoying their ride.

99 Chinese goose

CHINESE GOOSE *(Anser cygnoides)* PHOTO 99
Origin: China.

The Chinese goose we keep is a descendant of the wild swan goose which has been domesticated for the last 3 000 years. The domesticated Chinese geese no longer walk upright and have become so heavy that they can no longer fly. They also have much larger knobs on the nose than the wild kind, which has almost no knobs. They become marvellous pets and like to 'talk' to their owner. They need space to graze and are reared in the same way as ordinary tame geese.

Description: *Male* – Back of head, back of neck and back: brown. Underside of face and throat: light brown to white. Breast and belly: brown. Wings: grey and white which gives a streaky appearance. Beak: dark grey with a white edge where it joins the face. A knob appears above the nose. Legs and feet: orange. *Female* – As for the male, but she is smaller and the knob on her nose is also smaller or completely absent. Size: 120 cm.

Breeding habits: The female lays about eight eggs. She broods on her own while the male stands watch. The incubation period is a little over four weeks. They build a nest like ordinary farm geese, namely beneath a dense shrub where they arrange twigs and grass to their liking.

HAWAIIAN GOOSE *(Branta sandvicensis)*
PHOTO 100
Origin: Hawaii and surrounding islands.

In 1950 there were only about 50 of these geese left in the world, but through a breeding programme in England and Hawaii they were saved from total extinction in time. However, because so few were left with which to breed and there was only a small variety of genetic material available, the goslings inherited a type of down which results in many of them succumbing to wet conditions in nature.

100 Hawaiian goose

The Hawaiian goose is actually a descendant of the Canadian goose, but through evolution their webs adapted themselves to the volcanic rocks of Hawaii; in contrast to other geese, they walk very well on dry land and stones.

Description: *Male* – Face, head, throat, beak and back of neck: black. There is a dark ring around the bottom part of the neck. Breast and flanks: light brown. Rump: black. Rest of body: black and white and grey which appears streaky. Legs and feet: black. *Female* – As for the male. Size: 65 cm.

Breeding habits: The male courts the female by puffing up his neck feathers and nodding his head up and down. He is very aggressive and pugnacious. Brooding time is from October to February. The nest is built on the ground and is lined by the female with her own feathers. Three to six cream-coloured eggs are laid. The incubation period is 30 days.

MUTE SWAN (*Cygnus olor*) PHOTO 101

Origin: Europe and Asia.

Their habit of sailing across the water with uplifted wings is not copied by other northern swans. When they fly, their powerful wings make a loud swooshing sound which can be heard up to a kilometre away. Although the name may indicate that they are mute, they do make various sounds.

Description: *Male* – Snow white with a pinkish bill which has a black base. *Female* – As for the male, but smaller and more delicate. The knob on her nose is smaller than that of the male. Size: 150 cm.

Breeding habits: They breed during summer. Their nesting requirements are discussed on p. 89. Normally there are four to seven greyish white eggs which take about five weeks to hatch. The cygnets are often carried on the parents' backs. The cygnets stay with their parents for a long time, often up to nine months.

101 Mute swan

102 Golden pheasant

104 Reeves pheasant cock and hens

103 Silver pheasant

105 Ringneck pheasant

14

Pheasants

Of the 175 pheasant species and subspecies that occur in the world, only a few are found in our country, and then only in small numbers.

Yet everybody who regards himself as an aviculturalist has a duty towards pheasants. Because man is destroying the natural habitat of the pheasants, many have already become extinct or are in danger of extinction. In fact, many species occur only in captivity. To save what is left, the governments of countries such as Thailand, China, India and Taiwan have placed an outright ban on the export of pheasants.

Because wild pheasants may no longer be exported from their countries of origin, we are left with those bred in aviaries and those which may still be bred in the future. To import such pheasants is very expensive. The airfreight alone for such large, heavy birds runs into an enormous amount.

However, with our warm climate, we can breed the tropical pheasants on a large scale, and in the cooler areas we can breed the highland pheasants such as the Kalijs. Had we grasped the opportunity to breed pheasants on a large scale when they were still plentiful and cheap, we could have been exporting pheasants today, in particular the tropical species. People are so eager to get hold of the rarer species that the high costs of the airfreight will not deter them. However, we let that opportunity slip by.

Yet it is not too late. Those who really are interested can still buy some of the country's limited stock of ornamental pheasants and begin farming with them, and import new blood for breeding. Apart from ornamental pheasants, there is a market in South Africa for pheasants for the table and for hunting.

There are also those extremely exotic pheasants for which there is a market in America and Europe. They will do well in South Africa, as long as the necessary starting stock can be acquired and imported. In this regard you can think of the four species of junglefowl, the genus *Gallus*, which originated in the warmer regions of Sri Lanka, India, Burma and Malaysia, as well as the Firebacks from China and Malaysia. They require a warm climate and need to be in the hands of an expert who will devote himself to the challenging task of breeding these pheasants. Perhaps this is just the ticket for a retired bird lover.

All true pheasants (apart from one species) come from the East. What we in South Africa sometimes call a pheasant or francolin – that little grey bird with the red face found in the Bushveld – is not a true pheasant. The male of a true pheasant is showy and endowed with colourful feathers, while the female is often drab. In addition their legs are bare. The popular showy peacock found on some farms, for example, is an example of a true pheasant.

Beginners can choose from among the following pheasants:

GOLDEN PHEASANT   (*Chrysolophus pictus*)
PHOTO 102

From China, they are beautiful and become so tame that you can pick them up and stroke them.

LADY AMHERST   (*Chrysolophus amherstiae*)
A showy pheasant in its own right, tame and easy to breed.

SILVER PHEASANT   (*Lophura nycthemera*)
PHOTO 103

This large pheasant originally comes from Thailand and China. The easiest ornamental pheasant to keep and breed.

These three species are fairly common in South Africa and therefore easily obtainable. They are hardy as regards cold and heat, make a good nest even in captivity, hatch their eggs themselves and raise their chicks themselves. Other pheasants do not necessarily do this in captivity.

Unfortunately many of the available Lady Amherst pheasants are crossbred. The product is a most beautiful bird, but those who want the true pheasant must note the following: The birds must bear a small red crest with a green crown on the head, show no red on the breast or belly and have a tail with clear black and white bars. A pure Lady Amherst pheasant shows no hint of yellow in her feathers.

Pheasants begin laying in spring and sometimes continue to March. In the case of the above-mentioned three species a chicken nest in a sheltered spot will do. One male is assigned three to five females and only one such group is kept to an enclosure. During the breeding season pheasant males fight one another to the death.

Other pheasants which are hardy and suitable for the beginner but do not brood themselves are the Reeves (see photo 104) and the ringneck (see photo 105). These two pheasant are game pheasants, bred to be hunted or slaughtered for the table. The rule that there should be only one male to an aviary also applies in this case. The Reeves in particular is a formidable fighter and will sometimes even kill his own females.

The last-mentioned two pheasant species lay their eggs scattered all over the ground and therefore do not need a nest. One male can handle three to five females. The eggs must be hatched in an incubator or beneath bantam or silkie hens and the chicks raised artificially. If you have a number of laying pheasants, the males are switched every two weeks to ensure genetic variety.

Follow the instructions for the incubator and raise the chicks like chickens, using a hen or brooder.

Examples of hardy pheasants which are difficult to obtain but will do their bit even in the hands of a beginner are the Swinhoe, Elliot, brown-ear and any of the Kalij types (see photo 106). The Kalij females will often kill one another and it is better to have only one female per male and to keep each pair in their own pen.

Housing

In general pheasants are hardy birds, but because many species come from high mountain countries where it is cool, they are not very tolerant of the sun and great heat. Housing must therefore provide shade as well as shelter from the wind, rain or hail. A simple and relatively inexpensive housing method is the following:

Construct an enclosure of creosote or iron poles and chicken wire. A suitable size for one cock and three hens is 5 m x 5 m. Stretch a roof of shade netting over it and fix this securely. The shade netting roof must be high enough for a man to stand comfortably upright underneath it. Tie grass to the sides of the enclosure to a height of about 0,5 m to provide shelter from the wind. Place a number of branches in the enclosure so that the pheasants can hide beneath them, or plant shrubs such as cypresses in the enclosure. Spread a thick layer of grass or hay on the floor. When the floor becomes soiled, the grass is replaced.

Once or twice a year the top soil layer is removed and

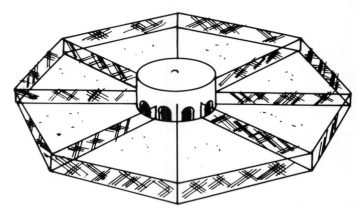

Fig. 24 A wagon-wheel type of enclosure designed for pheasants. Each division houses a male and his females.

replaced by clean soil or sand. Such a soil floor is warm and cheap. In very warm regions of the country tambookie grass or reeds can be placed on top of the shade netting for extra shade.

Where it is cold and wet, part of the roof could be covered with corrugated iron, asbestos or fibreglass.

Of course fancy enclosures can be built of brick. This all depends on the amount of money, time and labour available (see fig. 24 for an enclosure plan for pheasants). An important point to remember is that if pheasants pace nervously up and down along the wire, they are unhappy and need some kind of shelter. Therefore always ensure that there is some place to hide away in the enclosure, in the form of dense shrubs, large clumps of grass or loose branches.

Pheasants in an open run without a roof must have their wings pinioned or wing feathers clipped, otherwise they will fly away.

Feeding

Pheasants chicks need a high-protein ration (27-29% protein). The protein value of ordinary poultry growth meal is too low. Growth meal for turkeys is better, but seldom available. Large commercial pheasant farmers have a special high-protein ration made up, but the backyard breeder cannot do this.

Feed the pheasant chicks poultry growth meal and supplement it with hard-boiled egg. A word of warning, however: Beware of hard-boiled egg which is allowed to become old and warm. Give only as much egg as the birds can eat within an hour. Egg is a good breeding ground for harmful bacteria.

The pheasant chicks must also get plenty of greenstuff. Lucerne is good as greenstuff because it helps to supplement the protein.

Breeding birds are fed with a commercially available ration used for breeding hens. A brood mix usually contains more protein than laying meal.

106 A Nepal Kalij pheasant cock

94

107 Each pheasant enclosure accommodates one male and three to four females. The shade-netted roof, partially covered with tambookie grass, provides shelter from the rain. Grass standing upright against the wire prevents males from spotting one another and fighting through the wire. This also provides shelter from the wind. The floor is covered with a thick layer of grass or hay while dense, green branches provide shelter for females to lay their eggs.

108 A pheasant trap used to capture pheasants which have escaped from the enclosure. It is built into the wire of the pheasant enclosure. The back hatch is opened, while the front hatch can open only in one direction. As soon as the bird has passed through the front hatch, the hatch falls shut and the pheasant is safely in its enclosure.

Diseases

Pheasants can contract the same diseases as chickens, although they are hardier and do not fall ill as easily. Pheasants are also given exactly the same treatment as chickens. They must be dewormed regularly to combat roundworm, tapeworm and gapeworm. See chapter 8 for combating diseases or follow the instructions on the labels of poultry remedies.

Pheasants do not readily contract coccidiosis, particularly if the premises are kept clean, but the chicks must be inoculated against smallpox just like chickens. The vaccine is available from Onderstepoort or veterinarians. After a few days, check whether there is a scab on the inoculation site. If there is no scab, the vaccination has not taken and the process must be repeated. As is the case with chickens, pheasants can also contract bacillary white diarrhoea and the feared Newcastle disease.

The same remedy as for chickens is applied in the case of bacillary white diarrhoea. Newcastle disease is normally controlled by the authorities.

Pheasants for the pot

In South Africa pheasants are bred on a small scale for the pot (i.e. for hunting or slaughtering – the so-called game pheasants). The most popular pheasant for this purpose is the ringneck. The Reeves is bred on a smaller scale because it is so belligerent.

These pheasants do not hatch their eggs themselves and the eggs must be collected every day or twice a day. Only eggs which are no older than a week must be used for breeding purposes. The eggs must be kept in a cool place and only eggs which are not misshapen are placed in the incubator. If the very small type of incubator (60 eggs) is used, it is important to place it in a spot where the temperature is fairly constant and not in front of an open window.

Hatching times

The following gives an indication of the time it takes for pheasant eggs to hatch:

Lady Amherst: 22-24 days
Golden pheasant: 23-24 days
Nepal Kalij: 24-25 days
Reeves: 24-25 days
Silver pheasant: 26-27 days
Ringneck: 24-25 days
Swinhoe: 24-25 days

The young pheasants are hunted or slaughtered at four to six months. Because from three to seven females are kept to one male, there is a surplus of males and therefore mostly males are hunted or slaughtered.

When a pheasant is slaughtered, the head must not be chopped off. The neck is quickly broken below the head and the head is then pulled away from the body, but only enough to sever the arteries. The skin of the neck must remain intact. The pheasant then bleeds inside the unbroken skin of the neck. The whole pheasant, with feathers, entrails, blood, head, etc. is kept in the refrigerator in a plastic bag for about eight to ten days. The bird is then plucked and the entrails removed. The flesh has a delicate flavour which is not far removed from that of a chicken.

The meat of young birds and females is very tender and can be prepared like chicken.

Luxury liners calling at South African harbours, restaurants and hotels offer a market for slaughtered pheasants. Of course the packaging, transportation and marketing must be done very professionally.

Hunting farms

There are a number of hunting farms in South Africa for which a few thousand pheasant chicks need to be bred every year. The hunting farms are usually planted with rows of shrubs alternated with open patches of grass in between. A few hours before the hunters arrive, the pheasants are let loose, whereupon they take shelter among the shrubs. Hunting dogs are used to flush them, and as soon as they fly into the air or run across the open stretches, they are shot.

Although such pheasant hunts are an overseas custom which is still relatively unknown to South Africans, it is to the advantage of the ringnecks as a species. As soon as humans find a use for an animal (or bird), they will ensure that the species remains in existence and does not become extinct. As long as we hunt and eat ringnecks, their existence is assured.

109 A Chinese painted quail male

111 Californian quail male and female

110 Singing quail

112 Japanese rain quail

15

Quail

Quail can be successfully incorporated into an avicultural operation because they stay mainly on the ground and will consequently seldom bother the other birds in the aviary. There are also people who breed quail on a large scale for the slaughter market.

The smaller quail such as the Chinese painted and singing quail do not bother the other birds in the aviary at all. However, larger quail such as the Californian quail, which sleeps off the ground, may frighten the other birds if the aviary is too small.

The backyard farmer keeps ornamental or show quail for his pleasure. The following are some of the most popular types:

CHINESE PAINTED QUAIL (*Excalfactoria chinensis*)   PHOTO 109

They are very small and do not bother the other occupants of the aviary. The females hatch the chicks by themselves. Chinese painted quail become amazingly tame and are cheap. During the breeding season the males fight viciously among one another.

The male has white and black bars under the throat, while the female is completely brown-grey. A male without a female will start crying in the most heart-rending manner day in, day out – to such an extent that you will get into the car and drive many kilometres to find the poor chap a wife.

There are already a few mutations of the Chinese painted quail, of which the silver mutation is the easiest to obtain.

In the case of the silver quail it is sometimes difficult to determine the sex. However, the male's eyes are reddish, while those of the female are dark brown.

SINGING QUAIL (*Perdicula asiatica*)   PHOTO 110

The true singing quail originates from America and we do not find many of them in our aviaries. What we call the singing quail here is actually the jungle bush quail, *Perdicula asiatica*, from Asia. They are somewhat larger than the Chinese painted quail and hatch their chicks by themselves. They are reasonably priced. Unfortunately they remain quite wild.

The male has bars on the breast, while the female is coloured brown.

The chirring of quail all day long reminds one of the Bushveld and is not intrusive. They mix well with the other birds in an aviary.

CALIFORNIAN QUAIL (*Lophortyx californica*)
PHOTO 111

They are very pretty and sport a beautiful crest. The crest of the female is smaller than that of the male and her colours are rather duller. They are fairly large and like to sleep above ground on a branch or other perch (such as other birds' nests), and therefore they frighten small birds. They fight among one another and there should preferably be only one pair per aviary. Keep them with large parakeets such as redrumps, rather than with finches.

Quail for the pot

The Japanese rain quail, *Coturnix japonica* (photo 112), is raised for slaughtering purposes. The name 'rain quail' is incorrect, because the real rain quail comes from India. The so-called Siberian quail is nothing but a Japanese quail with a different colour, and the White Jap is a white mutation of the Japanese quail.

The Japanese rain quail has an interesting history. This is the quail we read about in the Bible. These quail occurred in gigantic swarms in ancient Egypt and on the grasslands of Europe and Asia. They thrived particularly on the grainfields. Because they matured within six weeks and could begin breeding a few weeks later, there were masses of these birds which gorged themselves on the Egyptian grain fields.

The Egyptians caught them in nets, and they provided an easy source of meat for all the people, from the poorest to the richest. It was often a difficult choice for the Egyptians – more grain or more quail? Because the quail were such an important source of food, they were called Pharaoh quail, and they occupy a prominent place in ancient drawings and writings.

When they stripped the grainfields bare, the swarms grew to thick clouds, and began to emigrate in their millions in their search for food. Some flew into the desert, where they eventually died. Others flew out over the sea, where they drowned when they became exhausted.

In this way nature redressed the imbalance. A case has been described where such a migrating mass of birds spotted a sailing vessel and descended on the rigging and masts in a heavy black cloud, eventually capsizing the ship!

The Japanese and Chinese began keeping these quail in cages and improved the race through selection of the largest eggs. Today many subspecies of the original quail exist, and the eggs are as much sought after as the meat.

The market for Japanese quail consists of top-class hotels, some restaurants and luxury liners calling at our ports. The slaughtering must be done strictly according to municipal regulations and a licence is needed for it.

Brooding process

When quail are bred for commercial purposes the eggs are hatched with the aid of an incubator. As is often the case with birds, the quail continue laying eggs if the female's eggs are removed every day to stop her from becoming broody.

Most quail hatch their own eggs very well. They prefer a dense clump of grass or shrub beneath which they build a sheltered nest. If the aviary has a concrete floor, place a small wooden box such as a budgie or cockatiel nest on its side on the floor. Open the lid and turn the opening to the wall so that it is well protected. Place a handful of grass inside. The quail will enter the box via the open lid.

Many quail, but in particular Chinese painted quail, lay far too many eggs to cover properly. The outer eggs then become cold and the embryos die. The female later rolls them to the inside and rolls the inside ones to the outside. In this process even more eggs become cold and their embryos also die. The end result is that one or two chicks may hatch from ten eggs.

Leave a quail female with only enough eggs for her to cover properly. For example, six eggs are plenty for a Chinese quail. Hatch the remaining eggs in an incubator, or beneath a bantam, silkie or large dove. However, chickens such as the silkies can quite easily trample the tiny quail to death.

If the quail are hatched with the help of an incubator, they naturally do not have a mother, and keeping them warm becomes a problem. If quail are hatched on a large scale, an artificial brooder used for chickens is worth the cost and trouble, but for the plain hobby breeder such a brooder is too expensive.

If the weather outside is not bitterly cold, one or two chickens of about three weeks old are ideal 'artificial mothers'. The quail creep in underneath the chickens and the two species keep one another warm. Furthermore the chickens teach the quail what to eat.

The wooden or cardboard box in which the quail are to be kept must be covered with chicken wire, gauze, a tea net or shade cloth. If not, the quail jump up and are out of the box in a flash.

Another method of keeping the small quail warm is to suspend an ordinary 60-watt globe above the box. The quail will, of their own volition, move as close to the bulb as is comfortable for them.

Just be very careful; a bulb can scorch a cardboard box badly and even set it alight if it touches the side of the box the whole night through. Using a loop, tie the bulb's flex to the chicken wire covering the box and let the bulb hang down in the centre. Of course an infra-red lamp is excellent, but is more expensive.

When quail are raised by their mother, the chicks must be allowed to stay with her even when she hatches the next nest of eggs.

The previous set of chicks make excellent foster parents for the new quail. The newcomers crawl in underneath their older siblings and are thus kept warm while their mother goes her own way. The young quail are so tiny that they easily crawl through the openings of ordinary chicken wire and then become lost. Make provision for this by stretching shadecloth or something similar around the chicken wire of the aviary.

Sometimes a male will start pecking at his chicks when he wants to mate again. When this happens he will have to be removed immediately.

Feeding

Adult quail

Quail eat all sorts of seeds such as mixed birdseed, grass seeds and other small seeds. These must be given together with a meal mix such as poultry growth mix, laying meal or dog meal. Quail do not dehusk seeds as canaries do, so you must always provide bird grit or coarse river sand. When the quail eat the grit, it grinds the husks from the seed in the crop. As is the case with all birds, greenstuff is essential.

Quail chicks

Young quail are amazingly independent. When walking about with their mother, they quickly learn what to eat. In nature they eat large quantities of live food such as worms while still very young. Only later do they switch to a diet consisting mainly of seeds. Fortunately they adapt well to the food we can provide for them.

Give them poultry growth meal, laying meal or dog meal, bird and shell grit, as well as finely chopped greenstuff and a bowl of fine seeds. Together with these foods, it is essential that the chicks get soft food such as rearing mix or at least a piece of wet brown bread, particularly during the first two weeks. A mixture of brown bread, mashed hard-boiled egg and finely grated carrot is, as always, a very good supplement for the chicks. Do not give more than they can eat within one hour, because the egg will soon spoil, particularly in a heated box or brooder. However, canary rearing mix may be left with the chicks in the box the entire night. The quail also eat chopped young white mealworms, but survive well without the worms.

If the quail are raised artificially, they learn what to eat with greater difficulty. Sprinkle the meal or soft food on the floor of the box in which they are kept. Close the box with chicken wire. Place a piece of an antheap on top of the chicken wire or inside the box (see fig. 25). As the ants fall

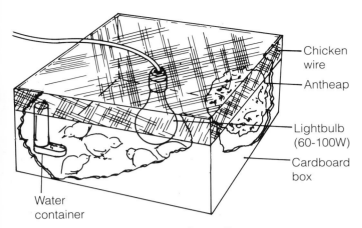

Chicken wire
Antheap
Lightbulb (60-100W)
Cardboard box
Water container

Fig. 25 A home-made brooder for quail

through, the movement catches the attention of the quail and they learn to peck at the food on which the ants are moving. (Keep the extra antheap under wet sacking until it is required.)

It really is a problem to supply young quail (particularly Chinese painted quail, which are hardly larger than moths) with water while at the same time keeping them dry. Only a few drops of water will wet them through and, if this happens, they can die of the cold within a short time, particularly if a cold wind blows on them. It is simply looking for trouble to place an open bowl of water in a small box with quail chicks. One solution to the water problem is to buy those automatic water bottles meant for caged birds or even the bottle meant for white mice. Suspend it so that the bottom rests on the ground. The spout is small enough for the quail not to be able to climb inside.

Two special characteristics of quail of which you must take note, are the following:

☐ The birds like bathing in sand and for this a large, flat container with clean sand is essential.
☐ Quail have the habit of flying up into the air very quickly when frightened. When doing so they bump their heads against the wire of the cage or the top of the travel box until they are bloody. Quail must therefore never be transported in a box with a top made of chicken wire – this will cut them to pieces. It is better to transport them in an almost dark travel box so that they will not be frightened. Even then it is better to glue a thin layer of foam rubber to the top of the box on the inside.

16

Wild doves

Aviculturalists have a choice of three types of doves, namely racing pigeons, fancy pigeons and wild doves. Fancy and racing pigeons were artificially bred from wild doves and rearing them is a specialised activity.

There are considerably more than a thousand different types of wild doves, of which only a few species are kept by aviculturalists. The reason is probably that although doves are generally peaceful and mix well with other birds, most are simply too large for the average bird keeper's aviary. A huge dove in a small aviary populated by finches can knock the wind out of the small birds with its flapping wings. Consequently only the smaller dove species are in demand.

In fact, the very smallest dove, the diamond dove, *Geopelia cuneata* (see photos 113a and 113b), from Australia, is the most popular. Other doves found in South African aviaries are the pygmy dove, *Columbina minuta*, from South America and the zebra dove, *Geopelia striata* (see photo 114), which originates from Australia and the islands of the East.

Larger doves which have also found favour with bird fanciers are the Barbary dove (photo 115), various types of Bleeding hearts which display a red patch on the breast, the green-winged dove, *Chalcophaps indica* (photo 116), and the bronze-winged types. The Barbary dove was long ago bred artificially by means of crossbreeding and does not occur in nature.

In general these doves are not brightly coloured and it is actually strange that the beautifully coloured fruit doves of the tropics, as well as the large variety of green doves, do not find greater favour among South African aviculturalists. This is probably a case of unknown, unloved.

The fact that doves do not need insects to raise their young means that they are easy to keep. Doves have the particular characteristic that they secrete a so-called 'milk' in the crop with which they feed their young. For the first three to four days the young receive this milk only, and thereafter they get a mixture of crop milk and food. Both the cock and the hen produce crop milk.

Any aviary is suitable for doves, as long as there is shelter from cold wind, rain and the burning sun. The doves will not try to chew the wire and can even be kept under shade netting.

The smaller types can share an aviary with any other species, while the larger types suit parakeets and parrots better.

Male doves put on a fine courting display. Apart from other displays, the cock bows before the hen while cooing to her. The courting display of the diamond dove, in particular, is very attractive, because he spreads his tail like a fan while bowing before the object of his admiration.

Breeding habits

Doves make an untidy nest using twigs and grass. This is an open platform and during hailstorms, driving rain or heat-waves the young may die or the nest may fall apart. Sometimes the nest is built so flimsily that the eggs fall right through.

It is therefore best to construct a platform or support on which they can build their nest beneath a roof. The flat trays in which one buys seedlings make good bases for nests. Suspend these in a corner under a roof. Place dry grass and thin twigs in the tray and also on the ground. The doves will soon finish off the nest to their taste. They like it when the nest is in a corner, so that there is shelter on two sides.

You can also buy commercial cardboard or plastic nests meant for racing pigeons. Place the nest on a shelf or suspend it. Wild doves will breed in these.

For a natural effect you can plant dense shrubs such as cypress species or lemon or orange trees in the aviary. Spread twigs and dry grass on the ground – the doves will build a nest themselves in the shrubs to their own taste.

In the case of most dove species the female incubates at night, while the male and female incubate during the day for equal periods of time. If the male dies, the eggs can't be saved.

Doves lay no more than one or two eggs and only one or two young are raised at one time. The incubation period is short – about 14 days (slightly longer in the case of the larger species).

Many of the smaller dove species are fully grown within eight or ten months and can then begin breeding, although such young birds often fail at their first attempt.

Doves do not recognise their own young before the young have feathers. It is therefore possible to give young orphaned doves to strange foster parents. The foster parents will raise them as long as the orphans do not yet have feathers.

When one dove species is raised by parents of another species, it identifies with the strange parents and on reaching sexual maturity will try to mate with the same species as the foster parents. However, if doves are raised by their own parents, different species can live together in the same aviary without any interbreeding taking place.

113a Diamond dove (red mutation)

113b Diamond dove (normal colour)

114 Zebra dove

115 Barbary dove

116 Green-winged dove

117 Tambourine dove

118 Chinese necklace dove from Asia

Feeding

Doves (like quail) cannot dehusk seeds as budgies can. They swallow the seeds whole and the husks must be rubbed off in the crop. It is absolutely essential that there should be coarse sand, bird grit or small stones in the aviary. The doves eat the grit and the grit abrades the husks from the seeds. For the rest they eat the same food as finches. They can therefore be incorporated with other aviary birds with little trouble or extra attention.

The smaller doves eat small seeds such as mixed birdseed, millet, canary seed, turnip, radish, sorghum, wheat, etc. Larger doves get larger seeds such as maize and peanuts. Laying or growing meal provides protein, vitamins and minerals. A container with minerals is essential. Special minerals for racing pigeons are for sale commercially and are suitable for all doves. If this is unobtainable, charcoal, a lump of salt and shell grit can be placed in the aviary. For the rest the doves get vitamins in their water once or twice a week. Daily greenstuff is also important.

When there are young, most doves will raise them well without extra food, but a piece of soaked brown bread or some rearing mix will make it easier for the parents to fill the hungry crops. Sprouted seeds are also good food.

The prevention of diseases is the same as for other birds.

Doves like to bath when it rains gently, or in a shallow dish of water. The dish for drinking water should therefore not be too deep. Diamond doves, on the other hand, hardly ever bath.

The dove aviary should not be overcrowded. More than one pair of the same species can be kept in one aviary, as long as there is enough space. Extra males may sometimes interfere and prevent successful mating. Various dove species can also occupy the same aviary and doves can share their aviary with parakeets, parrots or finches.

Sexing

Sexing can be a problem. The cock bows down before the hen, but when you enter the aviary to catch the birds, they no longer do this, and how do you then pick a pair?

In general the colours of the hen are duller than those of the cock. You can also capture one dove and place it in a wire cage inside the aviary. If it is a hen, the cocks will come and bow before her. Otherwise the following can serve as guidelines in sexing:

Diamond doves: During the breeding season the red ring round the eyes of the cock is larger and wider than that of the hen. Outside the breeding season (in winter) the rings look alike.

Zebra doves: It is extremely difficult and often impossible to determine the sex. The stripes of the hen are often less sharply delineated than those of the cock, and furthermore her breast has a duller colour.

Barbary dove: Although not always a hundred percent accurate, the cock's legs are purple while those of the hen are a lighter red.

Pygmy dove: The hen's colours are duller. The iridescent dots on the wings are dark purple in the case of the cock and brown in the case of the hen.

Green-winged dove: The hen is brown wherever the cock is purple. She does not show white on the shoulder. The grey and white on her head is limited to the forehead.

119 Swallow pigeon

120 Gimpel pigeon

121 Norwich cropper

122 Modena Magnani

123 Archangel

124 Crimpbacked or frilled pigeon

17

Fancy pigeons

Calm and peace fill your mind when you find yourself among fancy pigeons. Their restful cooing, stately preening and tame natures dispel all tension – until you get to the fancy pigeon show! In contrast to the peace you feel in the aviaries at home, the show exudes excitement and tension. And a fancy pigeon must go on show; why else would you keep such showy creatures?

Fancy pigeon lovers make up one of the largest single groups of bird breeders in the country. This is no wonder, because there is an astonishing variety of these pigeons – you could say one for every possible taste. Worldwide there are more than 800 types and colours.

It is unbelievable that there can be so very many variations on one basic theme. There are fancy pigeons which walk with such a backwards posture that they cannot see the ground. Others have such large feathered hoods that they can see nothing at all. The legs of some are covered with such long feathers that they strut about like frogmen. Others tumble when they should be flying. Some display huge 'warts' on their noses, or their bills are so short that foster mothers must raise their young. And then there are those which simply hatch only fat, large, good-for-the-pot squabs.

There are Modenas such as Schietti and Gazzi, owls, Jacobins, frills, Gimpels, Blondinettes, nuns, Mookees, tumblers, pouters, croppers, Mondains, rollers, Dragoons, Arabian laughing doves, fantails, and pages full of others. Some types are not common in South Africa.

For all these types set race standards are laid down for which the breeder must strive. The descriptions of race standards fill entire books, and furthermore differ from one country to the next.

Fortunately these birds are all only pigeons. Feeding and housing them is therefore quite simple, and the same rules apply more or less to all of them.

The beginner is advised to join a fancy pigeon society. Fortunately there are many clubs spread across the country. Specialist clubs concentrating on heavy races (e.g. for slaughtering or showing) or tumblers only, are also common. If there is no club in your vicinity at present, a few enthusiasts could get together and form their own club.

There are also clubs for slaughter pigeons. The South African Fancy Pigeon Society is alive and well and publishes a handy monthly newsletter which keeps people in contact with the pigeon scene throughout the country. Furthermore you can only get hold of rings through a club, and it is better to take part in the various shows through the auspices of a club.

Aviaries

The beginner must first have a look at the aviaries of a number of old hands before starting to build his own. In this way he will pick up many ideas and can then decide for himself what will best suit him and his circumstances.

Pigeons can be kept in anything from a box in a tree to a huge double-storey edifice with louvre windows, a ceiling and a wooden floor which will grace any suburb. It all depends on how much money and time you have and on your particular interests. The pigeons themselves expect only a balanced diet and a sheltered spot for their nest and chicks.

Because there are so many possibilities as regards building lofts and flights only a few guidelines are given. Start off with three aviaries. One is for the breeding pairs. Ten to 16 breeding pairs can be kept with ease in one aviary, as long as there are as many males as females. An unpaired male could try and take over the nest or female of another pigeon, and in the ensuing fight the eggs may be broken.

The other two aviaries are for the young birds only. The young are removed from the parents' aviary at about six weeks and the two sexes are further raised separately. Pigeons are sexually mature as early as about six months, but rather allow them to reach nine or twelve months before they are required to breed.

If you want to apply, e.g. colour breeding, a particular cock must be paired with a particular hen. You do this by placing the young pair in a separate enclosure for about two or three days. Once the male has fallen in love with his wife, he will stay with her for life. He will not begin to wander unless his partner is removed, or dies.

A number of pairing cages are therefore necessary. Wire cages will do for this purpose, but enthusiastic breeders build beautiful double wooden boxes with bars in front, and incorporating sliding doors. After the pairing off, these can then do double duty as nests.

The aviary in which the breeding pairs are kept consists of a shelter with a roof, which is enclosed on three sides, plus an open flight made of chicken wire. (See chapter 2 for more information on the building of aviaries.) Stack the nests in the shelter on top of each other like blocks of flats. The openings in the chicken wire must be small enough to ensure that few mice and no rats can slip through, and the entire structure must be high enough for someone to walk upright inside it. However, the birds should not be able to fly above your outstretched arms, because it is difficult to capture them. Two metres high is about right.

125 Polish Lynx

126 Dutch cropper

127 An almost perfect Mookee

Wet aviaries are unhealthy. They provide an environment for worms, snails and bacteria. Spread fine river sand or gravel over the floor to absorb water. Replace it as soon as it is soiled.

Nests

Pigeons normally lay two eggs at a time, and before the young are fully adult, the hen begins laying again. A pair therefore needs a double nest, with a shelf in front of the nest which is theirs only. It is advisable to construct a partition between the double nests of the various pairs so that they cannot see one another (see fig. 26).

There are also various other methods of building nests, and a club will be happy to help enthusiasts. If you do not know how to build a wooden nest, or there is too little money, or the effort is too much, you simply use two large tins of which the tops have been cut off, or two wooden boxes placed next to each other on the ground on their sides. The pigeons will soon enter these and build their nest, because they like their nests to be sheltered.

Pigeons like to build their nests in something which looks like a round bowl. The drip saucers used for pot plants are quite adequate.

If not, you can buy the cardboard nests used for racing pigeons. A nest like this is simply discarded when it becomes soiled. Also provide nesting material; use any kind of hay or grass that is available.

Feeding

Fancy pigeons are large birds and do not easily crawl through holes in the wire of their dovecote. The pigeons' food, water and grit containers can therefore be placed outside, next to holes in the wire so that they can stick their heads through to eat and drink. This means that the

Fig. 26 This is how a number of pigeon nests are accommodated. Each pair gets two nests partitioned from their neighbours so that they cannot see one another. The nest itself is a drawer which can be pulled forward for easy cleaning.

aviculturalist has no need to enter the aviary to clean the containers.

Such a system will work only where there are no rats and mice. In all other cases the containers are placed inside the flight or loft.

If you want to tame the pigeons properly, feed them by hand once or twice a day. If there is too little time or if you are going away, the seed is placed in a self-feeder. If the self-feeder has various compartments, the seeds do not mix and the pigeons can choose for themselves what they want, without spillage or mess. Self-feeders are available from pet shops, or from dealers who supply products for chickens. The handy aviculturalist will also be able to build one for himself.

Fig. 27 A screen around the container prevents the pigeons from fouling their drinking water, food or grit.

Some aviculturalists who breed pigeons for show purposes believe that pigeons should not bath. The reason is that the pigeons drink the dirty bathwater. Such breeders supply water bowls which are so small that the pigeons cannot bath in them, or water receptacles covered with a screen through which only the pigeons' heads can fit. The same kind of screen can also be placed over the grit and food so that these are not spilt (see fig. 27).

It is not essential for pigeons to bath. Their sweat is normally adequate to protect the eggs against drying out, with the possible exception of a heat wave. However, pigeons like to bath so much that you can certainly give them a large, flat dish of water in which to do so. It always gives great pleasure to watch their antics in the bath.

Ready-mixed food for pigeons can be bought in most food shops. If you wish to make up your own mix, the following works well: 35% yellow maize, 20% peas (for protein), 15% grain sorghum, 30% wheat.

Ensure that the seeds are not meant for sowing purposes. Such seeds are dusted or fumigated against insects and are poisonous. The seed must be fit for animal feed.

Pigeons need small stones or stone grit in the crop to grind down the grain. They swallow amazingly large stones for this purpose. The stones must be hard so that they do not break up in the crop. Fairly fine stone grit or granite chips (the type mixed with cement for building purposes) will do the job.

Pigeons must also get extra minerals such as calcium, which is needed for egg production. The seed they eat does not contain enough minerals. The minerals are often simply mixed with the grit. Such mixtures are available commercially. The following is a suitable mineral/grit mix-

ture you can mix yourself: 35% stone grit, 40% shell grit, 10% charcoal, 5% bone meal, 5% lime, 5% salt.

Pigeons must also get greenstuff. Because they are large birds, large green leaves can be fed whole. Spinach, lettuce, lucerne, cabbage and carrot leaves are generally used.

Young pigeons do not need a special feeding mix. Both parents produce milk in their crops with which the chicks are fed. The pigeon cock is a good parent. Not only does he help to feed the young, he also broods for about six hours during the day. If the hen is busy with her second set of eggs or if she dies, he will raise the young by himself. Pigeon eggs take about 18 days to hatch. Moulting time is in February/March.

Combating diseases

Pigeons are tough birds and if the loft and flight are kept clean, they do not easily fall ill. To prevent diseases, however, the following rules must be observed:

☐ Keep all newly purchased pigeons in quarantine for three to four weeks.
☐ Dust all new pigeons for external parasites.
☐ Delouse the lofts once a year, or more often if necessary.
☐ Dust or spray the pigeons for lice a few times per year.
☐ Deworm the pigeons a few times per year, particularly if they are free to walk about or fly outside. You can buy numerous special worm mixtures for pigeons from pet shops or other shops which supply animal medicines. You can also obtain a prescription for such remedies from a veterinarian.
☐ Do not dose the birds continually with antibiotics, vitamins and laxatives. This is not necessary.

Preparation for the show

Basically there are two types of show pigeons, namely those which fly free and are judged according to their flying ability, and those which are bred for their appearance (build, posture and colour).

First attend a few shows and then join a club. Then decide what kind of pigeon you like. Before you buy, you must ensure that you are *au fait* with the standards with which your race must comply.

Fancy pigeons are artificially bred birds and do not occur in nature. Never buy crossbreeds. Nobody wants the young and there are no categories for crossbreeds at exhibitions.

If you wish to show the birds, they must be extremely tame. The pigeons are shown in wire cages and therefore the young pigeon must grow accustomed to it.

Place the cage on the ground in the flight and place a few green leaves such as spinach inside it. The pigeon will enter the cage by itself. As soon as it feels safe and calm inside the cage, you can close the wire cage and carry it about with the pigeon inside. Do not catch the pigeon with a net and then place it inside the wire cage. This frightens it, and it associates the cage with something unpleasant.

The pigeon must also become accustomed to being captured and held in your hands. Remove the young pigeon from the cage and gently handle it; stroke it and smooth its feathers until it calms down.

The pigeon must also learn to pose for the judges inside the cage in a particular way. Place it in the wire cage and manoeuvre it with a rod until it stands correctly. The wings must be held just so; the neck must be bent just so. It quickly learns what is expected of it, and when its owner stands near the cage, it quickly assumes the required posture!

The pigeon is bathed before the show. Baby shampoo is just right for this purpose. Small feathers of the wrong colour are snipped out. The bill is filed so that the upper and lower mandibles fit over each other neatly. The toenails are neatly clipped and filed. Bill, legs and toenails are then oiled slightly, e.g. with baby oil, and the bird is ready for the show.

Tumblers and rollers are pigeons which fly freely. The aviary must always be closed and they are released only on an empty stomach. They get food only if they return. If the aviary is always left open, they will soon learn to forage for themselves in the veld or the neighbour's garden, and will not return home with such alacrity.

When releasing a group of free-flying pigeons for the first time, it is a good idea to partially clip one wing of one of them so that it can fly only a short distance. This helps to ensure that the others remain with him and do not fly too far.

Pigeons inherit colours, feather patterns and build according to Mendel's laws. It is therefore possible in certain cases to determine beforehand which colour, patterns or crest a pigeon will probably inherit. As there are so many types of pigeons as well as a great many colours and colour combinations, this is a specialised subject which must be studied thoroughly.

128 Mutations of the rosy-faced lovebird. On the left is the cream lutino and on the right a particularly fine example of the yellow lutino.

129 A good example of a pastel blue mutation of the rosy-faced lovebird.

Breeding for colour

Breeding birds of different colours is an intricate art and requires a sound knowledge of hereditable factors. You cannot simply mate a blue bird with a yellow one and hope that this will result in a green bird. For example, you must know or accurately guess at which colours occurred in the antecedents.

To achieve success in breeding various colours, you should make a thorough study of the subject. In this chapter we will therefore simply explain a few basic concepts which, it is hoped, will place the beginner on the bottom rung of the ladder to colour breeding.

To understand heredity, we must first learn the 'language' of heredity.

Definitions

Normal: This is the colour of the bird in its natural state and is strongly dominant.

Chromosome: For new life to come into existence, the chromosome of a male cell must fuse with the chromosome of a female cell. Chromosomes are the 'threads' on which the various characteristics of the bird are 'carried', e.g. the colours of the feathers.

Dominant: A dominant colour is the one which is strongest, even if other colours are present on the chromosome.

Recessive: A recessive colour is 'weak' and is overpowered by dominant colours if the latter are present on the chromosome. Recessive colours only come to the fore if no dominant colours are present.

Green is always dominant vis-à-vis blue. If a bird is blue, it therefore means that it carries only blue on its chromosomes and that the recessive blue is not dominated by anything else.

Say a pure green bird mates with a pure blue bird, we can represent the pairing of the chromosomes by means of the following diagram:

Bird A **Bird B**

gr ⤬ bl
gr ⤬ bl

The chromosomes of all the chicks are green/blue, in other words they contain both colours, but because green is dominant over blue, all the chicks will appear green, although they will carry the blue factor.

130 A beautiful yellow/green pied mutation of the rosy-faced lovebird.

131 The white-masked lovebird is a mutation of the well-known black-masked lovebird. This is not a very good example, as there is too much dark pigment in the wings.

107

Split: A bird which carries two (or more) colours in its chromosomes although it shows only the dominant colour. The chicks (gr/bl) referred to above are thus split for blue. We always state the dominant colour first and then the recessive colour after the slash, e.g. green/blue. Let's take a look at what happens when we mate a split bird (sex not important) with another split bird:

Bird A   Bird B

gr ⤬ gr
bl ⤬ bl

The result is: 25% are gr/bl
25% are gr/bl
25% are bl/bl
25% are gr/gr

We therefore started off with two birds but managed, through breeding, to ensure that for every 100 birds 25 of the chicks are blue, in other words a new colour. Fifty are gr/bl, therefore split for blue, and 25 are green. The split for blue birds therefore appears green, but can produce blue chicks in certain circumstances.

Unfortunately this is where many opportunities for cheating present themselves. An aviculturalist can sell a bird of a normal colour and claim that it is a split. There is absolutely no way in which the buyer can determine whether this is true or not.

On the other hand an honest seller may be selling a genuine split, but the bird produces only normal chicks, because it does not produce a hundred chicks, but only one or two, which can both quite easily be gr/gr or gr/bl.

The 25% and 50% indicate that of 100 chicks the *possibility* exists that their chromosomes will pair off in the manner mentioned above. This does not, however, mean that if there are only four chicks, the four will be divided in the same manner. With the first breeding one may perhaps achieve only two chicks (both green) and with the next breeding three chicks, all three of which are split for blue, but they will still be green.

Sex chromosomes: These chromosomes determine the sex of the bird. (Some colours are carried on the sex chromosomes.) Male birds have two similar chromosomes, which we indicate with XX. The sex chromosomes of female birds differ and are indicated with XY. (The chromosomes of birds and butterflies are the other way round to those of other animals. In mammals such as humans the male chromosome is the XY.)

Sex-linked: Certain colours occur only on the X chromo-somes. We call them sex-linked. In the case of budgies these are the opaline, cinnamon-wing, lutino, albino and lacewing. As both females and males have X chromosomes, the colour can be carried by both sexes in a form which is visible or invisible.

There are therefore five possible combinations of, e.g. the lutino factor which are sex-linked, namely:

1. *Lutino male:* The factor is visible, therefore both X chromosomes carry the lutino factor.
2. *Split lutino male:* The factor is invisible, therefore only one X chromosome carries the lutino factor, while the other X chromosome carries a dominant colour.
3. *Male without any lutino factor:* None of the X chromosomes in the male carry the lutino factor and he is therefore normal.
4. *Lutino hen:* Her one X chromosome carries the lutino factor and it is visible.
5. *Non-lutino hen:* She carries no lutino factor on her single X chromosome and she is therefore normal.

The following table shows which colours can be expected if any of the males 1, 2 or 3 mates with females 4 or 5.

1. Lutino male × lutino female
Expectation: 100% lutino males and females

2. Lutino male × normal female
Expectation: 50% normal/lutino males (i.e. splits)
50% lutino females

3. Normal male × lutino female
Expectation: 50% normal/lutino males (i.e. splits)
50% lutino females

4. Normal/lutino male × lutino female
Expectation: 25% lutino males
25% lutino females
25% normal/lutino males
25% normal females

5. Normal/ lutino male × normal female
Expectation: 25% lutino females
25% normal/lutino males
25% normal males
25% normal females

There are no other possible colour combinations. It is therefore clear that controlled colour breeding is an interesting but intricate specialist subject. The above information is meant only to give the beginner a basic idea of what it all entails.

Caged birds

It is distressing to a bird lover to see a parrot cooped up for life all by itself in a small cage – just for the pleasure of so-called animal lovers. Parrots are intelligent creatures. In their natural state they fly for kilometres, chew branches, seek food, consort with others of their own kind, build nests, mate, brood and raise chicks. They are busy and on the go, and there is no question of loneliness.

However, when a parrot becomes a caged bird, it is locked up in a small cage which allows it no room to fly and virtually no room to move. It is separated from its own kind and often sits cooped up alone for hours while its owners are off at work. It cannot give expression to its breeding instincts and usually does not even have a stick to chew on. It's no wonder that it pulls out its own feathers in pure frustration and misery. Cockatiels, budgies and lovebirds, too, are often subjected to this lot. Solitary confinement without a mate is cruel and such short-sightedness cannot be described as a love for animals.

Fortunately it is a fact that many parrots do adapt well to their human owners, become very attached to them and even appear happy – but then the humans also play their part. Such parrots are usually the ones which are allowed to clamber out of the cage, are given branches to chew and are seldom left alone. For example, parrots in pubs seldom pull out their own feathers because there are always people who take notice of them.

Once a parrot has become tame, it is not necessary for it to live its entire life in a cage. Unfortunately it is general practice in South Africa to keep tame parrots in a cage – usually for life.

In other countries such as America use is made of a T-bar on a single upright. The parrot's food and water are fixed to the ends of the bar and the parrot is not confined behind bars. It can even fly down to the ground and walk about. But what about the droppings it deposits everywhere? And it chews all the furniture to pieces! If there is no place outside where the parrot may move about, it must at the very least be taken out of the cage each day and allowed to move about.

The more attention and stimulation a parrot gets, the cuter it becomes. A parrot which is taken from a cage can be placed in a tree in the garden or on a platform on the stoep where it can move about freely.

It is often adequate simply to open the door of the cage. The bird will use the cage as base or place for resting, but will venture forth from there to explore the world outside. Tame parrots with clipped wings will not fly away or even run away.

Parrots which spend their lives in a cage, particularly in a room in which there are often no people for long periods of the day, often lapse into a passive, disconsolate state and pluck their own feathers.

A parrot which is handled often, is let out of its cage and receives a great deal of attention usually adapts very well to family life. It becomes an interesting member of the family and eventually prefers the company of humans above that of its own kind. The more stimulation a parrot experiences, the livelier it will remain in spirit.

General care

Birds which remain indoors soon lose the ability to adapt to the cold and become sensitive to draughts and cold wind. Therefore choose the place where the cage is to stand with great care. People often forget that the sun moves – a budgie or parrot which enjoyed the shade in the morning may fry to death in the afternoon sun.

The feeding requirements of caged parrots are a basic seed mix which must be supplemented with fruit, vegetables, peanut butter and even a bit of meat. Vitamin/mineral preparations can be given once or twice a week. Dissolve these in their water.

Far too many parrots end up at the vet because their owners only feed them seeds. A caged bird such as a budgie, lovebird, cockatiel or parrot cannot live on seed alone and must also get greenstuff and/or fruit.

Do not give a tame parrot too much unnatural food such as cake and sweets. Suspend a mineral block (available from pet shops) in the cage.

Good talkers like the African grey and Amazon parrots and cockatoos usually teach themselves words and tunes as time goes by. Parrots that have lived with humans for 20 years are still capable of learning new words.

Birds which learn to talk with greater difficulty, such as Senegals, budgies and cockatiels, can be helped along by constantly playing a tape recording of a few words to them.

Regurgitating

In their natural state parrots feed one another. This is normally a sign of love and affection. A parrot which loves its owner will often try to feed him and suddenly vomit on his hand. This regurgitation is quite natural and not a sign of illness.

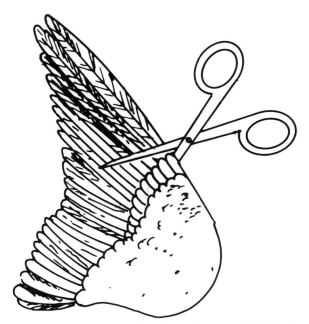

Fig. 28 Do not cut the wing feathers of a caged bird further than a little way in front of the next layer of feathers. If you cut through the shafts of the long feathers, they may bleed a great deal, infection could set in or new feathers could grow crooked.

Clipping of wings

Do not cut the wing feathers too short. Wing feathers cut off near the quick may regrow crookedly and the follicles, from which the feathers emerge, may become infected (see fig. 28).

Sometimes only a few feathers are cut, or each feather is cut lengthwise. These methods do not spoil the bird's appearance to a great extent, but it is still able to fly quite well, so it is better to cut off the feathers of one wing completely.

Plucking feathers

Parrots which spend most of their time outside their cages seldom pluck their feathers, unless they have lice or have picked up the bad habit earlier.

Parrots are birds which like to chew things and provision must be made for this deep-rooted instinct. A parrot in a cage must therefore be given fresh, non-poisonous branches to chew every day. The branches of fruit trees are normally safe, unless they have been sprayed with pesticide. Willow branches are also suitable. If this inborn desire to chew is satisfied, there is less chance that it will pull out its own feathers.

Unfortunately it is an extremely difficult habit to eradicate once a parrot has acquired it. What is often successful is to give it complete freedom by putting it in a tree in the garden by day. It also helps to buy a mate and to allow them to be with each other freely.

A cockatiel in a cage feels the absence of its own kind badly, because cockatiels are sociable birds which like living in a group. You often hear a cockatiel calling constantly for a mate, but its owners are too misinformed to know what it is all about. They think it's simply the cockatiel calling, without realising that it is an expression of loneliness. Always try to keep at least two cockatiels together.

Index

Page numbers in **bold type** indicate photographs and/or illustrations.

Abyssinian lovebird 47
African grey parrot 38, 44, 46, 47, **47**, 109
African ring-necked parakeet 44, 47-48
African silverbill 30, 33, 63, 64
Alexandrine parakeet 30, 48
Amazon parrot 16, 44, 109
Antibiotics 29, 40, 41-42
  warning 41
Arabian laughing dove 103
Archangel 102
Aviaries **6**, 7-14, **8-14**
  bacteria in soil 12
  beautifying 17
  breeding aviaries 7
  building 7-13
  cleaning 37, 39, 43
  collection of birds in 29-30
  design 7
  display aviaries 7
  floors 11-12
  flying area 7
  foundations 11

framework 7-9
gates 11
heating 13-14
measurements 9
moveable 9
number of birds in 30
plans 7-13
plants in 7, 17
shelter 7
shelters and roofs 12-13
siting 7
size 29
template 9
wire for 7, 9-10

Bacteria
  in aviaries 12
  salmonella 35
Bacterial infections 35-36
  coccidiosis 12, 36, 95
  paratyphus 35-36
  scour (diarrhoea) 12, 40-41
  tuberculosis 12, 36
Bahama pintail 83
Baraband 44
Barbary dove 100, **101**, 102

Bathing, necessity for 20
Bedbugs 39
Bengalese or society finch 29, 30, 33, 63, 64-65
Bicheno or owl finch 63, **65**, 65
Bird clubs 6, 103
Black-capped or blue-thighed lory **48**, 48
Black-masked lovebird 29, 30, 44, 45, **49**, 49
Black-necked swan **90**, 90-91
Black swan **90**, 90
Bleeding heart dove 100
Blondinette 103
Blue-fronted Amazon parrot **49**, 49
Blue-masked lovebird 49, **49**
Blue waxbill 63
Bones, broken 42
Border canary **76**, 76
Botulism 86
Bourke's parakeet 45, 49-50
Bronze-winged dove 100
Brooder
  for ducklings 88
  for pheasants 94
  for quail **99**

Brown-eared or brown-breasted conure **50**, 50
Brown-eared pheasant 94
Brush-tongues 44, 46-47
  bathing 46
  droppings 46
  feeding 22, 23, 26, 46
  lories 44
  lorikeets 44
  nests 19-20, **20**
  see also Psittaciformes
Budgies 18, 22, 30, 33, 38, **50**, 50-51, 80-82
  aviaries 80, **81**
  breeding 81
  caged birds 109, 110
  feeding 22, 26, 50-51, 80-81
  fertility 5
  nests 18, **19**, 51, 82
  record keeping 81-82
  show birds 50, **80**, **81**, 80-82
  show training 82
  see also Psittaciformes
Bumblefoot **42**, 42
Buying birds 27-30
  how to 27

points to consider 28-29
where to 28
see also Trade in birds
see also Imported birds

Caged birds 109-110
  care of 109, 110
  cockatiel 109, 110
  feather plucking 109, 110
  feeding 109
  mannikins 63
  mynah 68
  parrots 46, 109, 110
  Pekin robin 25, 26, 70
  regurgitation 109
  wing clipping 110
Californian quail 30, **96**, 97
Canaries 76-79
  aviaries 77
  Border **76**, 76
  breeding 77
  cages 77, **78**
  colour 76
  diseases 40
  feeding 77-79
  Frills 77, 77
  Gloster 76
  Lizard 76
  Norwich 76
  Red Factor **76**, 76, 77, 79
  Roller 77
  sexing 79
  show birds 76-79
  singing canaries 76
  Yorkshire 76
Canary-winged parakeet 30, **50**, 51
Candida albicans 26
Caninde macaw **51**, 51-52
Cardinals 64
  red-crested **71**, 71-72
  Virginian or scarlet **74**, 75
  see also Finches
Carolina duck 83-84, **84**, 87, 88
Chattering lory 52
Chicks,
  kicking out of nest 33
Chinese goose **91**, 91
Chinese necklace dove 101
Chinese quail 30, **96**, 97, 98, 99
CITES 5
Coccidiosis 12, 36, 95
Cockatiels 18, 30, 33, **37**, **38**, 38, 52-53, 109, 110
  caged birds 109, 110
  feeding 53
  fertility 5
  nests 18, 53
  see also Psittaciformes
Cockatoos 8, 10
  lesser sulphur-crested **55**, 55-56
  nests 18
  placing of food bowls 16
  see also Psittaciformes
Coelestial **53**, 54
Cold
  cause of nest deaths 33
  protection against 13-14, 29
Colour
  breeding for 107-108
  chromosome 107
  dominant 107
  lutino factor 108
  normal 107
  recessive 107
  sex chromosomes 108
  sex-linked 108
  split 108
Conures 44, 45-46
  brown-eared or brown-breasted **50**, 50
  flying area in aviaries 9
  Jenday **55**, 55
  peach-fronted **57**, 57

Queen of Bavaria 5, 44, 46
  sun or yellow 60-61, **61**
  see also Parakeets
Cordon Bleu 30, 63, 65-66, **66**
Crimpbacked or frilled pigeon **102**, 103
Cut-throat finch 65

Deworming 29
Diamond dove 30, 100, **102**, 102
Diamond sparrow 17, 30, 63, **66**, 66
Diseases
  anaemia 37, 38
  bacterial infections 35-36
  combating 35-43
  infections 40-41
  injuries 40-43
  parasites, external 38-40
  parasites, internal 36-37
  programme against 43
Doves 30, 100-106
  aviaries 8, 13, 100
  Barbary 100, **101**, 102
  bleeding heart 100
  breeding 100
  bronze-winged 100
  Chinese necklace **101**
  courting 100
  diamond 30, 100, **101**, 102
  feeding 100-102
  green-winged 100, **101**, 102
  milk in the crop 100
  nests 18, 100
  pygmy 29, 100, 102
  racing pigeons 18, 100
  sexing 102
  tambourine **101**
  wild 100-102
  zebra 100, **101**, 102
  see also Pigeons, fancy
Dragoon 103
Droppings 23
  brush-tongues 46
  cause of bacteria 12
  mynah 68
Ducks 30, 83-89
  botulism 86
  breeding 87
  enclosures 7, 8, 84-85
  feeding 86-87, 88, 89
  nests 87
  pinioning 84
  ponds 85-86
  rearing ducklings 87-88
  wet ducklings 89
  see also Waterfowl, ornamental
Dusky lory 46
Dutch cropper **104**

Egg 32
Egg blockages 41
Elegant grass parakeet 45, 54
Elliott 94
Endangered species 5

Fairy lorikeet 46
Fantail 103
Feather plucking 110
Feeding 22-26
  animal protein 23, 24-26
  bone meal 24
  branches 24
  bread 23
  chicks 34, 34
  coarse grit 24
  dog meal 23, 26, 46
  egg 23
  eggshells 24
  fruit and vegetables 23, 26
  fruit flies 25
  grasshoppers 25
  honey 26
  maggots 25
  mealworms 25

minerals 24, 26
  nectar 26, 44, 46
  peanut butter 23, 26
  ProNutro 23, 26, 34, 46, 88
  rearing mixture 23
  rock salt 24
  seed mixes 22
  seed sprouts 23-24
  shell grit 24
  spray millet 17, 24
  supplements 23-24
  termites and ants 25
  vitamins 24, 26
  see also Food
Fertility problems 5, 32
Fighting amongst birds 7
Finches 63-82
  aviaries 8, 15, 17
  Bicheno or owl 63, **65**, 65
  breeding 63
  cut-throat 65
  deaths from cold 29
  feeding 22-23, 24, 25, 63
  Gouldian 13, 20, 40, 63, **66**, 67
  long-tailed grass 30, 63, 68-69, **69**
  masked grass 69
  mynah 68
  nests 20-21, 63
  Parson 63, **70**, 70
  Pekin robin 25, 26, 70
  pin-tailed nonpareil parrot 71, 71
  placing of food containers 16
  red-headed aurora **72**, 72-73
  red-headed parrot 30, **73**, 73
  star 73-74
  three-coloured parrot 30, **74**, 74-75
  zebra 20, 21, 29, 30, 33, 38, 75
  see also Cardinals, Mannikins, Sparrows and Waxbills
Fischer's lovebird **31**, **32**, **54**, 54-55
Flukes, liver and other internal 36, 38
Flying area in aviaries 7, 9
Food
  containers 15-16, **16**
  placing in aviaries 7
  provision 15-16
  see also Feeding
Foster mothers 32-33
  bantam or silkie hens 88, 94
  Bengalese finch 64-65, 66
  cockatiels 33
  red-rumped parakeets 33
  waterfowl 88
Frills 77, 77
Fungal infections
  Candida albicans 26

Gapeworm 37-38, **38**
Geese 89-92
  Chinese **91**, 91
  feeding 90
  Hawaiian **91**, 91
  nests 89
  see also Waterfowl, ornamental
Gimpel pigeon 102
Gloster canary 76
Golden-mantled rosella 46, **54**, 55
Golden pheasant 92, 93, 95
Gouldian finch 13, 20, 40, 63, **66**, 67
Grand eclectus 19, 44
Grass parakeets 7, 9, 30, 44, 45-46
  Bourke's 45, 49-50
  Elegant 45, 54
  Splendid 45-46
  Turquoisine 45-46
  see also Parakeets
Greater hill mynah 68
Green avadavat 68
Green-winged dove 100, **101**, 102

Hand-rearing of birds 33-34
  feeding of 34
Hawaiian goose **91**, 91

Heat
  advice against 14
  cause of nest deaths 33
Heating of aviaries 13-14

Imported birds 28, 29
Inbreeding 5
Indian ring-necked parakeet 44, 54, 55
Indigenous birds 6
Infections 40-41
  pneumonia 40-41
  scour 40-41
Infertility 32
Injuries
  broken bones 42
  broken wings 42-43
  bumblefoot **42**, 42
  egg blockages 41

Jacobin pigeon 103
Japanese quail 38, **96**, 97
Java sparrow 38, 63, 68
Jenday conure **55**, 55

Kalij pheasant 93, 94, **94**, 95
Knemidocoptes mite **40**, 40

Lady Amherst 93, 95
Lesser sulphur-crested cockatoo **55**, 55-56
Lice
  cause of nest deaths 33
  treatment against 39
Lizard canary 76
Long-tailed grass finch 30, 63, 68-69, **69**
Lories 44
  black-capped or blue-thighed **48**, 48
  chattering 46, 52
  dusky 48
  see also Brush-tongues
Lorikeets 44
  fairy 46
  Swainson's Blue Mountain or rainbow 44, **61**, 61
  see also Brush-tongues
Lovebirds 33, 38, 44, 45
  Abyssinian 47
  beautifying aviaries 17
  black-masked 29, 30, 44, 45, **49**, 49
  blue-masked **49**, 49
  Coelestial **53**, 54
  death from cold 29
  feeding 16, 22, 26, 45
  Fischer's 29, 30, 44, 45, **54**, 54-55
  flying area in aviaries 9
  Madagascar 29, **55**, 56
  nests 20, 45
  Nyassa 45, 56-57
  rosy-faced or peach-faced 45, **58**, 59, **106**, 107
  see also Psittaciformes
Lutino factor 108

Macaws 5, 7, 8, 9, 10, 44
  Caninde **51**, 51-52
  nests 18
  placing of food containers 16
  scarlet 59-60
Madagascar or grey-headed lovebird 29, **55**, 56
Mandarin duck **83**, 83-84, 87, 88
Mannikins 63
  Bengalese finch 29, 30, 33, 63, 64-65
  silverbill (African) 30, 33, 63, 64
  spice or nutmeg finch 30, 73
  white-headed or white-headed nun 75
  see also Finches
Masked grass finch 69
Mealy rosella 46, 56, **57**
Mice 7, 10-11, 21
  carriers of bacteria 35

111

poisoning of 18
protection against 16, 18
Mites
cause of nest deaths 33
see also Parasites, external
Mixing of birds in aviaries 29-30, 44, 63
Modena **102**, 103
Mondain 103
Mookee 103, **104**
Moustached or banded parakeet 30, 56, 59
Mute swan **92**, 92
Mynah, greater hill 68
feeding 23, 26

Nature Conservation, Department of 6
Nest deaths 33
Nests 18-21, **18-21**
budgies 18, 51
cockatiels 18
lovebirds 20, 45
parakeets 18
quakers 19
waterfowl 87
New Zealand parakeet 6
Norwich canary 76
Norwich cropper **102**
Nun dove 103
Nyassa lovebird 45, 56-57

Orange-cheeked waxbill 21, 30, 63, **69**, 69-70

Parakeets 44, 45-46
African ring-necked 44, 47-48
Alexandrine 30, 48
aviaries 8, 9
Baraband 44
Bourke's 45, 49-50
breeding 45-46
canary-winged 30, **50**, 51
conures 44, 46
feeding 22, 23, 26
Grand eclectus 19, 44
grass parakeets 44, 45-46
Indian ring-necked 44, **54**, 55
moustached 30, 56, **57**
nests 19, **20**
New Zealand 6
placing of food containers 16
plum-headed **4**, 30, 44, **58**, 58
Princess of Wales 30, 44, 57-58, **58**
quaker 44, 45-46, 58-59
red-rumped or red-backed 30, 33, 44, 59
ring-necked 30, 44
rock pepler 44
rosella 44, 46
see also Budgies, Cockatiels and Psittaciformes
Parasites, external 38-40
bedbugs 40
lice 13, 33, 38, 39, 40
mites 13, 33, 38, 39-40
mites (knemidocoptes) **40**, 40
mites (sternostoma tracheacolum) 40
ticks 39, 40
Parasites, internal 15, 36-38
flukes, liver and other 36, 38
gapeworm 37-38, **38**
roundworm **36**, 36, 37
tapeworm 36, 38
Paratyphus 35, 36
Parrot family, see Psittaciformes
Parrots 44, 45, 46, 109, 110
African grey 38, 44, 46, **47**, 47, 109
Amazon 16, 44, 109
aviaries 8
blue-fronted Amazon 49, 49
caged birds 109, 100
feeding 22, 23, 24, 26
placing of food containers 16

Senegal 16, **60**, 60
yellow-fronted Amazon **62**, 62
see also Lovebirds and Psittaciformes
Parson finch 63, **70**, 70
Peach-fronted conure **57**, 57
Pekin robin 25, 26, 70
Pennant rosella 46
Perches 17-18
Pests
control of 10-11, 13
Peter's or red-throated twinspot 63, 70-71
Pheasant Trust of Norfolk, England 5
Pheasants 30, 93-96
breeding 95
brown-eared 94
diseases 94-95
Elliott 94
exotic 93
feeding 94
for the pot 95
golden **92**, 93, 95
housing 7, 8, 13, **94**, 94, **95**
hunting farms 96
hunting pheasants 93
Kalij 93, 94, 95
Lady Amherst 93, 95
nests 93
origin 93
ornamental 93
Reeves **92**, 93, 95
ringneck **92**, 93, 95
silver **92**, 93, 95
Swinhoe 94, 95
Philippine duck 83
Pigeons, fancy 100, 103-106
Arabian laughing doves 103
Archangel **102**
aviaries 103
bathing 104-105, 106
Blondinette 103
crimpbacked or frilled **102**, 103
disease combating 105
Dragoon 103
Dutch cropper **104**
fantail 103
feeding 104-105, **105**
gimpel **102**
Jacobin 103
Modena **102**, 103
Mondain 103
Mookee 103, **104**
nests **104**, 104
Norwich cropper **102**
nuns 103
Polish Lynx **104**
pouters 103
rollers 103
show preparation 105-106
swallow **102**
tumblers 103
see also Doves
Pygmy dove 29, 100, 102
Pin-tailed nonpareil parrot finch **71**, 71
Plants in aviaries 7, 17
Plum-headed parakeet **4**, 30, 44, 57-58, **58**
Pneumonia 40-41
Poison
branches 24
for mice 18
Polish Lynx **104**
Ponds for waterfowl 85-86
botulism 86
Porchard duck 83
Pouters 103
Princess of Wales 30, 44, **58**, 58
ProNutro 23, 26, 34, 46, 88
Psittaciformes 13, 44-61
beautifying aviaries 17
brush-tongues 44
disadvantages 44-45

feeding 25, 26
lovebirds 45
parakeets 44, 45-46
parrots 7, 9, 44, 45, 46
Pygmy dove 29, 100, 102

Quail 97-99
breeding 98
cages 8, 13
Californian 30, **96**, 97
Chinese 30, **96**, 97, 98, 99
feeding of adults 24, 98, 101
feeding of chicks 98-99
for the pot 97
Japanese 38, **96**, 97
rearing chicks 98
Siberian 97
singing quail 30, 96, 97
water for chicks 99
Quakers 44, 45-46, 58-59
nests 19
voices 44
see also Parakeets
Queen of Bavaria 5, 44, 46

Rainbow lorikeet 44, **61**, 61
Rare birds
breeding 5
smuggling 5
Rats 10-11
carriers of bacteria 35
protection against 16, 18, 84
Red-crested cardinal **71**, 71-72
Red-eared waxbill 21, 30, 63, **72**, 72
Red Factor canary **76**, 76, 77, 79
Red-headed aurora **72**, 72-73
Red-headed parrot finch 30, **73**, 73
Red-rumped or red-backed parakeet 30, 33, 44, 59
Red-throated twinspot, see Peter's twinspot
Reeves pheasant **92**, 93, 95
Ringed teal duck 83
Ring-necked parakeet 30, 44
Ringneck pheasant **92**, 93, 95
Rock pepler 44
Roller canary 77
Roller pigeon 103
Rosellas 44, 46
golden-mantled 46, **54**, 55
mealy 46, 56, **57**
Pennant 46
Stanley's parakeet 46, 60
see also Parakeets
Rosy-faced or peach-faced lovebird 45, **58**, 59
Roundworm, see Parasites, internal
Ruddy shelduck 83

Salmonella 35
Scarlet macaw **59**, 59-60
Scour (diarrhoea) 35, 40-41
Seed mixtures 22-23
Senegal parrot 16, **60**, 60
Sexing **31-32**, 31-32
Show birds
budgies 50, 80-82
canaries 76-79
fancy pigeons 105-106
Siberian quail 97
Silverbill (African) 30, 33, 63, 64
Silver pheasant **92**, 93, 95
Singing quail 30, **96**, 97
Snakes 9, 10-11
Sparrows
diamond 17, 30, 63, **66**, 66
Java 38, 63, 68
Spice or nutmeg finch 30, 73
Splendid 45-46
Stanley's parakeet 46, 60
Star finch 73-74
Sternostoma tracheacolum mite 40

Strawberry finch 5, 21, 26, 63, **74**, 74
Sun or yellow conure 60-61, **61**
Swainson's Blue Mountain or rainbow lorikeet 44, **61**, 61
Swallow pigeon **102**
Swans 83, 89-92
black **90**, 90
black-necked **90**, 90-91
feeding 90
mute **92**, 92
nests 89, **90**
see also Waterfowl, ornamental
Swinhoe pheasant 94, 95

Tambourine dove 101
Tapeworm 36, 38
Three-coloured parrot finch 30, **74**, 74-75
Ticks 39, 40
Trade in birds 5, 44
see also Buying birds
Transport of birds 27-28
by plane 27-28
by train 27-28
capture nets 28
quail 99
travel boxes **27**, 27-28
Tuberculosis 12, 36
Tumblers 103
Turquoisine 45-46

Virginian or scarlet cardinal **74**, 75

Water supply 15
dispensers 15, **15**
Waterfowl, ornamental 83-92
Bahama pintail 83
botulism 86
breeding 87
Carolina duck **84**, 83-84, 87, 88
ducks 83-89
enclosures for ducks 84-85, **85**
feeding of ducks 86-87, 88, 89
geese 83, 87, 89-92
greenwing duck 83
Mandarin duck **83**, 83-84, 87, 88
nests **87**, 87
Philippine duck 83
ponds 85-86, **86**
porchard duck 83
rearing of ducklings 87-88, **89**
ringed teal duck 83
ruddy shelduck 83
swans 83, 87, 89-92
Waxbills
blue 63
Cordon Bleu 30, 63, 65-66, **66**
feeding 22, 24, 25, 26, 63
nests 20-21
orange-cheeked 21, 30, 63, **69**, 69-70
Peter's or red-throated twinspot 63, 70-71
placing of food containers 16
red-eared 21, 30, 63, **72**, 72
strawberry finch 5, 21, 26, 63, **74**, 74
see also Finches
White-headed mannikin or white-headed nun 75
Wild doves 100-102
Wing clipping **110**, 110
Wings, broken 42-43
Wire for aviaries 7, 9-10
biting by macaws 10, 51
biting by parrots 7, 8, 44

Yellow-fronted Amazon parrot **62**, 62
Yorkshire canary 76

Zebra dove 100, **101**, 102
Zebra finch 20, 21, 29, 30, 33, 38, 75